Family

Family Law in Scotland

J M Thomson, LLB
Regius Professor of Law
University of Glasgow

Second edition

Edinburgh
Butterworths/Law Society of Scotland
1991

Butterworths

United Kingdom	Butterworth & Co (Publishers) Ltd, 88 Kingsway, LONDON WC2B 6AB and 4 Hill Street, EDINBURGH EH2 3JZ
Australia	Butterworths Pty Ltd, SYDNEY, MELBOURNE, BRISBANE, ADELAIDE, PERTH, CANBERRA and HOBART
Canada	Butterworths Canada Ltd, TORONTO and VANCOUVER
Ireland	Butterworths (Ireland) Ltd, DUBLIN
Malaysia	Malayan Law Journal Sdn Bhd, KUALA LUMPUR
New Zealand	Butterworths of New Zealand Ltd, WELLINGTON and AUCKLAND
Puerto Rico	Equity de Puerto Rico, Inc, HATO REY
Singapore	Butterworth & Co (Asia) Pte Ltd, SINGAPORE
USA	Butterworth Legal Publishers, ST PAUL, Minnesota, SEATTLE, Washington, BOSTON, Massachusetts, AUSTIN, Texas and D & S Publishers, CLEARWATER, Florida.

Law Society of Scotland
26 Drumsheugh Gardens, EDINBURGH EH3 7YR

First published 1987
Reprinted 1988

A CIP Catalogue record for this book is available from the British Library

ISBN 0 406 105766

Printed in Great Britain by Thomson Litho Ltd., East Kilbride, Scotland.

For
Mum and Dad

Preface

The purpose of this book is to provide a clear and concise account of the rules of Scottish private law which govern family relationships. In this second edition, I have tried to keep as much of the original text as possible while at the same time taking account of the developments in the subject which have taken place since the first edition. While primarily a student's text book, I have also provided full citation of authorities where these would be useful to legal practitioners, particularly in relation to the law on financial provision on divorce where there has been significant judicial activity. I have also added a new section on the legal aspects of international child abduction. I have tried to take account of legal developments up to 31st August 1990: however, I have been able to incorporate the legislative changes introduced by the Human Fertilisation and Embryology Act 1990 and the Law Reform (Miscellaneous Provisions) (Scotland) Act 1990. The Review of Child Care Law in Scotland, which makes important and valuable recommendations, was published too late for the detailed discussion it deserves.

I have been greatly assisted in the preparation of this edition by Miss Clare Lynch LLB who expertly organised much of the new material. I, of course, remain responsible for any errors in the text.

J M Thomson,
12th December 1990

Abbreviations

Bell, *Principles:*   Professor G J Bell, *Principles of The Law of Scotland* (10th edn, 1899)

Clive: Dr Eric Clive, *The Law of Husband and Wife in Scotland* (2nd edn, 1982)

Erskine, *Institute:*   Professor John Erskine, *The Institute of the Law of Scotland* (8th edn, 1870)

Stair: Sir James Dalrymple, Viscount Stair, *Institutions of the Law of Scotland* (Tercentenary edn, 1981)

Contents

Preface   vii
Abbreviations   viii
Table of statutes   xiii
List of cases   xxi

Introduction   1

Chapter 1   Getting married   6
  Engagements   6
  The formalities of marriage   8
  Regular marriages — formal marriages   8
  Irregular marriages   14

Chapter 2   Legal impediments to marriage — void and voidable marriages   20
  Introduction   20
  Void and voidable marriages   20
  Capacity to marry   21
  Defective consent   30
  Voidable marriages — incurable impotency   36

Chapter 3   The legal consequences of marriage I   40
  Introduction   40
  Personal effects   41
  Obligations   43
  Taxation   46
  Income support   46
  Aliment   47
  Succession   55

Chapter 4   The legal consequences of marriage II: moveable property   60
  Introduction   60
  Wedding presents   61
  Gifts between spouses   62
  Corporeal moveables bought by the spouses   63

Money and securities   69
Savings from housekeeping   70
Married Women's Policies of Assurance (Scotland) Act 1880   71

Chapter 5   The legal consequences of marriage III: the matrimonial home   73
Introduction   73
The ownership of the matrimonial home   74
The occupation of the matrimonial home   79
Tenancies   92
Matrimonial interdicts   93
Cohabitees   96

Chapter 6   Divorce   99
Introduction   99
Irretrievable breakdown of marriage   100
The grounds of divorce   102
Judicial separation   117
Procedural matters   117

Chapter 7   Financial provision on divorce   120
Introduction   120
The nature of the orders   123
The principles   126
Agreement for financial provision   144
Variations of periodical allowances awarded under the Divorce (Scotland) Act 1976   145
Procedural matters   146

Chapter 8   Parents and children   148
Introduction   148
Establishing parentage   150
Blood tests and DNA 'Fingerprinting'   153
Legitimacy and illegitimacy   157

Chapter 9   Children's rights and duties   164
Introduction   164
Pupils and minors: tutors and curators   164
Contractural obligations   166
Delict   168
Succession   169
Marriage   170
Criminal Liability   170
Aliment   170

Chapter 10 Parental rights in respect of the care and upbringing of children 177
Introduction 177
Who can exercise parental rights? 178
The duration of parental rights 179
The nature of parental rights 182

Chapter 11 Actions in relation to parental rights 194
Introduction 194
Procedure 194
The welfare principle 200
Conclusion 207
International aspects 208

Chapter 12 Adoption 212
Introduction 212
Adoption agencies 213
Welfare of children 214
Prospective adopters 215
Procedure 218
Parental agreement 219
The adoption order 228

Chapter 13 Children in need of care 230
Introduction 230
Children in care 231
Compulsory measures of care 240
Conclusion 251

Index 253

Table of statutes

PAGE

Abortion Act 1967
 s 1(1) 148, 149
Act 1573 99
Administration of Justice Act 1982
 s 8 45
 9 46
 14 44
Administration of Justice (Scotland) Act 1933
 s 12 166
Adoption (Scotland) Act 1978 212
 s 1(1) 213, 214
 (2) 213
 (3) 213
 (4) 214
 ss 3 to 5 214
 s 6 .... 215, 217, 221–226, 228
 7 215
 11(1) 214
 (3) 214
 12(1) 212
 (5) 215
 (7) 215
 (8) 215
 13(1)–(3) 218
 14(1) 215
 (1A), (1B) 215
 15(1)(a) 215
 (b) 216
 (3) 216
 16 237
 (1) 222
 (a) 221
 (b) 219, 222
 (2) 222, 225
 (a) 223
 (b) 222, 225, 226, 228
 (c) 225
 (4) 220
 (5) 222, 225
 18(1) 221
 (b) 222
 (2)(a) 220
 (b) 220

PAGE

Adoption (Scotland) Act 1978—
 continued
 s 18(3), (4) 220
 (5)–(8) 221
 19 221
 20 221
 (4), (5) 221
 22 218
 23 218
 25(1) 228
 26 229
 27(1) 220
 (2) 221
 28(1)–(3) 219
 30 229
 ss 32 to 35 218
 s 36(1)(b), (c) 218
 39(1), (2) 212
 40 212
 41(1), (2) 212
 (3)–(5) 213
 42 213
 45 229
 46 212
 56 219
 57 219
 58(1)(a), (b) 219
 65 196
 (1) 215, 219, 220
 Sch 1 229
Age of Majority (Scotland) Act
 1969 .... 22, 164, 167
Age of Marriage Act 1929 170
Bankruptcy (Scotland) Act 1985
 s 34 62
 40 86
 41 .... 86, 90
Betting, Gaming and Licensing Act
 1963
 s 10(1) 182
 Sch 4
 para 2 182
Blank Bonds and Trusts Act 1696 .. 75,
 76, 77

PAGE

British Nationality Act 1981
  s 8 41
Child Abduction and Custody Act
  1985 208
  s 3(1) 210
  4 210
  14(1) 209
  15 210
  18 210
  27(2) 210
  Sch 1 (Hague Convention) 210
  art 3 210
    12, 13 211
  Sch 2 (European Convention)
  art 10 210
      (1)(a), (b) 210
    11 209
Children Act 1975
  s 37(1), (2) 217
  47(2) 196
    (d) 197
    (5)(a) 196
  48(1) 197
    (3) 198
  49 197
  51 197
    (2), (3) 197
  53(1) 216, 228
    (a), (b) 217
  55(1), (2) 196
Children Act 1989
  s 108(7) 217
  Sch 10
  Pt 11 212
  para 33 215
  Sch 13
  para 62 209
  Sch 15 217
Children and Young Persons (Scotland) Act 1937
  s 12(1) 185
    (7) 185
  18 182
  21(1) 241
  28 182
  55 170
Civil Evidence (Scotland) Act 1988
  s 1(1) 103, 118, 152, 236, 247
    (2) 152
  8(1) 103, 118, 152
    (3) 103, 118

PAGE

Congenital Disabilities (Civil
  Liability) Act 1976 149
  s 1(1) 149
  2 149
Conjugal   Rights   (Scotland)
  (Amendment) Act 1861
  s 9(1) 198, 200
    (2)(a), (b) 198
Criminal Justice Act 1988
  Sch 15
  para 51 244
Criminal   Justice   (Scotland)   Act
  1980
  s 80 182
    (7) 244
Criminal Procedure (Scotland) Act
  1975
  s 170 170
  369 170
  Sch 1 .... 240, 244, 245, 247
Damages (Scotland) Act 1976 .. 45, 169
  s 1(3), (4) 44
  10(2) 44
  Sch 1
  para 1 44
    17 160
Divorce   Jurisdiction,   Court   Fees
  and Legal Aid (Scotland) Act
  1983
  s 2 114
  Sch 1
  para 18 117
Divorce Reform Act 1969 100
Divorce (Scotland) Act 1938 ..... 2, 99
  s 5 29
Divorce (Scotland) Act 1964
  s 5 .... 99, 108
    (1) 111
  6 47
Divorce (Scotland) Act 1976 .. 100, 145
  s 1(1) 101
    (2) 101, 102, 118
      (a) 42, 102
      (b) 32, 37, 42, 102,
                      107–109, 111
      (c) 110
      (d) 113, 115, 117–119
      (e) 32, 115, 118, 119, 143
    (3) 103, 105, 106
    (5) 115, 116
    (6) 103, 109, 112, 114
  2(1) 102
    (2) 105

PAGE

Divorce (Scotland) Act 1976—
continued
s 2(3) 113
  (4) 111, 114, 115
3 ....112, 114, 117
  (1) 109
4 117
5 ....3, 120
  (2) 47, 120
  (4) 145
6 146
7(2) 47
13(2) 105, 111, 113
Domicile and Matrimonial Proceed-
  ings Act 1973
s 1 41
  (2) 41
7 117
8(2) 117
Education (Scotland) Act 1980
ss 8–10 188
s 8(2) 188
28 186
ss 28A to 28H 186
30, 31 186
s 35 186
48A 186
135(1) 187
Employment Act 1989
s 10 182
Employment of Children Act 1973: 182
Family Law Act 1986
s 1 209
9 196
10 196
12 196
13 198
16 196
25(1) 209
26 208
27 209
29 209
32(1) 209
50 9
Sch 1
para 21 9
Sch 2 216
Family Law (Scotland) Act
  1985 ....5, 120, 121
s 1(1) 48
  (c), (d) 123, 170, 171,
                  172, 174
  (2) 48, 171

PAGE

Family Law (Scotland) Act 1985—
continued
s 1(2)(d) 47
  (5) 48, 143, 176
    (a) 123, 171
    (b) 171
2(1) 52, 174
  (2) 52, 174
    (a) 123
  (3) 52
  (4)(a)–(c) 173
  (5) 173
  (6) 51, 173
  (7) 51, 173
  (8) 50, 51, 173, 174
  (9) 50, 51, 174
3(1) 51
  (a) 174
  (b) 175
  (c) 173, 175
  (2) 51, 175
4 53
  (1) 48, 172
  (c) 48, 49
  (2) 172
  (3) 172
    (a) 48, 49, 54, 55, 172
    (b) 49, 51, 172
5(1) 52, 75
  (2) 48, 52, 175
6 147
  (1) 52
  (3) 147
ss 8 to 17 3
s 8(1) 123
  (a) 123, 124
  (aa) 123, 124
  (2) 126, 138, 139, 141
    (a) 126
    (b) 126, 131
9 ....126, 127, 144, 145
  (1)(a) 127, 129, 135–140,
              142, 143
    (b) 135–140, 142–144
    (c) 124, 125, 136–140
    (d) 124, 125, 139, 140,
              142–144
    (e) 125, 137, 141, 142, 144
  (2) 135, 136
10(1) 130, 131
  (2)(a), (b) 127
  (3) 127
  (4) 7, 129, 130

PAGE

Family Law (Scotland) Act 1985—
continued
s 10(5) 116, 129
    (6) 130
        (a), (b) 132
        (c) 132, 135
        (d), (e) 132
    (7) 127
    11(2) 136
    (3) 138
    (5) 141
    (6) 138, 140, 141
    (7) 135, 141
        (b) 140
    12(1)(a), (b) 123
    (2) 123
    (3) 124
    (4) 124
    13(2) 125, 138, 139, 141
    (3) 125
    (4) 125
        (b) 125
    (5) 125
    (7)(a) 125
        (b) 125, 143
    14 125
    (2)(a)–(d) 125
        (e)–(h) 126
        (j), (k) 126
    (5) 81
        (a) 126
    16 144
    (1)(a), (b) 145
    (2)(a), (b) 145
    (3) 145
    17 123
    (1) 21
    (2) 53
    18 .... 133, 146
    19 .... 146, 147
    20 147
    21 .... 174, 200
    24 60
    (1) 43
    25 .... 2, 64–68, 70, 71
    (1) 64, 68
    (2) 65
    (3) 64, 66
        (a) 64, 69
        (b) 64, 71
        (c) 64, 71
    26 .... 70, 71
    27 .... 48, 123, 137, 170

PAGE

Family Law (Scotland) Act 1985—
continued
s 27(2) 127, 129
    28(3) 145
    Sch 1
    para 11 93
Guardianship Act 1973
s 10 179
    (1) 179
    11(1)(a), (b) 198
    12(2) 198
Guardianship of Infants Act 1925
s 1 200
Health and Social Services and
    Social Security Adjudications
    Act 1984
s 7 239
Housing (Scotland) Act 1987 74
Housing (Scotland) Act 1988 74
Human Fertilisation and Embry-
    ology Act 1990 149
s 27(1) 150
    28 216
    (2) 152
    (4) 152
    (7) 152
    29 152
    34(1) 148
    Sch 4
    para 4 .... 212, 216
Hypnotism Act 1952
s 3 182
Incest and Related Offences (Scot-
    land) Act 1986
s 1 24
Land Tenure Reform (Scotland)
    Act 1974
s 8 73
Law Reform (Husband and Wife)
    Act 1962 44
Law Reform (Husband and Wife)
    (Scotland) Act 1984 .... 7, 8
s 1 43
    (1), (2) 6
    2 41
    (2) 44
    3(1), (2) 43
    4 41
    6 43
    7 43
Law Reform (Miscellaneous Pro-
    visions) Act 1970 7
s 1(1) 7
    3(2) 7

PAGE

Law Reform (Miscellaneous Provisions) (Scotland) Act 1949
s 4 . . . . 21, 158
Law Reform (Miscellaneous Provisions) (Scotland) Act 1966
s 5 213
  7 156
Law Reform (Miscellaneous Provisions) (Scotland) Act 1968 . . . 160
s 5 160
  10 . . . . 103, 109
  11 103
Sch 1 57
Law Reform (Miscellaneous Provisions) (Scotland) Act 1980
s 22 . . . . 8, 12
Law Reform (Miscellaneous Provisions) (Scotland) Act 1985
s 13(3) 80
  (5) 83
  (6)(c) 88
  (7) 89
  (8) 89
  (9)(a), (b) 97
  (10) 80
  25(1) 246
  (3) 247
  26 250
  27 214
  28 220
  29 248
Law Reform (Miscellaneous Provisions) (Scotland) Act 1990
s 61 156
  64 96
  69 45
  70 154
  (1) 156, 157
  (2) 156
  (3) 154, 155
  (4) 156
Sch 8
para 31(1) 88
  (2) 89
  34 . . . . 123, 124
Sch 9 . . . . 88, 89, 123, 124
Law Reform (Parent and Child) (Scotland) Act 1986 . . . . . . 4, 5, 178
s 1(1) . . . 157, 159, 160, 162, 196, 197
  (2) 160
  (4)(b), (c) 160
2 2
  (1) 21

PAGE

Law Reform (Parent and Child) (Scotland) Act 1986—*continued*
s 2(1)(a) 161, 165, 178
  (b) 161, 162, 165, 178, 194, 219
  (2) 21, 178
  (a), (b) 162
  (4) 178, 195
3 . . . . 2, 162, 165, 166, 183, 195, 196, 220, 250
  (1) . . . 162, 183, 187, 195, 196, 197, 200, 205, 221
  (2) . . . 162, 178, 184, 185, 200, 201, 205, 206, 208, 210
  (3) 166
4(1), (2) 165
5 . . . . 151, 152, 155, 157, 159, 161, 171
  (1) 20, 28, 155
  (a) 150, 151
  (b) 151, 161
  (2) 20, 28, 151
  (3) 152
  (4) 151, 159
6(1), (2) 154
  (3) 155, 156
  (4) 156
7 174
  (2) 152
  (3) 152
  (4) 137
8 . . . . . . 165, 178, 180, 185, 194–196
9(1)(a) 162
  (c) 161
  (d) 161
  10(1) 160
Sch 1 160
para 2 198
  7 160
  (2) 56
  8 151
  9 249
  10 160
  14 196
  15 . . . . 160, 169
  17 24
  18 160
  (1) 221
  (4) 196, 220
  21 170
Sch 2 . . . . 57, 58, 179, 196, 216

PAGE

Legitimation (Scotland) Act 1968 . . 158, 162
s 1 158
  (1) 159
  4 159
  8(1) 159
Licensing (Scotland) Act 1976
  s 68 182
Marriage Act 1977
  s 1 170
Marriage (Prohibited Degrees of Relationship) Act 1986 25
  Sch 2
  para 2(b) 24, 25
    (c) 24
Marriage (Scotland) Act 1856 15
Marriage (Scotland) Act 1939 15
  s 5 ....14, 15, 16
Marriage (Scotland) Act 1977 ....8, 25, 160
  s 1 170
  (1) 21
  (2) 22
  (3) 29
  2(1) 22
    (1A) 24
    (1B) 25
    (2)(a) 24
    (3) 22
    (a), (b) 22
    (5) 24
  3(1) 8
    (a) 9
    (b) 9
    (5) 9
    (b) 9
  4 9
  5(1) 9
    (2)(a) 9
    (b) 10
    (3) 10
    (4) 9
  6(3) 10
    (4)(a), (b) 10
    (5) 11
  8(1) 11
  9 ....11, 12
  12 12
  13 30
    (1) 12
  15(2) 12
  18(3), (4) 11
  19(1) 10

PAGE

Marriage (Scotland) Act 1977—continued
  s 19(2) 11
  21 18
  23A 12, 13, 20
  24 13
  Sch 1 23
  para 1 23
    2 ....23, 24
    2A 23, 24
    3 23
Married Women's Policies of Assurance (Scotland) Act 1880 71
  s 2 72
Married Women's Policies of Assurance (Scotland) (Amendment) Act 1980 72
Married Women's Property Act 1964 70
Married Women's Property (Scotland) Act 1881 60
  s 1(1) 60
Married Women's Property (Scotland) Act 1920
  s 1 ....43, 60
  3(2) 53
  4 47
  5 62
Matrimonial Causes Act 1973 100
  s 1 100
    (2)(b) 108
    (6) 113
  5 116
  6 101
  12(b) 37
    (c) 31
    (f) 32
  52(1) 171
Matrimonial Homes (Family Protection) (Scotland) Act 1981 ...66, 74, 79, 129
  s 1(1) 79, 80
    (1A) 80
    (5), (6) 87
  2 81
    (1) 81, 126
    (2) 81, 126
    (4)(a), (b) 90
    (5)(a) 68, 126
    (b) 68
    (6) 90
    (8) 93
    (9) 126

PAGE

Matrimonial Homes (Family Protection) (Scotland) Act 1981—
continued

s 3 .... 81, 92, 95, 97
  (1) 67
  (2) 67, 68, 69
  (3) 67, 69, 81, 82, 84, 85,
                          88, 91, 93
  (4) 67, 82
  (7) 82, 89
4 .... 82, 83, 86, 92, 95, 96, 97
  (1) 83
  (2) 82, 83, 84
  (3) 83
    (a), (b) 82
  (4) 96
    (a) 95
  (5) 96
    (a) 95
  (6) 82
  (7) 90, 95
6(1)(a), (b) 86
  (2)(a), (b) 86
  (3)(a)(i), (ii) 87
    (c) 88, 89
    (d) 88
    (e) 88, 89
    (f) 88
7 .... 89, 91
  (1), (2) 87
  (3) 88
8(1), (2) 89
9(1) 90
    (a) 92
13 .... 97, 124
  (1) 92, 93
  (2) 93
  (7)–(9) 93
14 .... 83, 94
  (1) 94
    (b) 88
  (2) 94
    (a) 94, 96
    (b) 95, 96
15(1)(a), (b) 96
  (2)–(4) 96
  (3) 96
18(1) 96, 97
  (2), (3) 97
  (6) 97
19 .... 91, 92
  (a), (b) 91
22 .... 64, 67, 68, 80

PAGE

Matrimonial Proceedings (Children) Act 1958
s 8 199
  (1), (2) 199
9 .... 198, 200
  (1) 174
10 200
11 199
12 200
Parent and Child (Scotland) Act 1986
s 3 189
Perjury Act 1911 136
Presumption of Death (Scotland) Act 1977 29
s 1(1) 29
  3(1) 29
  (3) 29
  4(5) 30
Prohibition of Female Circumcision Act 1985 190
Registration of Births, Deaths and Marriages (Scotland) Act 1965
s 28A(5) 9
Rent (Scotland) Act 1984 .... 74, 93
Road Traffic Act 1972
s 4(1) 182
School Boards (Scotland) Act 1988 .. 186
Sexual Offences (Scotland) Act 1976
s 2B 24
ss 3–5 182
s 7 244
Sheriff Courts (Scotland) Act 1907
s 5(2) 195
  (2C) 196
Sch 1 (Ordinary Cause Rules)
r 132F 200
Social Security Act 1986 55
s 20(11) 46, 54
  26(3) 54, 175
Social Work (Scotland) Act 1968 .... 4, 177, 185
s 12 231
  (2)(a), (b) 231
  15 .... 231–236, 240
  (1)–(3) 231
  (3A) 232
  (8) 231
  16 .... 232–238, 251
  (1)(a) 232
    (i) 234
    (ii) 234, 237

PAGE

Social Work (Scotland) Act 1968—
continued
s 16(1)(iii) 235
    (iv) 236
    (2) 234
        (a), (b) 234
        (c) 234, 235
        (e) 224, 235
    (3) 237
    (5) 236
    (6)–(8) 236
    (12) 234
17(3) 235
    (6), (7) 238
    (8) 232, 238
17A 251
    (1), (2) 239
    (4) 239
17B 239, 251
17C–17E 239
18(1), (2) 239
    (3) 240
18A 237, 239, 240
20 .... 231, 250
    (1) 238
20A 231, 238, 250
30(1)(a) 240, 243
    (2) 249
32(2) 243, 245
33(1) 242
34(1), (2) 242
34A 249
36(1) 242
    (5) 242
37(1) 241
    (1A) 241
    (2) 240
    (3)(c) 241
    (4) 241
    (5) 241
    (5A), (5B) 241
39(1)–(3) 242
40(1)–(9) 246
41(1) 246
    (2) 246
42(2)(a) 246
    (c) 246
    (3) 246, 247
    (4) 246

PAGE

Social Work (Scotland) Act 1986—
continued
s 42(5) 247
    (6) 247
    (6A) 247
    (7) 246
43 246
    (1) 247, 248
    (2) 248
    (3) 247
44(1) 248
    (5) 250
47(1) 248
    (2) 248
48(2), (3) 248
    (4) 248
        (a)–(c) 248
    (4A) 248
49(1) 248
    (5) 249
50(1) 249
    (3) 249
51(2) 249
58A 250
    (3) 250
ss 58B to 58G 250
s 94(1) 241, 249
Sch 8 200
para 43 199
Sch 9 200
Succession (Scotland) Act 1964 56,
                               160, 213
s 2 58
  5 58
  8(1) 57
  9 57
    (3) 58
  13 57
  20(5) 54
  23(1) 213
  24 54
ss 25 to 27 3
s 28 169
  36(1) 57, 58
Tattooing of Minors Act 1969
s 1 182
**Tenant's Rights Etc (Scotland) Act
    1980** 69
Wills (Soldiers and Sailors) Act 1918
s 3(2) 169

List of cases

PAGE

A v B (1987) 217, 224, 227
A v B and C (1971) 219, 226, 227
A v Children's Hearing for Tayside
  Region (1987) 214
A v G (1984) 151
A v N (1973) 205
A and B v C (1977) 224
A and B v C (1987) 219
AB v CB (1959) 108
AB v CB (1961) 39
AB v CD (1957) 22
AB Petr (1988) 195
Abernethy v Abernethy (1988) 204
Abrahams v Abrahams (1989) 175
Adam v Adam (1962) 76
Advocate, HM v Duffy (1983) 42
Advocate, HM v Paxton (1985) 42
Aitken v Aitken (1978) 250, 251
Akram v Akram (1979) 34, 35, 36
Allardyce v Allardyce (1954) 39
Allardyce v Johnstone (1979) 154
Amphtill Peerage, The (1977) 156
Andrews v Andrews (1971) 103
Annan v Annan (1948) 105
Atkinson v Atkinson (1988) 125

B v Harris (1990) 186, 244
B v Kennedy (1987) 243
B (minor), Re (1981) 189
B (minor), Re (1988) 189
Ballantyne v Douglas (1953) 159
Barbour v Barbour (1990) 84
Barclay's Bank v McGreish (1983) . . . 78
Baxter v Baxter (1947) 37
Beagley v Beagley (1984) 237, 238,
                             239, 240
Beaney v Beaney (1987) 200
Bell v Bell (1983) 82, 83, 84
Bell v Bell (1988) 125, 142
Bell v Bell (unreported) 174
Berry v Berry (1988) 91, 92
Berry v Berry (No 2) (1989) 91
Beveridge v Beveridge (1925) 62

PAGE

Blance v Blance (1978) 199, 206
Borders Regional Council v M
  (1986) 250
Borland v Borland (1990) 205
Boyd v Boyd (1978) 115
Boyle v Boyle (1977) 114
Boyle v Woodypoint Caravans
  (1970) 166
Bradley v Bradley (1973) 109
Bradley v Bradley (1987) 198
Brannigan v Brannigan (1979) 206
Briandon v Occidental Petroleum
  (Caledonia) Ltd (1990) 165
Britton v Britton (1973) 109
Britton v Central Regional Council
  (1986) 201
Brooks v Brooks (1990) 206
Brown v Brown (1985) . . . 82, 83, 84, 85
Brown v Ferguson (1990) 45
Buckland v Buckland (1965) 33
Buczynska v Buczynski (1989): 127, 129
Burke v Burke (1983) 28

C v C (1989) 211
C v Kennedy (1987) 249
C v S (1988) 149
C v S (1990) 211
CB v AB (1885) 38
C (minor), Re (1990) 189
Campbell v Campbell (1866): 16, 17, 18
Campbell v Campbell (1973) 109
Campbell v Cosans (1982) 185, 186
Campbell v Grossart (1988) 152
Campins v Campins (1979) 201, 209
Campins Coll (1989) 210
Canlon v O'Dowd (1987) 152
Carlyon v Carlyon (1987) 199, 204
Carpenter v Carpenter (1990) 134
Carroll v Carroll (1988) 136
Cato v Pearson (1990) 249
Central Regional Council v B
  (1985) 224, 225, 233, 235, 236,
                             237, 251

PAGE

Chalkley v Chalkley (1984) 120
Cheetham v Glasgow Corpn (1972): 183,
        200, 237
Clark v Clark (1978) 121
Clark v Clark (1987) 201, 203, 204
Clarke v Hatten (1987) 97
Clement v Clement (1987) 206
Colagiacomo v Colagiacomo (1983):   83
Coles v Homer and Tulloh (1895) .. 159
Collins v Collins (1989) 146
Cooper v Cooper (1987) 205
Cooper v Cooper (1989) 134
Corbett v Corbett (1970) 26, 27
Cosh v Cosh (1979) 193, 199, 206
Cossey v UK (1990) 27
Cowie v Cowie (1977) 121
Cowie v Tudhope (1987) 186
Crow v Crow (1986) 92
Crowley v Armstrong (1990) 206
Currie v Currie (1950) 153

D (infant), Re (1977) 227
D (minor), Re (1976) 188
D (minors), Re (1973) 224
D v Kennedy (1988) 245
D v Sinclair (1973) 249
D v Strathclyde Regional Council
        (1985) 250, 251
Denheen v British Railways Board
        (1986) 45
Denvir v Denvir (1969) 77
Dever v Dever (1988) 140
Dickson v Dickson (1982) 91
Docherty v McGlynn (1983) .. 154, 155,
        156, 157, 182, 190
Docherty v McGlynn (1985) ... 152, 157
Donaldson v Donaldson (1988): 53, 175
Donnelly v Donnelly (1959) 47
Dumfries and Galloway Regional
        Council v M (1990) 236
Dunbar v Dunbar (1977) 144
Dunn v Dunn's Trustees (1930) 15

E (minor), Re (1989) 211
Early v Early (1989) 204
Early v Early (1990) 201, 202
Edgar v Lord Advocate (1965) 45
Edmond v Edmond (1971) 111

PAGE

Elder v Elder (1985) 144
Elder's Trustees v Elder (1894) 149

F (Re) (1989) 189
F (R) (infant), Re (1969) 223
F v F (1945) 38
F v Kennedy (1988) 244
Ferguson v P (1989) 241, 247
Fergusson v Fergusson (1977) 121
Findlay v Findlay (1988) 109
Finlayson (Applicant) (1989) .. 189, 244
Finnie v Finnie (1984) 164
Firth v Firth (1990) 49
Ford v Stier (1896) 31
Forsyth's Curator Bonis v Govan
        Shipbuilders (1988) 45
Fowler v Fowler (1981) 199
Fraser v Fraser (1976) 136
Fullarton v Fullarton (1976) 107
Fuller v Fuller (1973) 114
Fyfe v Fyfe (1987) 87

G v H (1976) 200
Gallacher v Gallacher (1928) 103
Gallacher v Gallacher (1934) 104
Gardner v Gardner (1876) 151, 158
Geddes v Geddes (1987) 204
Gillick v West Norfolk and Wisbech
        Area Health Authority (1985) ... 191,
        192
Girvan v Girvan (1988) 184
Gold v Hume (1950) 7
Grant v Grant (1974) 107
Gray v Gray (1979) 121
Gribben v Gribben (1976) 94

H (minor), Re (1982) 228
H v H (1953) 33
H v H (1968) 108
H and H v Petitioners (1976) 224
Hall v Hall (1987) 91
Hampsey v Hampsey (1988) 84
Hannah v Hannah (1971) 202, 203
Hannah v Hannah (1988) 52, 175
Hardie v Sneddon (1917) 169
Harper v Adair (1945) 63
Harris v E (1989) 244
Harvey v Harvey (1860) 180, 181
Hastie v Hastie (1985) 108, 204
Hastie v Magistrates of Edinburgh
        (1907) 169

PAGE

Hastings v Hastings (1941) 107, 111
Hay's Trustee v Hay's Trustees
  (1951) 78
Henry v Henry (1972) 49, 55
Higgins v Higgins (1989) 204
Hill v Hill (1990) 202, 211
Hirani v Hirani (1982) 33
Hogg v Gow (1812) 6
Horak v Lord Advocate (1984) 30
Howarth v Howarth (1990) 170
Huggins v Huggins (1981) 174
Hume v Hume (1926) 201
Humphrey v Humphrey (1988) 142
Humphries v S (1986) 241

Imre v Mitchell (1958) 151, 154,
                               155, 165
Inglis v Inglis and Mathew (1987) .. 170,
                                    172

J v C (1969) 183, 184, 186, 200, 201
J v J (1978) 37
J F v McGregor (1981) 246
Jack v Jack (1962) 47
James v McLennan (1971) 151, 158
Jamieson v M'Leod (1880) 62
John's Assignment Trusts, Re,
  Niven v Niven (1970) 71
Johnson v Francis (1982) 205
Johnstone v Brown (1823) 31
Johnstone v Johnstone (1990): 141, 143
Jordan v Jordan (1983) 204
Jowett v Jowett (1990) 171, 173

KD (minor), Re (1988) 185
Keeney v Strathclyde Regional
  Council (1986) 186
Kennedy v A (1986) 243, 249
Kennedy v B (1973) 243, 247
Kennedy v H (1988) 249
Kennedy v M (1989) 249
Kennedy v S (1986) 243
Kennedy v Weir (1665) 167
Kerr v Martin (1840) 158
Kerrigan v Kerrigan (1988) 133
Kilgour v Kilgour (1987) 211
Kirkwood v Kirkwood (1970) 171
Kyte v Kyte (1987) 50

L v Central Regional Council
  (1990) 222, 224–226

PAGE

L v L (1931) 36, 39
Lambert v Lambert (1982) 48, 120
Lang v Lang (1921) 32
Latter v Latter (1990) 127, 129, 131, 133
Lennie v Lennie (1950) 110
Lewisham LBC v Lewisham Juv-
  enile Court Justices (1979): . 232, 233
Little v Little (1990) 123, 124, 125,
                  127, 129, 130, 134, 136
Livingstone-Stallard v Livingstone-
  Stallard (1974) 108
Long v Long (1950) 30
Longmuir v Longmuir (1985) 88
Lothian Regional Council v H
  (1982) 237
Lothian Regional Council v R
  (1988) 227
Lothian Regional Council v S
  (1986) 251
Lothian Regional Council v T
  (1984) 234
Low v Gorman (1970) 17

M v W or M (1966) 37
M v Lothian Regional Council
  (1989) 195
M v Lothian Regional Council
  (1990) 250
M v McGregor (1982) 244
M (minor), Re (1987) 217
McAlinden v Bearsden and Miln-
  gavie District Council (1986) 97
McAuley v McAuley (1968) 49
McCabe v Goodall (1989) 205
McCafferty v McCafferty (1986) . 84, 85
McCarrol v McCarrol (1966) 49
McCash v Toal (1990) 205
M'Clements v M'Clements (1958): . 187,
                                    202
McCluskey v Gardiner (1988) 203
McCormack v McCormack (1987) .. 137
McCrae v McCrae (1988) 146
McDevitt v McDevitt (1988) 204
Macdonald v Macdonald (1863) 15
M'Donald v M'Donald (1875) 51
McDonald v McDonald (1953) .. 61, 62
McEachan v Young (1988) 206
M'Feetridge v Stewarts & Lloyds
  Ltd (1913) 167, 168
McGeachie v McGeachie (1989) 53

PAGE

McGowan v McGowan (1986) 93
McGregor v H (1983) 244
McGregor v L (1981) 243
MacInnes v MacInnes (1990) 53
MacIntyre v MacIntyre (1962) 199
Mackay v Mackay (1957) 188, 202
McKay v McKay (1980) 174
McKechnie v McKechnie (1990) ... 208
Mackenzie v Hendry (1984) 208
Mackenzie v Scott (1980) 17
McKeown v McKeown (1988) 126
McKinnell v White (1971) 169
Maclean v Maclean (1976) 146
Maclellan v Maclellan (1988) 129
McLennan v McLennan (1958) 102
M'Leod v Adams (1920) 31, 35
McLeod v Cedar Holdings Ltd
   (1989) 78
MacLeod v MacLeod (1990) 108
MacLure v MacLure (1911) 79, 93
Macmillan v Macmillan (1989) 211
McNaught v McNaught (1955): 187, 202
Macpherson v Macpherson (1989) .. 146
McRobbie v McRobbie (1983) 80
Mahmud v Mahmud (1977) 34
Mann v Glending (1990) 206
Marckx v Belgium (1979) 159
Marshall v Lyall and Marshall
   (1859) 76
Mason v Mason (1980) 109
Mason v Mason (1987) 199
Mather v Mather (1987) 85
Matheson v Matheson (1986) 84
Matheson v Matheson (1988) ... 52, 175
Meikle v Meikle (1987) 108
Michlek v Michlek (1971) 95
Middleton v Middleton (1987) 205
Millar v Millar (1940) 79
Mills v Mills (1989) 145
Mitchell v Gartshore (1976) 45, 47
Monkman v Monkman (1988) 139
Montgomery v Lockwood (1987) ... 206
Mooney v Mooney (1987) 199, 204
Morris v Morris (1987) 18
Morrison v Monoghan (1969) 137
Morrison v Morrison (1989) ... 134, 139
Muhammad v Robertson or Kettle
   or Muhammad (1972) 29
Muir v Muir (1989) .. 129, 134, 136, 140
Mulhern v Mulhern (1987) 132
Munro v Munro (1986) 49
Murdoch v Murdoch (1973) 94, 95

PAGE

N v C (1933) 15
Naismith v Naismith (1987) 205
National Assistance Board v Wil-
   kinson (1952) 54
Neill v Neill (1987) 52
Nelson v Nelson (1988) 81
Newton v Newton (1923) 77
Newton v Newton (1925) 77
Nicol v Bell (1954) 17
Nixon v Nixon (1987) 52, 175
Nolan v Lindsay (1990) 195
Nolan v Nolan (1979) 116

O v Central Regional Council
   (1987) 227
O'Donnell v Brownieside Coal Co
   (1934) 167
Oliver v Oliver (1988) 84
O'Neil v O'Neil (1987) 80, 88
O'Neill v O'Neill (1975) 108
Orlandi v Castelli (1961) 34

P (infant), Re (1977) 222, 226
P (minor), Re (1982) 192
P v Lothian Regional Council
   (1989) 215, 222, 226
P (R) v P (P) sub nom P v P (1969) ... 171
Paton v Trustees of BPAS (1978) .. 149
Paton v UK (1980) 149
Patrick v William Baird & Co
   (1926) 168
Peebles v MacPhail (1990) 186
Perrett's Trustees v Perrett (1909) ... 78
Petrie v Petrie (1911) 17
Petrie v Petrie (1988) 133, 134, 136
Phillip v Phillip (1988) 136
Phillips v Grampian Health Board
   (1989) 44
Polland v Sturrock's Exors (1952) .. 175
Porchetta v Porchetta (1986) 184,
                               205, 206
Preston v Preston (1950) 63, 70
Preston-Jones v Preston-Jones
   (1951) 153
Price v Watson (1951) 90
Puddini v Puddinu (1987) 205
Pugh v Pugh (1951) 22
Purves' Trustees v Purves (1896) ... 158
Pyatt v Pyatt (1966) 71

R v Children's Hearing for the Borders Region (1984) 214

PAGE

R v Lothian Regional Council (1987) ...227
Raeburn v Raeburn (1990) ...84
Rees v UK (1987) ...27
Reiterbund v Reiterbund (1975) ...116
Robertson v Henderson & Sons Ltd (1905) ...167
Robertson v Robertson (1990) ...204
Robertson v Turnbull (1982) ...45
Rukat v Rukat (1975) ...116
Russell v Russell (1977) ...120
Russell v Woods (1987) ...160

S v HM Advocate (1989) ...42
S v Kennedy (1987) ...244
S v S (1967) ...195
S v S (1970) ...154, 156, 190
S v S (1977) ...151
S (minor), Re (1987) ...217
Saleh v Saleh (1987) ...13
Salman's Trustee v Salman (1989) ...86
Sandison's Exrx v Sandison (1984) ...125
Sands v Sands (1964) ...102
Santos v Santos (1972) ...113
Savage v M'Allister (1952) ...7
Scott v Sebright (1886) ...33
Scott's Trustee v Scott (1887) ...166
Scrimgeour v Scrimgeour (1988) ...91
Scully v Scully (1989) ...170
Secretary of State for Social Services v McMillan (1987) ...54
Shaw v Henderson (1982) ...17, 18
Silver v Silver (1955) ...33
Sinclair v Sinclair (1987) ...204, 208, 209
Singh v Singh (1971) ...33
Singh v Singh (1988) ...117
Sloss v Taylor (1989) ...206
Smith v Smith (1933) ...69, 70
Smith v Smith (1983) ...82, 83, 84
Smith v Smith (1988) ...146, 204
Smith v Smith's Trustees (1884) ...62
Snow v Snow (1972) ...171
Speirs v Peat (1988) ...207
Sproat v McGibney (1968) ...154
Steele v Caldwell (1979) ...78
Stein v Stein (1914) ...32
Stevenson v Adair (1872) ...167
Stewart v Stewart (1959) ...41
Stewart v Stewart (1987) ...108
Stewart v Thain (1981) ...180, 186

PAGE

Strathclyde Regional Council v M (1982) ...236
Syme v Cunningham (1973) ...195

Tattersall v Tattersall (1983) ...93, 95
Tayside Regional Council v Thaw (1987) ...238
Temple v Mitchell (1956) ...93
Terry v Murray (1947) ...52
Thirde v Thirde (1987) ...125
Thomson v Thomson (1908) ...104
Thomson v Thomson (1982) ...144
Thomson v Thomson (1990) ...135
Thurlow v Thurlow (1975) ...107, 108
Torrie v Turner (1990) ...154, 155, 156
Traill v Traill (1925) ...62
Tymoszczuk v Tymoszczuk (1964) ...71
Tyrrell v Tyrrell (1990) ...129, 136, 140

Valier v Valier (1925) ...31
Viola v Viola (1988) ...211

W (infant), Re (1971) ...225, 228
W (minor), In re (1985) ...228
W v A (1981) ...193
W v Glasgow Corpn (1974) ...250
WY v AY (1946) ...38
Walker v Walker (1911) ...106
Walker v Walker (1990) ...124
Wallace v Fife Coal Co Ltd (1909) ...17
Ward v Ward (1983) ...82, 83
Watson v Nikolaisen (1955) ...224, 234
Weissenbruch v Weissenbruch (1961) ...75
Welsh v Welsh (1987) ...81
Wemyss v Creditors (1637) ...167
White v White (1966) ...109
Whitecross v Whitecross (1977) ...203
Whitehall v Whitehall (1958) ...155
Whyte v Hardie (1990) ...195
Wilkinson v Wilkinson (1943) ...111
Williams v Williams (1964) ...108
Wilson v Wilson (1987) ...145, 173
Winton v Winton (1987) ...205
Wood v Wood (1935) ...149, 168

X-Petitioner (1957) ...26

Young v Rankin (1934) ...149, 168

Introduction

In this short introduction, it is proposed to explain the selection of subjects chosen for extended treatment and to discuss the policies underlying some of the most important features of contemporary family law.

Since the end of the eighteenth century, the nuclear family has become the essential family unit in Scotland.[1] This comprises a man and a woman who have a sexual relationship and their children. Before their relationship can give rise to mutual legal rights and obligations, as a general rule, the couple have to marry. More importantly, it is only when a couple have been married that the law regulates their income and capital when their relationship breaks down, in the form of financial provision on divorce. Similarly, a spouse, but not a cohabitee, has important legal rights in respect of succession to a proportion of the deceased spouse's estate.[2]

In spite of evidence that a considerable number of couples are now living in stable sexual relationships outside marriage,[3] the vast majority of couples eventually marry. Accordingly, the law of husband and wife remains of fundamental importance. Scots law, however, has begun to recognise that non-married couples (cohabitees) face similar problems to married couples, especially when their relationships break down. While there has been no attempt to create a legal status of cohabitee, the legislature has provided cohabitees with certain rights in relation to particular matters, for example, the occupation of the home in which the cohabitees are, or have been, living.[4]

While marriage retains its fundamental importance in Scots family law, it should be noted that it is of very little legal significance for the spouses *during* the marriage. Until the later years of the nineteenth

---

1 Before that time the extended family in the form of clans was important, at least in the Highlands of Scotland.
2 On the spouses' rights to succession, see *infra* Ch 3.
3 Statistical information on this subject is notoriously inexact, but approximately 14% of couples who live together are unmarried. For statistical data, see *The Effects of Cohabitation in Private Law* SLC Discussion Paper No 86, para 1.3.
4 See *infra* Ch 5. For further proposals for reform of the law in relation to cohabitees, see generally *The Effects of Cohabitation in Private Law* SLC Discussion Paper No 86.

1

century, a woman lost many important rights on marriage, for example, in relation to her property. Since then, the law has endeavoured to achieve legal equality between the spouses by enacting that for various purposes, for example, contract, delict and property, the spouses should be treated as though they were unmarried.[1] But while legal equality may have been achieved, the application of rules which ignore the fact that the persons concerned are married, leads, particularly in relation to property matters, to results which are both artificial and unjust. Consequently, recent reforms have introduced special rules for spouses which take into account the fact that they are married.[2]

Of course, marriage does continue to give rise to rights and obligations for the spouses. Spouses, but not cohabitees, owe a duty to aliment (ie maintain) each other during the marriage.[3] Moreover, when parents are married at the date of a child's conception or subsequently, the father will automatically have parental rights in relation to the child:[4] if the couple never marry, only the child's mother will have parental rights unless and until the father obtains parental rights under s 3 of the Law Reform (Parent and Child) (Scotland) Act 1986. But the most important legal consequence of marriage is that a court can award financial provision for the spouses if the marriage ends in divorce.[5]

Judicial divorce has been possible in Scots law since the Reformation in 1560, but divorce was not a prevalent feature of Scottish society until this century. The reasons for this are complex. While the grounds for divorce were restricted to the defender's adultery or desertion until the Divorce (Scotland) Act 1938, religious disapproval of divorce must also have acted as a considerable restraint. As a result of the increasing secularisation of Scottish society in the twentieth century, the social upheavals of two world wars and the emphasis on personal fulfilment in sexual relationships, divorce has become an accepted part of contemporary Scottish society. The law has responded to the demand for easier divorce with the introduction of a system based, theoretically at least, on the non-fault principle of irretrievable breakdown of marriage.[6] It is estimated that in Scotland at least one in four marriages now end in divorce. As a divorced person

1 On contract and delict, see *infra* Ch 3: on property, see *infra* Chs 4 and 5.
2 See, for example, s 25 of the Family Law (Scotland) Act 1985: discussed *infra* Ch 4.
3 On aliment, see *infra* Ch 3.
4 Section 2 of the Law Reform (Parent and Child) (Scotland) Act 1986: discussed *infra* Ch 9.
5 On financial division on divorce, see *infra* Ch 7.
6 Divorce is discussed *infra* Ch 6.

will often enter a second marriage, it is not too cynical to suggest that we now live in a society where serial polygamy is common.

Given this high incidence of divorce, it is crucial that the law provides a system of financial provision which will enable the income and capital of the spouses to be redistributed in a fair manner after divorce. Until 1964, divorce was treated as judicial death: financial provision took the form of treating the defender as though dead and awarding the pursuer the legal rights to which a spouse would have been entitled from the defender's estate. That system was replaced[1] by one which gave the judge who was hearing the claim discretion to make financial provision which appeared just in the circumstances. Any advantages of flexibility which this system may have had were outweighed by the uncertainty that ensued. A much more sophisticated system has been introduced which provides a set of principles to be used in determining the financial provision which should be awarded in the circumstances of a particular marriage.[2] This gives greater certainty on the outcome of possible litigation and so enables spouses and their legal advisers to negotiate a settlement without recourse to the courts.

The current divorce law can be criticised on the ground of its complexity which inhibits the parties from being able to end their marriage with the minimum of legal intervention. On the other hand, the reform of the law on financial provision should, because of the increase in certainty as to the outcome of litigation, enable the parties or their legal advisers to reach a settlement more frequently than in the past. It is generally accepted that modern family law should encourage spouses to settle the property and other issues which arise when their marriage breaks down without recourse to litigation, thereby saving scarce legal aid resources. Scots law, at present, only does this to a limited extent and it is the present writer's view that the grounds of divorce should be further simplified and that more support should be given to conciliation services to help spouses reach agreement on such issues as property, financial provision and custody of children.[3]

While marriage continues to remain a condition for the legal regulation of the relationship between a man and a woman who are living together, Scots law has always recognised that parents owe duties towards their children, albeit that the parents have never married.

---

1 Part V of the Succession (Scotland) Act 1964; later replaced by s 5 of the Divorce (Scotland) Act 1976.

2 Sections 8–17 of the Family Law (Scotland) Act 1985, discussed *infra* Ch 7.

3 The Scottish Law Commission has recommended further simplification of the grounds of divorce: see *Report on the Reform of the Ground of Divorce* (SLC No 116). At the time of writing, these reforms have not been enacted. For discussion of the proposals, see *infra* p 119.

However, the extent of a child's rights which were exigible from his or her parents – and remoter relatives – depended for centuries upon whether or not the child was legitimate. A child is legitimate if he or she was conceived or born during the parents' marriage. During this century, piecemeal reforms have alleviated the legal position of the illegitimate child but as a result of the Law Reform (Parent and Child) (Scotland) Act 1986,[1] the legal position of an illegitimate child has, for all but a few minor purposes, been equated with that of a legitimate child. But since an illegitimate child is more likely to be a member of a one-parent family than a legitimate child, he or she will more often suffer social disadvantages stemming from impoverished economic circumstances.

While parents owe obligations towards their children, for example, the duty of aliment, they enjoy important rights in respect of the care and upbringing of their child. The nature and extent of these parental rights is one of the most controversial aspects of modern family law – in particular, the question of when these rights cease and children can assert their liberty to make their own decisions on such important matters as contraception or medical treatment. There are not many modern Scottish decisions which are in point and the approach taken by the present writer must be used with caution.[2]

Given the prevalence of divorce, the custody of the children is an important issue for modern family law. Scots law has adopted the welfare principle as the criterion for the determination of custody disputes.[3] In practice, however, the courts are reluctant to disturb the custody arrangements which have *de facto* been operative prior to the divorce, thus preserving the *status quo ante*: this is generally thought to be in the best interests of the child. Thus the law of custody merely underpins the self-regulation by the parents themselves of the custody of their children. Since in the vast majority of cases the mother will have *de facto* custody of any children when the marriage breaks down, the preservation of the *status quo* which is currently endorsed by the courts when applying the welfare principle, reinforces the traditional view that the care of a child is primarily the responsibility of the mother.

In a modern society, the state has a crucial role in relation to the care of children who are at risk when their families have become dysfunctional. State agencies have certain powers and duties to intervene in

1 The 1986 Act is discussed in detail, *infra* Chs 8 and 9.
2 See *infra* Ch 10.
3 See *infra* Ch 11.

this situation.[1] There is also a system of children's hearings introduced by the Social Work (Scotland) Act 1968 which is remarkable because the hearings are concerned not only with care proceedings but also with juvenile offenders. The danger of a welfare-based system is, of course, that a parent's prima facie right to bring up a child and the child's prima facie right to be brought up in his or her family environment may be given insufficient weight when it is thought that the removal of the child from the family is desirable for the child's welfare. A delicate balance has therefore to be found and procedural safeguards must exist so that the rights of parents and children to each other are given proper consideration in care proceedings.

One of the most remarkable features of contemporary Scottish family law is that much of the law is of very recent origin. The last few years have, for example, seen the full scale reform of financial provision on divorce[2] and illegitimacy.[3] These reforms are the result of the work of the Scottish Law Commission which is largely responsible for having provided Scotland with a system of family law which is capable of meeting the needs of contemporary Scottish society.

The Scottish Law Commission is now considering proposals for the codification of Scottish Family Law.[4] But family law cannot be a panacea for all the social ills which currently face families in Scotland. In particular, the financial needs of one-parent families cannot be met by a system of private law. Only when sufficient resources are made available to introduce a non-means tested benefit for one-parent families as recommended by the Finer Commission,[5] will there be any marked improvement in the lot of those families whose poverty arises inter alia from matrimonial breakdown.

1 See *infra* Ch 13.
2 By the Family Law (Scotland) Act 1985: discussed *infra* Ch 7.
3 By the Law Reform (Parent and Child) (Scotland) Act 1986: discussed *infra* Chs 8 and 9.
4 This is taking the form of a series of discussion papers: see *Family Law: Preconsolidation Reforms* SLC Discussion Paper No 85; *The Effects of Cohabitation in Private Law* SLC Discussion Paper No 86. The proposals for reform are discussed *infra* in the context of the current substantive law. *Parental Responsibilities and Rights, Guardianship and the Administration of Children's Property* SLC Discussion Paper No 88 was published too late for discussion in this edition.
5 *Report of the Committee on One-Parent Families* (Cmnd 5629) (1974). See Hoggett and Pearl *The Family, Law and Society* (2nd edn, 1987) Ch 4.

1 Getting married

ENGAGEMENTS

It is customary for a couple to become engaged for a period before they marry. At common law, an engagement was a contract and wrongful failure to implement the promise to marry gave rise to an action in damages.[1] These damages included not only compensation for pecuniary loss arising from the breach, for example, the cost of preparations for the wedding, but also for *solatium* to compensate the innocent party's injured feelings and wounded pride.[2] The Scottish Law Commission took the view that actions for breach of promise had become anachronistic in the late twentieth century and recommended abolition.[3]

By s 1(1) of the Law Reform (Husband and Wife) (Scotland) Act 1984, it is declared that:

> 'No promise of marriage or agreement between two persons to marry one another shall have effect under the law of Scotland to create any rights or obligations; and no action for breach of any such promise or agreement may be brought in any court in Scotland, whatever the law applicable to the promise or agreement.'[4]

The extent of this provision is wide. First, an engagement is no longer a legally enforceable contract. Therefore any contractual remedies for breach of promise are no longer competent in Scottish courts.[5] Second, by stipulating that a promise or agreement to marry does not create any rights or obligations in Scots law, it would appear that the section excludes any delictual liability which might arise from a breach of promise. For example, if a man deliberately lied when he promised to

---

1 For full discussion of the common law on engagements, see *Clive* p 198.
2 *Hogg v Gow* May 27, 1812 F C.
3 Report of the Scottish Law Commission on *Outdated Rules in the law of Husband and Wife* (1983) SLC No 76.
4 By s 1(2) the provision is expressly made retrospective but it does not affect any action commenced before the Act came into force.
5 This is so, whatever the proper law of the promise or agreement.

marry a woman, she would appear to have no right to sue him in delict on the ground of his fraudulent misrepresentation.[1] Thus, unlike the parallel English legislation,[2] which only prevents agreements to marry operating as contracts, the Law Reform (Husband and Wife) (Scotland) Act 1984 prohibits delictual as well as contractual remedies.

The 1984 Act does not address itself to any of the property issues which can arise between engaged couples. Where the marriage does not take place, any property dispute, for example, over the ownership of a house which was bought with a view to marriage, will be governed by the general principles of the law of property. Where the couple do marry, however, any property acquired during the engagement for use as a family home, or to be used in the home, will be regarded as matrimonial property for the purpose of financial provision on divorce.[3]

There are no special property rules in relation to gifts between engaged couples. If the gift is intended to be outright, for example, a birthday present, it need not be returned if the engagement is broken off. Where a gift is made expressly or impliedly conditional[4] on the marriage taking place, it must be returned if the condition fails: and the donor may use the *condictio causa data causa non secuta*[5] to recover the property.

Unlike the position in England,[6] there are no specific provisions in respect of gifts of engagement rings. In one sheriff court case it was held that the gift of an engagement ring is made unconditionally[7] but in another,[8] it was thought that the ring was returnable if the marriage did not take place – unless the donor had unjustifiably broken off the engagement.[9] A third possibility is that the ring is given on the implied condition that it should be returned if the marriage does not take place

---

1 Similarly there would be no right to sue in negligence, if the promise was made carelessly, for example, if without taking reasonable care to discover whether he had the capacity to marry the promisee, a man gives a promise to marry which he cannot fulfil.
2 Section 1(1) of the Law Reform (Miscellaneous Provisions) Act 1970.
3 Section 10(4) of the Family Law (Scotland) Act 1985 discussed, *infra* Ch 7. Similarly, moveable property obtained in prospect of the marriage is subject to the presumption of equal shares in household goods: s 25 of the Family Law (Scotland) Act 1985, discussed *infra* Ch 4.
4 For example, the gift of family jewellery.
5 Stair I 7.7.
6 See s 3(2) of the Law Reform (Miscellaneous Provisions) Act 1970, where there is a rebuttable presumption that the gift of the ring is made unconditionally.
7 *Gold v Hume* (1950) 66 Sh Ct Rep 85.
8 *Savage v M'Allister* (1952) 68 Sh Ct Rep 11.
9 This was the English position before the 1970 Act.

for any reason. Given that engagements now give rise to no legal rights or obligations between the parties, it is thought that it would be consistent with the policy of the 1984 Act, if engagement rings were presumed to be outright gifts; but that this presumption should be able to be rebutted on proof that the gift was intended to be subject to the condition that it should be returned if the marriage did not take place.

Where a couple receive engagement presents from third parties, it is thought that these are returnable if the marriage does not take place.[1]

THE FORMALITIES OF MARRIAGE

A marriage will not be valid unless the parties have capacity to marry and the marriage conforms to the formalities required by the law of the place where the marriage is celebrated. In this section, the formal requirements of a valid marriage celebrated in Scotland are discussed. Scots law recognises two possible methods of marrying *viz* regular or formal marriages and irregular or informal marriages.

REGULAR MARRIAGES – FORMAL MARRIAGES

The law on the formalities of regular marriages was the subject of the Kilbrandon Committee's Report in 1969[2] and in the light of the Committee's recommendations, the law was radically altered and simplified by the Marriage (Scotland) Act 1977.[3]

There are two types of regular marriage in Scotland, a civil ceremony and a religious ceremony. But before either can take place, the parties must follow certain civil preliminaries.[4]

Civil preliminaries

(i)   *Marriage notices*

Each of the parties to a marriage which is intended to be solemnised in Scotland, whether it is to be a religious or civil ceremony, must submit a notice of intention to marry – a marriage notice – to the district registrar for the registration district in which the marriage is to be solemnised.[5] There is no need for either party to be resident in that

---

1 Stair I 7.7.
2 *The Marriage Law of Scotland* Cmnd 4011.
3 As amended by Law Reform (Miscellaneous Provisions) (Scotland) Act 1980, s 22. See generally *Clive* Ch 4. References in this section are to the 1977 Act, unless otherwise stated.
4 Accordingly, the proclamation of banns has no legal significance in Scots law.
5 Section 3(1).

registration district nor, indeed, in Scotland, but as one of the parties must appear to finalise arrangements for a civil ceremony or, alternatively, collect the marriage schedule for a religious ceremony, in practice, one of the parties must be present in Scotland before the date of the ceremony.

The marriage notice is accompanied by the prescribed fee and the birth certificate of the party submitting it. If either party has been married before and the marriage has been dissolved, a copy of the decree of divorce or declarator of nullity must be included: similarly, if either party is a widow, or widower, the death certificate of the former spouse must be submitted.[1] If one of the parties is domiciled abroad,[2] he or she must 'if practicable' submit a certificate issued by a competent authority in the state in which the party is domiciled that he or she 'is not known to be subject to any legal incapacity (in terms of the law of that state) which would prevent his marrying':[3] this is known as a certificate of capacity.[4]

On receipt of the marriage notice, the registrar enters the following prescribed particulars in a marriage notice book *viz* the party's name, address, marital status, date of birth and the proposed date of the marriage.[5] The names – but not the addresses – of the parties and the proposed date of the marriage are then displayed in a 'conspicuous' place at the registration office.

Any person claiming that he may have reason to submit an objection to an intended marriage, can inspect any entry relating to the marriage in the marriage notice book. The objection to the marriage must be submitted in writing to the district registrar.[6] Where the objection is concerned with a trivial matter, for example, an inaccuracy as to the age of the parties, the district registrar can, after notifying the parties, make the correction.[7] However, if the objection goes to the capacity of either party to marry,[8] for example, if it is alleged that one of them is already a party to a subsisting marriage, then the district registrar must

---

1 Section 3(1)(a) and (b). An extract of an entry in the Register of Divorces is sufficient evidence of the decree of divorce or declarator of nullity: s 28A(5) of the Registration of Births, Deaths and Marriages (Scotland) Act 1965.
2 And has not been resident in the UK for more than 2 years.
3 Section 3(5).
4 Where the *lex domicilii* does not recognise the party's divorce, but the divorce would be recognised in Scotland, a marriage can go ahead without a certificate of capacity: s 3(5)(b) as added by para 21 of Sch 1 to the Family Law Act 1986. See also ibid, s 50.
5 Section 4: the particulars are prescribed in the Marriage (Prescription of Forms) (Scotland) Regulations 1977 (SI 1977/1671) para 4.
6 Section 5(1).
7 Section 5(2)(a).
8 Section 5(4).

notify the Registrar General, and the completion or issue of the marriage schedule is suspended until the matter has been investigated by the Registrar General.[1] If after investigation the Registrar General is satisfied that there is no legal impediment, he will inform the district registrar and the marriage can go ahead: but if there is a legal impediment, the Registrar General must direct the district registrar to take all reasonable steps to ensure that the marriage does not take place.[2]

It will be obvious that there must be sufficient time for objections to be made and any subsequent investigations to be carried out. As a general rule, there is a minimum waiting period of fourteen days from the receipt of the marriage notice and a civil ceremony[3] or the issue of a marriage schedule for a religious ceremony.[4] However, the Registrar General has a dispensing power to allow a marriage to be celebrated within a shorter period if the circumstances justify it. This power is used sparingly.[5]

(ii)   *Marriage schedule*

After the usual waiting period has expired and the district registrar is satisfied that the parties have capacity to marry, he makes up the marriage schedule. The schedule contains the details of the parties and serves as an initial record of the marriage for registration purposes. Where there is to be a religious ceremony, in addition, the marriage schedule acts as a licence authorising the celebrant to proceed. If more than three months have elapsed since the receipt of a marriage notice, the Registrar General has discretion to direct the district registrar not to complete the marriage schedule unless a new marriage notice is submitted.[6] A marriage schedule for a religious ceremony will not be issued to the parties earlier than seven days before the ceremony.[7]

Civil marriage

If there is to be a civil ceremony, the district registrar retains the marriage schedule till the date of the marriage. The ceremony is usually conducted by the registrar and takes place in his office. Where,

1 Section 5(2)(b).
2 Section 5(3).
3 Section 6(4)(a).
4 Section 19(1).
5 Nevertheless there was a case known to the author where a marriage had been arranged for two years but the parties failed to submit their marriage notices: after some frantic telephone calls, the Registrar General was prepared to issue the marriage schedule on the morning of the wedding!
6 Section 6(3).
7 Section 6(4)(b).

however, one of the parties is unable to attend the registrar's office because of serious illness or serious bodily injury, then, provided delay of the wedding is undesirable, the registrar can, on application by either party, solemnise the marriage anywhere in his registration district, for example, a hospital.[1] There is no restriction on the time when the ceremony must take place but in practice it will be during the registrar's normal office hours.

Both parties must be present with two witnesses professing to be over sixteen.[2] The marriage schedule is completed and the district registrar explains to the parties the nature of marriage in Scots law. The parties declare there are no legal impediments and are then asked if they take each other as husband and wife. The registrar declares them to be married and the marriage schedule is signed by both parties, the witnesses and the registrar. The marriage is then registered.

Religious marriage

If there is to be a religious ceremony, the district registrar issues the marriage schedule *to the parties*. This is because the schedule acts as a licence to the celebrant to solemnise the marriage. A religious ceremony can be carried out at any time, for example, in the evening if the couple come from a farming community, and any place, for example, in a hotel. But the date and place chosen must be specified in the marriage schedule.[3]

The authorised celebrant is a person who is[4]

a) a minister of the Church of Scotland; or

b) a minister, clergyman, pastor, priest or other marriage celebrant of a religious body prescribed in regulations made by the Secretary of State: the religious bodies prescribed are the major Christian churches and denominations;[5] or

c) celebrants nominated by other religious bodies as a marriage celebrant and registered as such by the Registrar General under s 9 of the 1977 Act. Only religious bodies can nominate celebrants, who need not be priests but must be over 21. The nominee is authorised for three years in the first instance. A religious body is defined as 'an organised group of people meeting regularly for common

---

1 Sections 18(3) and (4).
2 Section 19(2).
3 Section 6(5).
4 Section 8(1).
5 See The Marriage (Prescription of Religious Bodies) (Scotland) Regulations 1977 (SI 1977/1670).

religious worship'. Non-Christian religions, such as Moslems or Hindus are clearly included, but as they must engage in religious worship, groups such as Humanists would appear to be excluded; or

d) temporarily authorised by the Registrar General under s 12 of the 1977 Act. There is no restriction on these persons except that they must be over 21. In practice, they are celebrants who are registered under s 9 but whose area of operation does not extend to the place where the marriage is to be celebrated, ministers from outside Scotland who have been asked to solemnise a marriage in Scotland, or ministers who are in Scotland on pulpit exchange with a recognised religious body. The authorisation must be in writing and is limited either to the marriage specified in the authorisation or for a specified period.

In the case of a) and b), the celebrant must follow the form of ceremony approved by his church: in the case of c) and d), the ceremony must be in an appropriate form which includes and is not inconsistent with (i) a declaration of the parties, in the presence of each other, the celebrant and two witnesses, that they accept each other as husband and wife and (ii) a declaration thereafter by the celebrant that they are husband and wife.

In all religious marriages, the approved celebrant must not proceed unless (i) the parties produce a marriage schedule issued in accordance with the Act, (ii) *both* parties are present, and (iii) there are two witnesses professing to be over sixteen.[1] After the ceremony, the marriage schedule is signed by both parties, the witnesses and the celebrant. The schedule must be returned to the district registration office for registration within three days of the ceremony.[2] This is traditionally the task of the best man who pays the registration fee as part of his wedding gift!

Effect of irregularities

A marriage solemnised under the Marriage (Scotland) Act 1977 will not be invalidated by non-compliance with these formalities provided both parties were present at the ceremony and the marriage was duly registered.[3] There must be some form of ceremony, but otherwise the marriage will not be invalidated by formal defects. The scope of s 23A

---

1 Section 13(1).
2 Section 15(2).
3 Section 23A, inserted by s 22 of the Law Reform (Miscellaneous Provisions) (Scotland) Act 1980.

was considered by Lord Clyde in *Saleh v Saleh*.[1] The pursuer sought a declarator of nullity. The parties had originally intended to be married by a Church of Scotland minister in Grangemouth. Marriage notices were lodged but the registrar was unable to issue a marriage schedule as there was doubt as to the defender's freedom to marry. Faced with this difficulty, the couple decided to be married in a mosque in Edinburgh. No marriage notices were lodged with the appropriate district registrar nor was any marriage schedule completed, far less issued. Nevertheless the ceremony took place and the matour issued a certificate recording the ceremony. But because of the absence of a completed marriage schedule, the marriage could not be, and was not, registered. In granting the declarator, Lord Clyde held that this was not a case where s 23A was applicable because, while the parties were present at the ceremony, there was no registration. Lord Clyde thought that s 23A could save a marriage when, for example, the schedule had been issued prior to the time limits or if the person who conducted the ceremony was not an approved celebrant or a marriage schedule was not produced at the ceremony, always provided that the parties were present and the schedule had been issued, signed and registered.

However, even if the marriage can be saved by s 23A, the parties and the celebrant may be liable to criminal sanctions for breach of the Act, for example, if a person falsifies or forges a marriage schedule.[2] However, the validity of a marriage is still challengeable on such grounds as lack of legal capacity of the parties or absence of true consent.

Conclusion

The purpose of legal preliminaries to the solemnisation of marriage is to ensure that the parties to a marriage have legal capacity to marry. As a result of the Marriage (Scotland) Act 1977, all persons who wish to enter into a regular marriage in Scotland must follow the same preliminary procedure whether or not they intend to have a civil or a religious ceremony. This makes for simplicity and uniformity.

Moreover, it is submitted that the current rules give sufficient time for objections to be made and appropriate investigations to take place. The procedure itself is admirably simple, without the complexities of residence requirements for the parties.

In relation to the ceremony itself, there are for religious marriages no limitations on the time or place of the wedding. It is thought, however, that the restriction of civil ceremonies to the district regis-

1   1987 SLT 633.
2   See s 24 for a full list of offences.

trar's office, unless one of the parties is seriously ill or injured, is unnecessarily restrictive and it is hoped that steps will be taken to enable a couple to have a civil ceremony when and wherever they wish.

IRREGULAR MARRIAGES[1]

(i)   *Introduction*

Before the Reformation in 1560, Scots law recognised the validity of irregular marriages. These involved no ecclesiastical formalities whatsoever. There were three kinds.

a) A declaration by the parties that they took each other as husband and wife: marriage *per verba de praesenti*. The consent of the parties was sufficient to constitute the marriage and there was no need for the presence of an episcopally ordained priest or witnesses.

b) A promise to marry at some future date followed by sexual intercourse on the faith of that promise: marriage *per verba de futuro subsequente copula*. The sexual intercourse on the faith of the promise was deemed to be agreement to marry. Not surprisingly, perhaps, there was no need for the presence of an episcopally ordained priest or witnesses.

c) Marriage constituted by the tacit agreement of the parties to marry presumed from a period of cohabitation with habit and repute that they were husband and wife: marriage by cohabitation with habit and repute.

After the Reformation these forms of irregular marriage continued to be recognised as constituting valid marriages in Scots law. The first two forms of irregular marriage were abolished by s 5 of the Marriage (Scotland) Act 1939 which came into force on 1 July 1940.[2] However, the third form, marriage by cohabitation with habit and repute, remains a valid method of constituting marriage in Scotland.

Because many of the older cases involved irregular marriages, it is proposed to outline the salient features of *de praesenti* and *de futuro* marriages and then to consider marriage by cohabitation with habit and repute in some detail.

(ii)   *Marriage by declaration de praesenti*

The essence of this form of marriage was that the parties seriously and genuinely exchanged present consent to marriage. The couple were

---

1 For full discussion see *Clive* Ch 5.
2 The section was not retrospective.

married as soon as consents were exchanged. Consummation was not required: *consensus non concubitus facit matrimonium*. Because there was no need for witnesses, there could be formidable problems of proof, particularly where one of the alleged spouses had died and the issue arose in a claim by the other for rights of succession.[1]

The exchange of consents had to take place in Scotland.[2] This explains the popularity of elopements from England to marry at Gretna Green. Eventually, a residence requirement of at least 21 days was introduced by the Marriage (Scotland) Act 1856. The *de praesenti* marriage has not been a competent form of contracting a marriage since 1 July 1940.[3]

(iii) *Marriage by promise subsequente copula*

In this form of irregular marriage, if a promise was made of marriage at some date in the future and sexual intercourse took place on the faith of the promise, the couple were taken to be married at the date of the intercourse. The theory was that while mutual consent was essential to marriage, where a woman permitted sexual intercourse in reliance on a man's promise to marry her, it was to be presumed that there and then the parties had exchanged consents to present marriage and, if this presumption was not rebutted, a marriage was constituted by promise *subsequente copula*.[4] Both the promise and the sexual intercourse had to take place in Scotland.

In time, this form of marriage was treated with scepticism. As Lord Sands explained in *N v C*:[5]

'According to the theory of the law, when two persons who are engaged to be married indulge in sexual intercourse, presumably they there and then exchange matrimonial consent and become married persons. But, according to the view which prevails in those sections of the community in which antenuptial fornication is most apt to occur, they do nothing of the kind. They yield to desire and indulge in immoral intercourse, robbed doubtless of some of its danger by the prospect of future marriage . . . Parents, employers and clergymen in rural Scotland have often had occasion to deal sorrowfully with a girl whose betrothed had got her in the family way. I much doubt if it has ever happened that the girl advanced the plea in excuse that she was a married

---

1 See, for example, *Dunn v Dunn's Trustees* 1930 SC 131.
2 *Macdonald v Macdonald* (1863) 1 M 854.
3 Section 5 of the Marriage (Scotland) Act 1939.
4 See *N v C* 1933 SC 492.
5 Ibid at 501.

woman ... Marriage by promise *cum subsequente copula* is a plant nourished by the law which has never taken root in the understanding or the conscience of the common people'.

It is therefore not surprising that this has not been a competent form of contracting a marriage since 1 July 1940.[1]

(iv)   *Marriage by cohabitation with habit and repute*

The Marriage (Scotland) Act 1939 did not abolish the third form of irregular marriage, marriage by cohabitation with habit and repute. The theoretical basis of the doctrine has been the subject of controversy.[2] It is not simply a matter of evidence. While there is a presumption from long cohabitation as husband and wife, that a couple have been married,[3] this is rebuttable by evidence that the alleged ceremony did not take place. However, marriage by cohabitation with habit and repute is not merely a rule of evidence that the parties are prima facie to be presumed to have married by declaration *de praesenti* or promise *cum subsequente copula*, for if that were so, marriage by cohabitation with habit and repute would have been impliedly abolished by the Marriage (Scotland) Act 1939. Instead, the basis of the doctrine is that the parties' *tacit* consent to marry, inferred from, and combined with, cohabitation with habit and repute constitutes marriage: a legitimate enunciation by the parties to themselves and others of their matrimonial consent which has never expressly been put into words.[4] Because of their cohabitation with habit and repute that they are married, the law presumes that the parties have *tacitly* agreed to be married, with the result that they *are* married unless evidence is led that they never intended to take each other as husband and wife.

The requirements

  (i)   There must be cohabitation, ie the couple must live together: merely to have sexual intercourse is not enough.[5]

 (ii)   The cohabitation must be as husband and wife: not as man and mistress or man and housekeeper. However, cohabitation which began on an indeterminate footing can ripen into a marriage if the

---

1 Section 5 of the Marriage (Scotland) Act 1939.
2 See, for example, Ashton-Cross 'Cohabitation with Habit and Repute' (1961) JR 21.
3 Or before 1 July 1940, that the couple had married by *de praesenti* consents or promise *cum subsequente copula*.
4 *Campbell v Campbell* (1866) 4 M 867 at 924–925.
5 *Quaere* whether a couple can cohabit for this purpose if they do not have sexual intercourse.

couple later cohabit as husband and wife.[1] However, where a couple live together with the intention that they will marry at a future date, since they are not cohabiting as husband and wife, they cannot become married as a result of the doctrine of marriage by cohabitation with habit and repute.[2] *A fortiori* the doctrine does not apply when a couple live together without any intention of ever marrying.

(iii) The cohabitation must take place in Scotland.

(iv) The cohabitation must be sufficiently long for the court to infer that the parties tacitly agreed to marry. At one time it was thought that this must be at least a year,[3] but in *Shaw v Henderson*[4] Lord Stott emphasised that there was no hard and fast rule: all that is required is that the evidence of cohabitation is sufficient for an inference of tacit agreement to be drawn. Eleven months cohabitation was enough in that case.

(v) The parties must be reputed to be husband and wife and this reputation must be 'uniform and undivided'.[5] But it is not fatal if some persons know that the couple are not married, provided they are generally thought by friends and society in general to be husband and wife.[6] But if a substantial number of relatives and friends do know that the couple are not married[7] or are merely contemplating marriage, the doctrine will not apply.[8]

(vi) The parties must have legal capacity to marry.[9] If, for example, one of the parties is already married to a third party, the doctrine cannot apply: but, once the impediment is removed by the death or divorce of the existing spouse then, as the party will now have capacity to marry, the doctrine is applicable. But the parties can only rely upon the cohabitation with habit and repute which occurs after the impediment has been removed.[10] Thus if A who is married to B begins to cohabit with C in 1970 and B dies in 1990,

---

1 See, for example, *Nicol v Bell* 1954 SLT 314 (woman began as man's housekeeper, became his mistress but on the birth of his child was treated as his wife: they were married as a result of 20 years' cohabitation as his wife).

2 See, for example, *Low v Gorman* 1970 SLT 356; *Mackenzie v Scott* 1980 SLT (Notes) 9.

3 See, for example, *Campbell v Campbell* (1866) 4 M 867; *Wallace v Fife Coal Co Ltd* 1909 SC 682.

4 1982 SLT 211.

5 *Petrie v Petrie* 1911 SC 360 per Lord Dundas.

6 *Shaw v Henderson* 1982 SLT 211.

7 *Low v Gorman* 1970 SLT 356.

8 *Mackenzie v Scott* 1980 SLT (Notes) 9.

9 Legal capacity is discussed in detail *infra* Ch 2.

10 *Low v Gorman* 1970 SLT 356.

the period of relevant cohabitation only begins with B's death in 1990: the period of cohabitation – albeit with habit and repute – between 1970 and 1990 is irrelevant. Where a relationship begins illicitly, it may, of course, be difficult to establish the necessary repute that the couple are living as husband and wife. But the doctrine will still be applicable once the parties are aware that the impediment has been removed.[1] Little, if any, weight is now given to the old idea that a relationship which begins illicitly should prima facie be presumed to continue illicitly. In *Shaw v Henderson*[2] Lord Stott felt that this had

'no practical relevance to the present day situation where a working-class couple who at the time when neither is free to marry begin to live together ... [and] continue in the same relationship after they have obtained their respective divorces. In that state of affairs if the inference of consent to marriage is sufficiently clear the presumption of marriage must in my opinion arise at least as strongly as in those cases where the parties were free to consent to marriage from the start'.

Procedure

A party to the alleged marriage by cohabitation with habit and repute will raise an action in the Court of Session for a declarator of marriage. It should be emphasised, however, that the couple are married by virtue of the doctrine: there is no need for a declarator to establish the marriage. A declarator has been granted where the couple were married by cohabitation with habit and repute albeit that they had separated before the husband's death.[3] By the nature of the doctrine it will be difficult to establish exactly when the couple were married. While the matter is not free from difficulty, there is force in Clive's view that the date should be when there was sufficient relevant cohabitation with habit and repute, for the inference of tacit consent to be drawn.[4] When a declarator has been granted, the Principal Clerk of Session will intimate the relevant details to the Registrar General to enable him to register the marriage.[5]

---

1 *Campbell v Campbell* (1866) 4 M 867. The case proceeded on the assumption that the parties knew of the death of the first husband. Thus it would appear that the presumption of tacit consent would be rebutted if the parties continued to believe that the impediment existed.
2 1982 SLT 211 at 213.
3 *Morris v Morris* 1987 GWD 39–1437.
4 See *Clive* p 67 ff.
5 Section 21 of the Marriage (Scotland) Act 1977.

Conclusion

Marriage by cohabitation with habit and repute is a distinctive feature of Scots family law but it is not a common occurrence. There are only about two declarators a year. The question arises whether the doctrine is worth retaining. While Scots law continues to consider a valid marriage – as opposed to cohabitation per se – as a condition *sine qua non* of the legal regulation of the property of the parties to a sexual relationship when it comes to an end, it is probably of value. Its illogicalities cannot be denied. For example, it requires the parties to *pretend* that they are married. Accordingly, it cannot provide a solution to the legal problems of a couple who openly cohabit as unmarried persons.

Where the doctrine is valuable is in the situation where a couple purport to enter a regular marriage but, unknown to the parties, they do not have legal capacity to marry at the time of the ceremony. As we shall see in the next chapter, in these circumstances the marriage is void. If, however, the impediment is subsequently removed and the couple continue to cohabit as husband and wife, they will *become* married as a result of the doctrine.[1] Thus marriage by cohabitation with habit and repute can be useful in creating the status of husband and wife when the couple's original marriage was void as a result of a legal impediment at the time of the original ceremony.

Nevertheless, it has been recommended that the doctrine be abolished.[2]

---

1 This certainly follows if the parties know that the impediment has been removed: *quaere* if they thought (wrongly) that the impediment continued.
2 *Family Law: Pre-consolidation Reforms*, SLC Discussion Paper No 85, paras 2.1–2.19.

2 Legal impediments to marriage – void and voidable marriages

INTRODUCTION

As we saw in the last chapter,[1] as a result of s 23A of the Marriage (Scotland) Act 1977, non-compliance with the formalities for regular marriages laid down in the Act will not affect the validity of the marriage provided both parties were present at the ceremony and the particulars of their marriage were duly registered. However, a marriage may be defective if the parties lack legal capacity to enter into the contract or if there is not true consent or the marriage cannot be consummated as a result of the incurable impotency of one or both of the parties. In this chapter we shall examine the impediments to marriage which are recognised by Scots law.

VOID AND VOIDABLE MARRIAGES

As a general rule where such an impediment exists, the marriage will be void in Scots law. There is one exception to this principle, namely, where the marriage has not been consummated as a result of the incurable impotency of one or both of the parties. In this case, the marriage is voidable.

Where a marriage is void, it prima facie has no legal effect whatsoever. There is no need for the parties to obtain a declarator of nullity of marriage in the Court of Session. However, any person who has a legitimate interest may seek a declarator of nullity from the Court of Session on the ground that the marriage was void. In certain circumstances, a void marriage may have legal consequences. For example, a child conceived during a void marriage is presumed to be the child of the mother's 'husband'[2] and he will have parental rights over the child if he entered into the marriage believing in good faith at that time that

---

1 *Supra* pp 12, 13.
2 Sections 5(1) and (2) of the Law Reform (Parent and Child) (Scotland) Act 1986, discussed *infra* Ch 8.

the marriage was valid.[1] Moreover, if a declarator of nullity is obtained by one of the parties, the court has the same powers to award financial provision for the parties as it does in actions of divorce.[2]

In the case of a voidable marriage, the marriage subsists unless and until a declarator of nullity of marriage is obtained from the Court of Session. Only a party to the marriage can seek declarator and, unlike the case of a void marriage, declarator cannot be obtained if one of the parties is dead. However, the effect of the decree is to declare that the marriage has never existed, ie it has retroactive effect. Nevertheless, the court can award the parties financial provision in the same way as in an action of divorce.[3] Nor does the retroactive effect of the decree affect the status of any children of the marriage.[4] Given that the sole ground of a voidable marriage is the incurable impotency of one or both of the parties, the number of children affected will be small, but, as we shall see, with modern reproductive techniques, the existence of children of a voidable marriage is not impossible.[5]

CAPACITY TO MARRY

We shall now consider the grounds on which a marriage is void in Scots law as a result of the parties' lack of legal capacity to enter into the marriage.

Non-age

By s 1(1) of the Marriage (Scotland) Act 1977, no person domiciled[6] in Scotland may marry before he or she attains the age of sixteen. Thus, for example, a fifteen year old girl who is domiciled in Scotland has no legal capacity to contract a marriage in Scotland or any other country in the world, even if the law of the foreign country allows its domiciliaries to marry below the age of sixteen. However, where a Scottish domiciliary is over the age of sixteen, he or she has legal capacity to marry a foreign domiciliary who is under the age of sixteen, provided the ceremony takes place abroad and the foreign party has capacity

---

1 Sections 2(1) and (2) of the Law Reform (Parent and Child) (Scotland) Act 1986, discussed *infra* Ch 8.
2 Section 17(1) of the Family Law (Scotland) Act 1985. Financial provision on divorce is discussed in detail *infra* Ch 7.
3 Ibid.
4 Section 4 of the Law Reform (Miscellaneous Provisions) (Scotland) Act 1949.
5 See *infra* p 39.
6 Domicile is a complex legal concept: its essence is a person having his or her permanent home in Scotland or who has a Scottish domicile of dependence as a result of his or her parent being domiciled in Scotland.

under his or her *lex domicilii* and the law of the country where the ceremony takes place (the *lex loci celebrationis*).[1]

By s 1(2) of the Marriage (Scotland) Act 1977, a marriage solemnised between persons either of whom is under the age of sixteen is void. Consequently, even if one or both of the parties have capacity to marry under the age of sixteen under their *lex domicilii*, the marriage is void if the ceremony takes place in Scotland. However the 1977 Act specifically refers to a marriage 'solemnised' in Scotland. It is open to argument, therefore, that provided the parties have capacity to marry below the age of sixteen under their *lex domicilii*, they can become married by cohabitation with habit and repute and a period of cohabitation prior to attaining the age of sixteen would be relevant for the purpose of the doctrine. However, in the case of a Scottish domiciliary who purports to marry under the age of sixteen, only periods of cohabitation after the impediment has been removed, ie after he or she has reached the age of sixteen, will be relevant in establishing a new marriage by cohabitation with habit and repute.[2]

Where a party is still a minor,[3] ie in this context between the ages of sixteen and eighteen, there is no requirement of obtaining parental consents to the marriage.[4]

Forbidden degrees of relationship

By s 2(1) of the Marriage (Scotland) Act 1977, a marriage between a man and any woman related to him in a degree specified in column 1 of Schedule 1 to the Act, or between a woman and any man related to her in a degree specified in column 2 of that Schedule, shall be void if (a) either the marriage is solemnised in Scotland or (b) either party is domiciled in Scotland at the time of the ceremony. The list is exclusive in the sense that where the relationship is not mentioned in the Schedule, the parties may validly marry[5] unless it would be contrary to their *lex domicilii* or the *lex loci celebrationis* for them to do so.[6] The lists are as follows:

---

1 Contrast the position in English law: see s 2 of the Marriage Act 1949; *Pugh v Pugh* [1951] 2 All ER 680, [1951] P 482.
2 *AB v CD* 1957 SC 415: see generally *Clive* pp 89–90.
3 Minority ends at the age of 18: the Age of Majority (Scotland) Act 1969. For a discussion of pupillarity and minority, see *infra* Ch 9.
4 In English law, parental approval of a marriage of a minor is still relevant in relation to the ecclesiastical and civil preliminaries of marriage.
5 Section 2(3) of the Marriage (Scotland) Act 1977. Similar principles apply to marriages by cohabitation with habit and repute: see *Clive* pp 33–4.
6 Section 2(3)(a) of the Marriage (Scotland) Act 1977. The marriage is also void if either of them is validly married to a third party at the time of the ceremony: s 2(3)(b) of the Marriage (Scotland) Act 1977.

1 – Relationships by consanguinity

Column 1	Column 2
Mother	Father
Daughter	Son
Father's mother	Father's father
Mother's mother	Mother's father
Son's daughter	Son's son
Daughter's daughter	Daughter's son
Sister	Brother
Father's sister	Father's brother
Mother's sister	Mother's brother
Brother's daughter	Brother's son
Sister's daughter	Sister's son
Father's father's mother	Father's father's father
Father's mother's mother	Father's mother's father
Mother's father's mother	Mother's father's father
Mother's mother's mother	Mother's mother's father
Son's son's daughter	Son's son's son
Son's daughter's daughter	Son's daughter's son
Daughter's son's daughter	Daughter's son's son
Daughter's daughter's daughter	Daughter's daughter's son

2 – Relationships by affinity

Daughter of former wife	Son of former husband
Former wife of father	Former husband of mother
Former wife of father's father	Former husband of father's mother
Former wife of mother's father	Former husband of mother's mother
Daughter of son of former wife	Son of son of former husband
Daughter of daughter of former wife	Son of daughter of former husband

2A – Relationships by affinity

Mother of former wife	Father of former husband
Former wife of son	Former husband of daughter

3 – Relationships by adoption

Adoptive mother or former adoptive mother	Adoptive father or former adoptive father
Adopted daughter or former adopted daughter	Adopted son or former adopted son

The prohibited relationships arise from (a) blood ties (consanguinity), (b) marriage (affinity), and (c) adoption. For the purposes of consanguinity, half-blood is treated as full-blood[1] and illegitimacy is irrelevant.[2]

Thus, for example, a man cannot marry his half-sister, ie his mother's daughter by a man who was not his father or his father's daughter by a woman who was not his mother. Similarly, a woman cannot marry her illegitimate son or her legitimate son's illegitimate son.

A degree of affinity is only created by marriage and not merely by the fact that sexual intercourse has taken place between the persons concerned. Thus a man cannot prima facie marry his mother in law ie the mother of his former wife, but he can marry the mother of his former or, indeed, current mistress. Similarly, he cannot prima facie marry his father's former wife, but he can marry his father's mistress even if she has cohabited with his father for many years and borne him children.

However, in certain circumstances, a marriage between persons related by affinity is not prohibited. First, persons who are related within the degrees of affinity in paragraph 2, may marry provided that both parties have attained the age of 21 at the time of the marriage and the younger party has not at any time before attaining the age of eighteen lived in the same household as the other party and been treated by the other party as a child of the family.[3] Thus, for example, a man may now marry his father's former wife provided both are over the age of 21 and, if he is the younger party, has not lived in the same household as his stepmother and been treated by her as a child of the family before he had reached the age of eighteen. If he has been so treated, the parties cannot marry.[4] In other words, provided the parties related within the degrees of affinity specified in paragraph 2 have never assumed, in effect, the roles of parent and child, they are free to marry if both are over the age of 21. Secondly, persons who are related within the degrees of affinity in paragraph 2A, may marry provided

---

1 Section 2(2)(a) of the Marriage (Scotland) Act 1977.
2 Para 17, Sch 1 to the Law Reform (Parent and Child) (Scotland) Act 1986.
3 Section 2(1A) of the Marriage (Scotland) Act 1977, as inserted by para 2(b) of Sch 2 to the Marriage (Prohibited Degrees of Relationship) Act 1986. Either party can petition the Court of Session for declarator that the conditions are satisfied which enable them to marry: see s 2(5) of the Marriage (Scotland) Act 1977, as inserted by para 2(c) of Sch 2 to the Marriage (Prohibited Degrees of Relationship) Act 1986: on the 1986 Act, see Nichols 1986 SLT (News) 229.
4 Sexual intercourse between the couple would also be a criminal offence: s 2B of the Sexual Offences (Scotland) Act 1976 as inserted by s 1 of the Incest and Related Offences (Scotland) Act 1986.

both parties have attained the age of 21 and the marriage is solemnised (a) in the case of a man marrying his mother-in-law or his daughter-in-law, after the deaths of his former wife and her father or the deaths of his son and his son's mother and (b) in the case of a woman marrying her father-in-law or her son-in-law, after the deaths of her former husband and his mother or the deaths of her daughter and her daughter's father.[1] Thus, it is still only in very exceptional circumstances that parents-in-law and children-in-law will be able to marry.

It should be noted that first cousins and step-brothers and step-sisters are free to marry.

There are two major policy reasons for having prohibited degrees. The first, in relation to consanguinity, is biological. Marriage to a close relative greatly increases the risk of conceiving a physically or mentally handicapped child. However, marriage between first cousins is permitted even though there is an enhanced risk of conceiving a physically or mentally handicapped child, particularly if the woman is in her mid-thirties or older. Secondly, it is argued that to allow marriage between persons who are closely related will give rise both to feelings of disgust in society generally and possible disruption within the family concerned. This can be the only justification for prohibitions in respect of affinity and adoption. However, if this were thought to be an important policy objective, why does the law, for example, permit adopted brothers and sisters to marry, even if for many years they believed they were siblings by blood? Moreover, it is thought that a total prohibition of marriage between persons who are only related by affinity is difficult to defend in modern society. The amendments to the Marriage (Scotland) Act 1977 made by the Marriage (Prohibited Degrees of Relationship) Act 1986 are therefore to be welcomed[2] but they do not, in the present writer's view, go far enough. It is, for example, difficult to believe that there would be objections in allowing a step-daughter to marry her mother's former husband when her mother had died, even if he had treated her, before the age of 18, as a child of the family.[3] The prohibition on the grounds of affinity survives only for historical reasons and it is submitted that it is an intrusion on personal liberty which serves little, if any, purpose.[4]

1 Section 2(1B) of the Marriage (Scotland) Act 1977, as inserted by para 2(b) of Sch 2 to the Marriage (Prohibited Degrees of Relationship) Act 1986.
2 Discussed *supra* p 24.
3 If the parties in this example wished to marry, they would have to obtain a private Act of Parliament to enable them to do so.
4 It has been recommended that the remaining limitations on marriage between a person and the parent of his or her former spouse should be abolished: *Family Law: Pre-consolidation Reforms* SLC Discussion Paper No 85, paras 3.6–3.13.

Parties of the same sex

Marriage in Scots law has always been regarded as a union between a man and a woman.[1] A marriage will therefore be void if the parties purporting to marry are of the same sex.

In the leading case of *Corbett v Corbett*,[2] the High Court in England had to consider the criteria for determining a person's sex for the purpose of the law of marriage. The couple went through a ceremony of marriage which was never consummated. Their relationship deteriorated and the 'husband' sought a declaration that the marriage was void on the ground that the respondent was also male. Evidence was brought that the respondent had been born with male external genitalia and gonads but was a transsexual, ie psychologically he regarded himself as a woman imprisoned in a man's body. Prior to the ceremony he had undergone sex realignment surgery and as a result of this and hormone treatment, his physical appearance approximated to that of the gender which he had always psychologically considered himself to be, ie a woman. Ormrod J held that, in spite of the sex realignment surgery, the respondent was nevertheless male. In the cells of biological males, there is present Y, as well as X, chromosomes: no Y chromosomes are present in the cells of a biological female. The sex realignment surgery had not altered the respondent's cell structure and, as there was a Y chromosome present, he remained biologically male.

Having been satisfied that the respondent was biologically male, Ormrod J went on to hold that for the purpose of the law of marriage, the parties biologically had to be of different sexes. He maintained that the concept of marriage as hitherto understood required that one party had to be biologically male and the other biologically female.[3] Accordingly, as both parties in this case were biologically male, he granted decree of nullity.

It is thought that Scottish courts would follow the approach taken by Ormrod J in this case. Marriage in Scots law has traditionally been considered to be exclusively a heterosexual relationship. More controversially, perhaps, it is submitted that Scots law would also regard biological criteria, including chromosomal or cellular make up, as determinative of sex for this purpose.[4]

---

1 Stair I 4.1–I 4.6.
2 [1970] 2 All ER 33, [1971] P 83.
3 Ibid at 106, per Ormrod J.
4 See, for example, *X-Petitioner* 1957 SLT (Sh Ct) 61.

However this criterion has been criticised as giving insufficient weight to psychological factors as a determinant of a person's sex.[1] But, unless and until there is a fundamental re-assessment of the nature and purpose of marriage in contemporary Scottish society, there is force in the contention that marriage in Scots law presupposes that only parties of different biological sexes can fulfil the traditional obligations arising from the status. The criterion laid down in *Corbett v Corbett*[2] at least has a measure of certainty even if it has the unfortunate result of denying post-operative transsexuals the right to marry persons whom they regard as being of the opposite sex.[3]

Underlying the decision in *Corbett* was the fear that if post-operative transsexuals were held to have capacity to marry, the question would arise whether a pre-operative transsexual could marry a person of the same biological sex, and if so, the way would then be open for homosexuals to argue that they were free to marry persons of the same sex. While the psychology of the transsexual is, of course, fundamentally different from that of the homosexual, there is no doubt that a considerable body of public opinion would not countenance the possibility of homosexual 'marriages'. By restricting marriage to biologically heterosexual couples, the decision in *Corbett* prevents this development. But for as long as Scots law regards marriage as a condition *sine qua non* for the legal regulation of cohabitation, parties to a homosexual relationship remain deprived of the right to have the economic and other consequences of their cohabitation governed by appropriate legal rules.

Prior subsisting marriage

A person who is already a party to a valid marriage lacks legal capacity to enter into a subsequent marriage while the first marriage continues to subsist.[4] There is no legal impediment if the first marriage is void: if, however, it is only voidable, it will operate as a bar to a second

---

1 See, for example, Kennedy, 'Transsexualism and Single Sex Marriage' (1973) Anglo American Law Review 112; Thomson, 'Transsexualism – A legal perspective' (1980) 6 Journal of Medical Ethics 92.
2 [1970] 2 All ER 33, [1971] P 83.
3 This has been held not to constitute a breach of article 12 of the European Convention on Human Rights (the right to marry and found a family): see *Rees v UK* 1987 9 EHRR 56; *Cossey v UK* 27 September 1990, ECHR.
4 See generally *Clive* pp 88–89.

marriage unless and until a declarator of nullity of marriage has been obtained.[1]

Even although the parties entered into marriage with the belief held in good faith that any prior marriage had ended as a result of the death of the spouse or divorce, the marriage will still be void if, in fact, the prior marriage was subsisting at the time of the ceremony.[2] However, if a decree of declarator of nullity were obtained, financial provision for the spouses is available.[3] Moreover, once the prior marriage is dissolved and the impediment to marriage is thereby removed, the parties may become married as a result of subsequent cohabitation with habit and repute.[4]

Where one of the parties is aware of this impediment, the innocent party may obtain damages for fraud. This can be illustrated by the case of *Burke v Burke*.[5] In this case H was living with W1. He went through a ceremony of marriage with the pursuer, W2. He told her that he was divorced from W1. He also informed W2 that he was working night shifts but he spent his evenings with W1. When W2 discovered that no divorce had taken place, she sought declarator of nullity and aliment for her child which had been conceived during the 'marriage'.[6] The court held that W2 did not have to prove the validity of the first marriage: she could rely on the presumption *omnia rite et solemniter acta esse*. The onus lay on the defender to establish, which in the circumstances he was unable to do, that the first marriage was void. Accordingly, she obtained declarator and aliment for the child. In addition, the court held that the pursuer was entitled to damages in delict as a result of the defender's fraud, and the court awarded her £2,500.

As we have seen, a marriage will be void even although the parties believed, in good faith, that a prior marriage had been dissolved as a result of the death of the spouse. This can raise difficulties for a person whose spouse has disappeared and wishes to enter a second marriage. At common law, there was a very strong presumption of life and a

---

1 Even although a declarator of nullity of marriage renders the marriage retrospectively null, it will probably not operate to validate a second marriage which was entered into before declarator was obtained.
2 In these circumstances, the marriage, while void, will be a putative marriage and any children conceived during it will be presumed to be the children of the 'husband'. Sections 5(1) and (2) of the Law Reform (Parent and Child) (Scotland) Act 1986, discussed *infra* Ch 8.
3 *Supra* p 21.
4 *Supra* pp 17, 18.
5 1983 SLT 331.
6 This child was legitimate as a result of the doctrine of putative marriage, see *infra* Ch 8.

person who had disappeared was presumed to live to a ripe old age.[1] This presumption could be rebutted by evidence establishing beyond reasonable doubt that a spouse was dead but even so, a subsequent marriage was still void if the spouse was in fact still alive.

This unsatisfactory position was resolved as a result of the Presumption of Death (Scotland) Act 1977.[2] Under this statute, any person with sufficient interest may petition the Court of Session[3] or the sheriff court[4] for a declarator of death. The court may grant decree if satisfied on a balance of probabilities that either—

a) the missing person is dead – including the date and time of death; or
b) the missing person has not been known to be alive for a period of at least seven years: in this case, the court will declare the missing person to have died at the end of the day occurring seven years after the date on which he was last known to be alive.[5]

The 1977 Act therefore covers two situations. In the first, a person has disappeared in circumstances which point to his death at a particular time, for example, if a person was travelling in an aeroplane which disappeared. Here, there is no need to wait seven years before bringing the action. In the second, a person has simply gone missing and there are no circumstances to suggest that he is dead. Here no action can be raised until seven years have elapsed during which there is no evidence that the missing person is alive.

A declarator of death is effective 'for all purposes including dissolution of a marriage to which the missing person is a party'.[6] Once a marriage has been dissolved as a result of a decree, 'the dissolution of the marriage shall not be invalidated by the circumstance that the missing person was in fact alive at the date specified in the decree'.[7] Thus if a person has obtained a declarator of death of a missing spouse,

---

1 Stair IV 45.17. See, for example, *Muhammad v Robertson or Kettle or Muhammad* 1972 SLT (Notes) 69.
2 See generally *Clive* Ch 28. By s 5 of the Divorce (Scotland) Act 1938, it was possible to obtain a decree of dissolution of marriage arising from the presumed death of a spouse after an absence of seven years or more.
3 The Court of Session has jurisdiction if a) the missing person was domiciled in Scotland, or habitually resident in Scotland for one year, at the date when last known to be alive, or b) if the pursuer is the spouse of the missing person and is domiciled in Scotland or habitually resident in Scotland for one year, at the date when the action is raised: s 1(3) of the 1977 Act.
4 The sheriff court has jurisdiction on the same grounds but in addition where jurisdiction is based on a) *supra* the last known place of residence of the missing person must have been in the sheriffdom and where it is based on b) *supra* the pursuer must have been resident in the sheriffdom for at least 40 days before the date of the action.
5 Section 1(1) of the Presumption of Death (Scotland) Act 1977.
6 Section 3(1) of the Presumption of Death (Scotland) Act 1977.
7 Section 3(3) of the Presumption of Death (Scotland) Act 1977.

he will have capacity to enter a subsequent marriage and this later marriage is not affected even if the missing spouse was in fact alive at the date of the later ceremony.

Although there are provisions for the variation or recall of the declarator if the missing person is found to be alive within five years of the date of the decree, no variation or recall 'shall operate so as to revive a marriage of the missing person dissolved by virtue of a decree in an action of declarator'.[1]

It should be noted that any person, for example, a beneficiary under the missing person's will, may apply for declarator. If it is granted, it will have the effect of dissolving the missing person's marriage, even although the missing person's spouse continues to entertain the belief that the missing person is still alive and does not wish the marriage to be dissolved.

Finally by s 13 of the 1977 Act, it is a defence to a charge of bigamy for the accused to prove that at no time within a period of seven years immediately preceding the date of a subsequent 'marriage' had he or she any reason to believe that a prior spouse was alive.[2]

DEFECTIVE CONSENT

Marriage is a contract and like any other contract requires consent. Accordingly, it will be null if the parties did not truly consent to take each other as husband and wife. Defective consent can arise for several reasons.

Mental illness or defect

As a result of mental illness or defect, one or both parties to a marriage may not be capable of understanding the nature of marriage and giving true consent thereto. However, the fact that a person is suffering from a mental illness, for example, depression, does not necessarily prevent the giving of a valid consent provided the necessary capacity is present at the time. Marriage has been said to be a simple contract. Accordingly persons of limited intelligence can validly consent to marriage.

It has been held[3] that there is a very heavy burden on any person denying the validity of a marriage to establish that one or both parties were incapable of understanding the nature of marriage as a result of

---

1 Section 4(5) of the Presumption of Death (Scotland) Act 1977.
2 It is possible to call the Lord Advocate as a defender in an action of declarator of death, but as a general rule the missing person should be called as defender: *Horak v Lord Advocate* 1984 SLT 201.
3 *Long v Long* 1950 SLT (Notes) 32.

feeble mindedness or mental illness at the time of the ceremony. However, if this burden can be discharged, the marriage will be void in Scots law.[1]

Intoxication

A party may lack capacity to consent as a result of drunkenness or abuse of drugs at the time of the ceremony. The effect of alcohol or drugs must be extreme before capacity is lost. However, in *Johnston v Brown*,[2] the pursuer, Mary Brown, obtained declarator of nullity of marriage on the ground that at the time of the ceremony and for three days thereafter she was so inebriated that she lacked capacity to consent to the marriage. Accordingly, the marriage was void.

Error

The parties' apparent consent may be vitiated by error with the result that the marriage is void. However, the scope of operative error in relation to marriage is strictly limited.

It is accepted that where a party is in error as to the nature of the ceremony, the marriage is void. Thus, for example, if A goes through a ceremony of marriage with B, believing it to be merely a betrothal, the marriage is void.[3] Similarly, if there is an error as to the identity of the other party, the marriage is void.[4] The error is only operative in cases of impersonation. Thus when Jacob married Leah, believing he was marrying Rachel, the marriage would have been void in Scots law as a result of error.[5]

However an error as to identity was held not to have arisen in the case of *M'Leod v Adams*.[6] The defender had deserted from the army. Using a false name to avoid detection by the authorities, he told a young and gullible widow that he was a sergeant in the Black Watch. The couple married by exchanging *de praesenti* consents whereupon the defender promptly deserted his wife, taking her savings with him. Lord Sands held that there was no operative error as the widow clearly intended to marry the man before her and accordingly there was no error as to the identity of the parties to the marriage.[7]

---

1 Cf the position in English law, where absence of true consent merely renders a marriage voidable: s 12(c) of the Matrimonial Causes Act 1973.
2 (1823) 2 S 495.
3 See, for example, *Ford v Stier* [1896] P 1; *Valier v Valier* (1925) 133 LT 830.
4 Stair I 9.9.
5 *Gen* Ch 29 v 21–30.
6 1920 1 SLT 229.
7 Declarator of nullity was however granted on the grounds that the marriage was a sham: see *infra* p 35.

It is settled that an error as to the qualities of a party to the marriage does not operate to vitiate consent. 'Errors in qualities or circumstances vitiate not: as if one supposing he had married a maid, or chaste woman, had married a whore.'[1] In the contract of marriage parties take each other 'for better or worse' and the Scottish courts have refused to imply resolutive conditions into the contract which would be inconsistent with this fundamental principle.[2] Moreover, in *Lang v Lang*,[3] the Inner House of the Court of Session held that it was irrelevant that an error as to qualities was induced by the fraudulent misrepresentation or concealment of facts by the spouse concerned.

The pursuer in this case sought a declarator of nullity on the ground that he had been induced to marry the defender as a result of her representation that she was pregnant by him when, in fact, she was carrying another man's child. The Court maintained that neither concealment of pregnancy *per alium* nor a fraudulent misrepresentation of the true source of a disclosed pregnancy was a ground of nullity in Scots law as these merely gave rise to errors as to qualities of the spouse and were therefore not sufficiently essential to vitiate consent.[4] The contract of marriage therefore constitutes an exception to the general law of contracts where a contract is voidable if it was induced as a result of a fraudulent misrepresentation.

The limited scope of operative error in relation to marriage can be the cause of considerable injustice. While a person in the position of the pursuer in *Lang v Lang*[5] could seek divorce, he may well have to wait five years before he has a relevant ground.[6] The fraudulent misrepresentation cannot constitute grounds for divorce as behaviour for this purpose is restricted to the defender's conduct '*since the date of the marriage*'.[7]

Force or fear

As a matter of principle, a marriage will be void if a party's consent was obtained as a result of force or fear.[8] There is an absence of Scottish

1 Stair I 9.9.
2 There is one exception: the marriage is voidable if one or both of the parties are unable to consummate the marriage as a result of incurable impotency. See *infra* p 36.
3 1921 SC 44: overruling *Stein v Stein* 1914 SC 903.
4 Cf the position in English law: s 12(f) of the Matrimonial Causes Act 1973.
5 1921 SC 44.
6 Ie 5 years non-cohabitation: s 1(2)(e) of the Divorce (Scotland) Act 1976. See *infra* Ch 6.
7 Section 1(2)(b) of the Divorce (Scotland) Act 1976: see *infra* Ch 6.
8 Stair I 4.1; I 4.6.

authority on the point, but it is submitted that Scottish courts would adopt the following principles.

First, the will of the party must have been overcome as a result of force or fear. Put simply, the party must be terrified at the time of the ceremony. The test should be a subjective one, ie was this particular person overcome by force or fear, not whether a person of reasonable fortitude would have been terrified.[1] As Clive has pointed out:[2]

'There is a built-in protection against abuse of a subjective standard. The more trivial the force or fear, the more difficult it will be to convince the court that it did in fact overcome the will of the person subject to it'.

Thus, for example, in *Singh v Singh*[3] consent was not vitiated when a young girl went through an arranged marriage out of deference to her parents' wishes as opposed to fear of the consequences if she did not do so. In contrast, where a young girl was threatened that she would be thrown out of the house if she did not agree to an arranged marriage, her will was held to have been overborne and the marriage was rendered void.[4]

The force or fear may emanate from a third party, for example, state authorities. It has been held that fear of incarceration for political reasons can be sufficient.[5] In the leading English case of *Buckland v Buckland*[6] Buckland was accused of corrupting a young girl in Malta. These charges were false but in order to avoid imprisonment, Buckland went through a ceremony of marriage with the girl. His petition for a decree of nullity was granted but the Court of Appeal emphasised that it would not have succeeded if he had actually been guilty of defiling the girl. In other words, the fear must have been unjustifiably imposed. Accordingly, if a man is forced to marry a girl whom he has made pregnant because of the threat that affiliation proceedings would be brought against him unless he did so, he could not rely on the fear as it was justly imposed.

Clive has argued[7] that this distinction is hard to justify as the consent is no more free where the fear is justly imposed. However, this may

---

1 A subjective approach was taken by the English courts in *Scott v Sebright* (1886) 12 PD 21, [1886–90] All ER Rep 363.
2 *Clive* p 100.
3 [1971] 2 All ER 828, [1971] P 226, CA.
4 *Hirani v Hirani* (1982) 4 FLR 233, CA.
5 *H v H* [1953] 2 All ER 1229, [1954] P 258. Cf *Silver v Silver* [1955] 2 All ER 614.
6 (1965) [1967] 2 All ER 300, [1968] P 296.
7 *Clive* p 101.

well be a case where reasoning from legal principle must give way to considerations of public policy.[1]

Sham marriages

Parties may enter into marriage, not because they intend to live together as husband and wife, but for some ulterior purpose, for example, to avoid deportation. In England, in the absence of force or fear, such marriages are valid.[2] However, in Scotland, such marriages may be treated as void on the grounds that the parties did not have real consent to marry.

In the leading case of *Orlandi v Castelli*[3] the pursuer, a Scots woman of Italian origin, met the defender who was an Italian. In order to enable him to remain in Scotland when his residence permit expired, the couple went through a civil marriage ceremony. Both were Roman Catholics and held the view that a civil ceremony did not constitute a valid marriage and a religious ceremony was necessary. The marriage was never consummated. Lord Cameron held that if the pursuer could establish her averments, declarator of nullity would be granted. In his Lordship's opinion:

> '. . . *where it can be established* that there is no true matrimonial consent and that the ceremony was only designed as a sham or as an antecedent to true marriage, it is competent to found upon the absence of that consent for the purpose of setting aside a marriage regularly celebrated'.[4]

This decision was followed in *Mahmud v Mahmud*[5] where Lord Kincraig held that a civil marriage was void where it was satisfactorily proved that a Moslem couple did not regard themselves as married until a religious ceremony had taken place. In *Akram v Akram*[6] Lord Dunpark expressed the principle as follows:[7]

> '. . . there is no doubt that Scots civil law has always applied the consensual principle to the contract of marriage so that *if it be proved* that, notwithstanding the trappings of a formal marriage ceremony, the parties thereto did not exchange their consent *for the purpose of obtaining married status*, the ceremony must be denied the legal effect it was designed to produce.'

1 See generally Davies 'Duress and Nullity of Marriage' (1972) 88 LQR 549.
2 See, for example, *Silver v Silver* [1955] 2 All ER 614.
3 1961 SC 113.
4 Ibid at 120; italics added.
5 1977 SLT (Notes) 17.
6 1979 SLT (Notes) 87.
7 Ibid at 88; italics added.

It is accepted that given a regular marriage ceremony, prima facie the parties' consent is presumed. There is therefore a heavy onus on the pursuer to establish that the parties did not consent to be married. While the parties' religious beliefs will be important evidence of the absence of true consent, it is thought that the principle will apply even in the absence of a religious element, though the difficulty of rebutting the presumption of consent will be formidable. However, if it can be shown that the parties' predominant purpose when going through the ceremony was some ulterior motive, for example, to evade immigration rules, and not to enter upon the status of husband and wife, the marriage is void for absence of true consent.

Clive has argued[1] that a marriage will only be void as a sham, if it can be shown that at the time of the ceremony, the parties had a positive intention not to be married. Proof that they had a predominant ulterior motive for entering upon the marriage is not sufficient. But as he himself admits,[2] it is doubtful whether the parties would draw the distinction between having an intention not to marry and marrying for a predominant ulterior motive. It is submitted that Clive's distinction is too subtle. Instead it is thought that a marriage is void as a sham if it is established that at the time of the ceremony the parties purported to consent to marriage, not for the purpose of living together as husband and wife, but for some other ulterior motive.[3]

In *Akram v Akram*[4] Lord Dunpark granted decree with reluctance. He was concerned that it might well be contrary to public policy to annul a marriage on proof of a predominant ulterior motive when, as a result of the ceremony, the parties had achieved their aims, for example, to avoid deportation. Indeed he suggested that the principle of personal bar 'might well be extended to cover cases in which the proved ulterior purpose was to circumvent any law of the land'.[5] It is thought, however, that the solution to the problem is to reduce even further the importance of marriage in, for example, the immigration rules, so that there is no advantage in being parties to a sham marriage.

There is authority for the view that a marriage is void as a sham where one party did not withhold true consent. In *M'Leod v Adams*,[6] for example, although the marriage was not void as a result of the

---

1 *Clive* p 104.
2 Ibid.
3 This is certainly the thrust of Lord Dunpark's reasoning in *Akram v Akram* 1979 SLT (Notes) 87, cited *supra* p 34.
4 1979 SLT (Notes) 87.
5 Ibid 89.
6 1920 1 SLT 229.

young widow's error,[1] declarator of nullity was granted on the ground that the soldier did not intend to marry her when they purported to exchange *de praesenti* consent. Lord Sands held that the defender did not intend to marry her and only wished to discover the whereabouts of the widow's money, steal it and leave:

> 'The marriage ceremony was a detail in the execution of this crime.... His statement that he took her as his wife was a falsehood, and the marriage was simulate on his part.'[2]

However, a person is personally barred from pleading his or her own unilateral and uncommunicated reservation of true consent in an action of declarator of nullity.[3]

It has, however, been recommended that sham marriages should no longer be treated as void.[4]

Validation of marriages void for absence of consent

There is some authority for the principle that a marriage which is void as a result of absence of consent will be validated if the parties choose to overlook the impediment and continue to live as husband and wife.[5] However, it is thought that the better view is that a couple will become married as a result of the doctrine of marriage by cohabitation with habit and repute, in the same way as if their original marriage was void because of a temporary impediment to their marriage.

VOIDABLE MARRIAGES – INCURABLE IMPOTENCY

The parties' consent is the essential element of marriage in Scots law: *consensus non concubitus facit matrimonium.* However, a marriage is voidable if, and only if, one or both of the parties is at the time of the ceremony permanently and incurably impotent. As Lord President (Clyde) explained in *L v L,*[6] *potentia copulandi* is a resolutive condition of the contract of marriage: if it is not fulfilled the marriage is a nullity. But before the marriage will be treated as null, a party to the marriage must obtain a declarator of nullity of marriage from the Court of Session whereupon the marriage is retrospectively void from

---

1 *Supra* p 31.
2 1920 1 SLT 229 at 231.
3 *Akram v Akram* 1979 SLT (Notes) 87 at 88, per Lord Dunpark; *Clive* p 106.
4 *Family Law: Pre-consolidation Reforms* SLC Discussion Paper No 85, paras 3.16 ff.
5 *Clive* pp 110–111.
6 1931 SC 477 at p 481.

the date of decree.[1] It has been recommended that impotency should cease to be a ground on which a marriage is voidable.[2]

The meaning of incurable impotency

Impotency means incapacity to have sexual intercourse. The Scottish courts have taken the view that sexual intercourse involves full and complete sexual intercourse: *vera copula perfecta* accomplished *modo naturalis*. Partial penetration by the husband of the wife is not enough.[3] However, once full penetration has been achieved, the marriage has been consummated. It is irrelevant that the husband has used a contraceptive sheath.[4] Moreover, impotency is incapacity for sexual intercourse not capacity to procreate. Consequently, sterility does not amount to impotency. If a spouse is capable of sexual intercourse but refuses to consummate the marriage, that is not a ground of nullity in Scots law[5] though it could give rise to grounds for divorce.[6]

The impotency may be the result of physical or psychological causes. It may exist only in relation to the other spouse: *quoad hanc* (vis à vis the wife) or *quoad hunc* (vis à vis the husband). Indeed, both spouses may be impotent in relation to each other: *quoad hanc et quoad hunc*!

The impotency must exist at the date of the marriage and must be permanent and incurable at the date of the action for declarator of nullity. The courts have taken a realistic approach on the question of incurability and have held that the issue is whether the impotency is incurable in the context of the particular marriage. Thus, for example, in *M v W or M*,[7] the husband suffered from a nervous or psychological inability to consummate the marriage. He was advised by his doctor that the impotency was curable if he had hormone treatment and had the full support and help of his wife. After the hormone treatment was administered, his wife refused to have sexual intercourse with him.

1 *Supra* p 21.
2 *Family Law: Pre-consolidation Reforms* SLC Discussion Paper No 85, paras 3.20–3.29. There are only about 8 declarators of nullity a year and it is doubtful whether they are all concerned with incurable impotency. The numbers concerned are therefore very small. It is true that specific matrimonial relief on the ground of incurable impotency is anomalous: there is no specific relief, for example, if a spouse marries when suffering from sterility or an incurable or infectious disease. It is argued by the Commission that divorce on the ground of irretrievable breakdown should be a sufficient remedy in cases of incurable impotency.
3 *J v J* 1978 SLT 128.
4 *Baxter v Baxter* [1947] 2 All ER 886, [1948] AC 274, HL, an English case which it is thought would be followed in Scotland.
5 Cf the position in English law: s 12(b) of the Matrimonial Causes Act 1973.
6 On the behaviour ground: s 1(2)(b) of the Divorce (Scotland) Act 1976, see *infra* Ch 6.
7 1966 SLT 152.

The Inner House held that the husband's impotency was incurable *quoad hanc* as the cure involved both the hormone treatment and the wife's help which had not been forthcoming.[1]

While this decision illustrates the court's sympathy towards the pursuer, it must be restricted to its own special facts: a potent spouse cannot argue that he is impotent *quoad hanc* merely because his wife refuses to have sexual intercourse with him since this would, in effect, be recognising wilful refusal to consummate as a ground of nullity.

If the impotency is curable, where the action is brought by the potent spouse, decree is not granted until the impotent spouse has had an opportunity to undergo the necessary treatment: if the defender refuses treatment, decree will then be granted.[2] If the impotent spouse is the pursuer, the action will fail if reasonable steps could be taken to effect a cure. Where the treatment carries a risk to life or intolerable pain, the impotent spouse is not expected to undergo such an ordeal, and the impotency will be regarded as incurable.[3]

The potent spouse can obviously bring an action. But in *F v F*,[4] the Inner House held that because impotency was an involuntary condition, the impotent spouse can also seek a declarator of nullity on the ground of his or her own incurable impotency.

Personal bar

A spouse may be personally barred from obtaining declarator of nullity on the ground of incurable impotency. Personal bar will arise if with knowledge of the impotency and the availability of a legal remedy, the pursuer has either approbated the marriage or taken advantage of, or derived benefits from, the matrimonial relationship with the result that it would be unfair or inequitable to permit the pursuer to treat the marriage as null.[5]

Two points should be noticed. First, personal bar will only arise if the pursuer knows of the facts and the availability of a legal remedy. But knowledge of the law will prima facie be assumed and the onus should therefore be on the pursuer to show that he did not have knowledge of a legal remedy. Secondly, it is the pursuer's *conduct* which constitutes approbation or the taking of advantages etc which

---

1 But the Lord President (Clyde) thought that the question was whether the husband was impotent throughout the marriage rather than whether it was curable at the date of the action: see *Clive* pp 112–113.
2 *WY v AY* 1946 SC 27.
3 Such risks are unlikely to arise in the context of modern medicine.
4 1945 SC 202.
5 *CB v AB* (1885) 12 R (HL) 36 at 38, per Lord Selborne.

renders it unfair or inequitable to grant decree. The following are illustrations of the principle.

Delay

Delay per se is not enough,[1] but if it would result in serious prejudice to the defender, it could be so.[2]

Knowledge of impotency

Where the pursuer entered into the marriage with knowledge of the defender's impotency this will result in personal bar. By marrying in these circumstances, the pursuer has adopted or homologated the defender's failure to perform a condition whose failure would otherwise have entitled the pursuer to have the marriage resolved.[3] Conversely, an impotent spouse who has allowed the potent spouse to enter the marriage with knowledge of the impotency is personally barred from seeking declarator on the ground of his or her own impotency.[4]

Children

Personal bar will arise where the pursuer has homologated or adopted the voidable marriage by agreeing to adopt a child or have a child by artificial insemination.[5]

1 See, for example, *Allardyce v Allardyce* 1954 SC 419.
2 *AB v CB* 1961 SC 347.
3 *L v L* 1931 SC 477 at 481, per Lord President (Clyde).
4 It is submitted that this is an example of *rei interventus*.
5 *AB v CB* 1961 SC 347. *Quaere* if the child was conceived by *fecundatio ab extra* during an unsuccessful attempt to consummate the marriage.

3 The legal consequences of marriage I

INTRODUCTION

In this and the following two chapters it is proposed to discuss the major legal consequences of marriage for the spouses. This chapter is concerned with a miscellaneous range of subjects but the treatment is not intended to be exhaustive and certain important matters, for example, evidence and bankruptcy, are thought to be outwith the scope of a student text on family law. In Chapters 4 and 5, the implications of marriage on the law of property is discussed in some detail.[1]

The twentieth century has seen a drastic decline in the legal consequences of marriage.[2] In the interests of equality between the spouses, many changes in the law have taken the form of treating the spouses as though they were unmarried. But, particularly in relation to property, as long as our society continues to perceive that the primary responsibility for child rearing should be the mother's, formal legal equality will often result in a wife's economic dependence on her husband, as in fact she does not have the same opportunities to acquire property during the marriage. However, as we shall see,[3] under our system of financial provision on divorce the courts can compensate a wife for economic disadvantages suffered by her as a result of the marriage. Moreover, when a marriage is terminated by death, Scots law protects the surviving spouse by providing the survivor with legal rights to a proportion of the deceased's estate which cannot be defeated by the deceased. It is perhaps not too cynical to observe that during the marriage the legal consequences of being married are, with some important exceptions such as aliment[4] and the right to occupy the

---

1 *Infra* p 60 and p 73.
2 See generally, *Clive* Part II and Ch 29.
3 *Infra* Ch 7.
4 Discussed *infra* p 47.

matrimonial home,[1] relatively insignificant compared with being married when the marriage is terminated by divorce or death.

PERSONAL EFFECTS[2]

Nationality

Marriage has no effect on nationality. If a wife is a citizen of the United Kingdom and Colonies before marriage she remains so: if not, she retains her existing nationality. A foreign spouse of a British citizen can acquire British citizenship by naturalisation. [3] Marriage does, however, remain important in the context of immigration.[4]

Adherence

It is the duty of the spouses to live together, ie adhere. But, it is a duty which could never be specifically implemented and actions of adherence are no longer competent.[5] Where a spouse refuses to adhere without reasonable cause, that spouse is, however, regarded as being in desertion.[6]

At one time, the husband had the right to choose where the matrimonial home should be, and provided his choice was genuine and reasonable, a wife was in desertion if she refused to live there with him.[7] This right has now been abolished.[8]

Domicile

Arising from the wife's duty to live with her husband, the rule developed that a wife's domicile depended on that of her husband. Accordingly, while the marriage subsisted, a wife could not have a domicile which was different from her husband's. The wife's domicile of dependency was abolished by s 1 of the Domicile and Matrimonial Proceedings Act 1973 and a wife can now acquire an independent domicile.[9]

1 *Infra* Ch 5.
2 See *Clive* Ch 11.
3 The previous system whereby a foreign spouse could, on marriage to a British citizen, acquire British citizenship by registration has been phased out: see, generally, the British Nationality Act 1981, s 8; *Clive* pp 167–68.
4 *Clive* pp 168–171.
5 Section 2 of the Law Reform (Husband and Wife) (Scotland) Act 1984.
6 Discussed in the context of divorce, *infra* Ch 6.
7 See, for example, *Stewart v Stewart* 1959 SLT (Notes) 70.
8 Section 4 of the Law Reform (Husband and Wife) (Scotland) Act 1984.
9 By s 1(2) of the 1973 Act, a wife who had a domicile by dependence retains that domicile unless and until it is changed by acquisition or revival of another domicile, on or after the Act came into force.

Sexual relations

If a spouse is unable to consummate the marriage as a result of incurable impotency, the marriage is voidable. Similarly, if a spouse wilfully refuses to have sexual intercourse, this could give rise to an action of divorce.[1] If a spouse voluntarily has sexual intercourse with a third party during the subsistence of the marriage, this can give rise to an action of divorce on the ground of adultery.[2]

At one time, it was thought that a husband could not be guilty of raping his wife if he had sexual intercourse with her without her consent: this was based on the view that, on marriage, a wife is prima facie deemed to have surrendered her person to her husband. Where there was evidence, for example, if the couple were *de facto* separated, from which it could be inferred that the wife was no longer prepared to surrender her body to her husband, then he could be convicted of rape and not merely indecent assault.[3] The High Court of Justiciary has now held that these rules are anachronistic and that a husband can be guilty of raping his wife even although the couple are living together.[4] In the course of his judgment the Lord Justice-General (Emslie) said:[5]

> 'Nowadays it cannot seriously be maintained that by marriage a wife submits herself irrevocably to sexual intercourse in all circumstances. It cannot be affirmed nowadays, whatever the position may have been in earlier centuries, that it is an incident of modern marriage that a wife consents to intercourse obtained only by force. There is no doubt that a wife does not consent to assault upon her person and there is no plausible justification for saying today that she nevertheless is to be taken to consent to intercourse by assault.'

Of course, even although a husband can now be charged with the rape of his wife, there remain formidable problems of proof.

On marriage, a spouse lacks capacity to enter into another marriage, unless the existing marriage is terminated by divorce or death.

Name

There is no legal requirement for a wife to take her husband's surname on marriage. It is, however, still common for a wife to use her husband's surname but this is mere usage. In formal legal documents a

---

1 Based on s 1(2)(b) of the Divorce (Scotland) Act 1976, discussed *infra* Ch 6.
2 Section 1(2)(a) of the Divorce (Scotland) Act 1976, discussed *infra* Ch 6.
3 *HM Advocate v Duffy* 1983 SLT 7; *HM Advocate v Paxton* 1985 SLT 96.
4 *S v HM Advocate* 1989 SLT 469.
5 *Ibid* at 473.

married woman will sign using her maiden name and her husband's surname, for example, Mrs Elizabeth Smith (maiden name) or Brown (husband's name).[1]

OBLIGATIONS

Contract

At common law a wife had no contractual capacity. However, in time the courts recognised exceptions to the general rule and in a series of statutes culminating in the Married Women's Property (Scotland) Act 1920, a married woman was deemed to 'be capable of entering into contracts and incurring obligations . . . as if she were not married'.[2] Now s 24(1) of the Family Law (Scotland) Act 1985 provides that subject to the provisions of any enactment marriage shall not of itself affect 'the legal capacity of the parties to the marriage'. Thus marriage per se has no effect on the contractual capacity of the spouses.

When a spouse is a minor, he or she is no longer subject to the curatory of his or her parent.[3] Moreover, the rule that a wife who was a minor entered into the curatory of her husband has been abolished.[4]

At common law, a wife was presumed to have been placed by her husband in charge of his domestic affairs and consequently she could pledge his credit for household expenses, for example, food, clothing etc. This was known as the wife's *praepositura*.[5] The *praepositura* was thought to have become anachronistic and has been abolished.[6] However, it is, of course, possible that one spouse may expressly appoint the other to act as his or her agent in a particular transaction. Moreover, one spouse may impliedly authorise the other to act as his or her agent by acquiescing in a series of transactions. For example, if a husband has paid the accounts incurred by his wife at a dress shop, he will remain liable to pay future accounts unless he has informed the shopkeeper that he will no longer be prepared to pay her accounts in the future: merely to tell his wife no longer to pledge his credit is not sufficient to avoid liability.[7]

1 For the form of names used in court proceedings, see *Clive* pp 177–179.
2 Section 1: for a full account of these developments, see *Clive* pp 260–261.
3 Section 3(1) of the Law Reform (Husband and Wife) (Scotland) Act 1984. For full discussion of minors and curators, see *infra* Ch 9.
4 Section 3(2) of the Law Reform (Husband and Wife) (Scotland) Act 1984.
5 For discussion of the *praepositura* see *Clive* pp 267–276.
6 Section 7 of the Law Reform (Husband and Wife) (Scotland) Act 1984.
7 The husband's liability to pay his wife's debts incurred before marriage has been abolished: s 6 of the Law Reform (Husband and Wife) (Scotland) Act 1984.

Thus, as a result of recent reforms, spouses enjoy the same contractual capacity as they would have had if they were unmarried.[1]

Delict

At common law, spouses could not sue each other in delict. The anachronistic nature of this rule can be illustrated by the case where, as a result of a husband's negligent driving, the wife was injured: it was indefensible that she could not sue her husband, particularly as the loss would ultimately fall on her husband's insurance company. This position was modified by s 2 of the Law Reform (Husband and Wife) Act 1962 which provides that each of the spouses has 'the like rights' to bring proceedings against the other in respect of a delict 'as if they were not married': however, where the action is brought during the subsistence of the marriage, the court has a discretion to dismiss the proceedings if it appears that no substantial benefit would accrue to either party if the action continued.[2] The court's discretion is unlikely to be invoked as the action must proceed if a benefit accrues to the *pursuer*, even although the couple, as a family unit, will not benefit.[3]

Under the Damages (Scotland) Act 1976, where a spouse has died as a result of a delict by a third party, the surviving spouse has a right to damages for loss of support, including a reasonable sum for loss of the deceased's personal services, funeral expenses and loss of society (a loss of society award).[4] A surviving *divorced* spouse can only obtain damages for loss of support and funeral expenses.[5] However, claims under the Damages (Scotland) Act 1976 can also be brought by members of the deceased's 'immediate family', for example, children. In an important step towards the recognition of cohabitation, the deceased's 'immediate family' includes, 'any person, not being the spouse of the deceased, who was immediately before the deceased's death, living with the deceased as husband and wife.'[6] As a member of the deceased person's immediate family, the cohabitee is entitled to damages for

---

1 With the exception that on marriage, a spouse who is a minor ceases to be in the curatory of his or her parent.
2 Law Reform (Husband and Wife) Act 1962, s 2(2).
3 It has been proposed that since the discretion in s 2(2) is anomalous and unnecessary, it should be repealed: *Family Law Pre-consolidation reforms* SLC Discussion Paper No 85, paras 5.1–5.7.
4 Sections 1(3) and (4) of the Damages (Scotland) Act 1976. Compensation for loss of society and support is not reduced where a wife married her husband knowing that he was suffering a fatal disease allegedly caused by the negligence of the defender: *Phillips v Grampian Health Board* 1989 SLT 538.
5 Sections 1(4) and 10(2) of the Damages (Scotland) Act 1976.
6 Section 14 of the Administration of Justice Act 1982, amending para 1 of Sch 1 to the 1976 Act.

loss of support, funeral expenses and loss of society. This important innovation is the result of the acceptance by Parliament that 'a significant minority of caring and stable relationships exist outside marriage.'

While it is not necessary that the deceased was under a legal obligation to aliment the claimant, the relative must show that loss of support has been or is likely to arise as a result of the delict. Thus, where both spouses work and pool their wages and enjoy an enhanced standard of living, but each is *in fact* supporting himself or herself, there may be little, if any, damages for loss of support: 'the loss of jam on the family bread and butter does not give rise to what can currently be termed a claim for loss of support.'[1] Where a housewife was killed, her husband and child obtained damages for the loss of her services as a housekeeper.[2]

The Damages (Scotland) Act 1976 is concerned with the situation where the delict results in death. Where a person is injured, it was held at common law that the defender did not owe a duty of care to the victim's spouse or relatives if they suffered loss as a result of the delict. Accordingly, the family could not sue for damages.[3] Moreover, the victim could not sue for losses sustained by a relative, for example, a spouse, who had given up his or her job to nurse him.[4] As a result of s 8 of the Administration of Justice Act 1982,[5] where a person has sustained personal injuries, the injured person can now recover damages which amount to reasonable remuneration for necessary services rendered to him or her by a relative.[6] For these purposes, a relative includes a cohabitee. The pursuer ie the injured person, will then account to the relative for any damages recovered under this provision.[7]

When the victim is not earning, at common law, he or she had no right to sue for loss of earnings. This was particularly unfair to wives

1 *Mitchell v Gartshore* 1976 SLT (Notes) 41 per Lord Grieve at 42. The case was concerned with the analogous action at common law but it is submitted it still applies to a claim under the Damages (Scotland) Act 1976.
2 *Brown v Ferguson* 1990 SLT 274.
3 *Robertson v Turnbull* 1982 SLT 96.
4 *Edgar v Lord Advocate* 1965 SC 67.
5 As amended by s 69 of the Law Reform (Miscellaneous Provisions) (Scotland) Act 1990.
6 Damages can also be awarded as reasonable remuneration for necessary services to be rendered by a relative after the date of the action: s 8(3). This reverses the decision in *Foryth's Curator Bonis v Govan Shipbuilders* 1988 SLT 321.
7 Section 8(2). Damages will not be paid if the relative has expressly agreed that no payment should be made for these services: s 8(1) and (3). For an example of the operation of the provisions, see *Denheen v British Railways Board* 1986 SLT 249. There is, however, no equivalent to s 8(2) in respect of recovery of damages for future services under s 8(3).

who had given up their job to look after the home or children. Section 9 of the Administration of Justice Act 1982 now provides that an injured person who has been providing *unpaid* personal service to a relative, can sue for damages if as a result of the injuries, he or she is unable to continue to do so. For these purposes, a relative includes a cohabitee. The personal services must be services which a) were or might have been expected to have been rendered by the injured person before the injury; b) were of a kind which when rendered by a person other than a relative would ordinarily be obtainable on payment; and c) the injured person but for the injuries in question might have been expected to render gratuitously to a relative. These would include a wife's or cohabitee's unpaid housekeeping services to her husband or cohabitee, a mother's unpaid child rearing services to her children or a husband's unpaid DIY maintenance for the benefit of his wife and family. Because the personal services must have been rendered gratuitously before s 9 applies, the Act recognises the fact that work at home is still prima facie unpaid, but that its economic value to the community is such that justice demands that the injured person receive compensation even though he or she has not suffered patrimonial loss.[1]

TAXATION

Marriage has important fiscal consequences. However, the law on this subject is complex and full treatment is not thought suitable for a student text on family law.[2]

INCOME SUPPORT

For the purpose of obtaining income support it is necessary to aggregate the needs and resources of certain persons who are living together. The requirements and resources of a married couple who are members of the same household are aggregated but so also are those of an unmarried couple who are living together as husband and wife.[3]

The relationship between the system of state support and the private law obligation of aliment is discussed in the next section.

---

1 Of course, if the victim was being paid for his or her services, they could recover damages for loss of wages in the usual way.
2 For a discussion of the law, see the *Laws of Scotland: Stair Memorial Encyclopaedia* vol 10, paras 890–894.
3 Section 20(11) of the Social Security Act 1986.

ALIMENT

Introduction: the common law

It was an axiomatic principle of Scots common law that a husband was under an obligation to aliment ie maintain, his wife. A wife was not under a corresponding obligation to aliment her husband. Even in 1976, Lord Grieve could observe[1] that '... it is not yet the law of Scotland that a wife is under an obligation to support her husband and family, when the husband is in a position to afford such support.' But where a husband was in fact unable to maintain himself, his wife could be liable to aliment him provided she had 'a separate estate or ... a separate income more than reasonably sufficient for her own maintenance.'[2] Such cases were rare and in practice it was only a wife who was entitled to aliment.

At common law a wife was entitled to aliment unless she was, without just cause, unwilling to adhere.[3] Thus, for example, a husband had a duty to aliment his adulterous wife, provided she was willing to continue living with him.[4] But if a wife refused to adhere, then her right to aliment was lost unless she had just cause for living apart from her husband. At first, the concept of just cause was narrow,[5] but it was extended by s 6 of the Divorce (Scotland) Act 1964 to include a husband's 'grave and weighty' misconduct and desertion. Further reforms were necessary as a result of the Divorce (Scotland) Act 1976, in particular to ensure that a wife could obtain aliment when she and her husband had agreed to separate and apply for a divorce on the ground of two years non-cohabitation with the parties' consent.[6]

These rules as to entitlement were hideously complex.[7] But, to add insult to injury as it were, s 7(2) of the Divorce (Scotland) Act 1976 provided that in determining the amount of aliment, *if any*, to be awarded the court had to consider the factors listed in s 5(2) of the Act *viz* 'the respective means of the parties to the marriage and ... all the circumstances of the case'. Accordingly, even if a wife, who had been guilty of adultery and was willing to adhere, was prima facie entitled to aliment, the amount she would in fact obtain depended upon all the

---

1 *Mitchell v Gartshore* 1976 SLT (Notes) 41 at 42.
2 The Married Women's Property (Scotland) Act 1920, s 4.
3 On adherence see *supra* p 41.
4 *Donnelly v Donnelly* 1959 SC 97.
5 *Jack v Jack* 1962 SC 24.
6 Section 1(2)(d) of the Divorce (Scotland) Act 1976, discussed *infra* Ch 6.
7 For full discussion of the difficulties, see *Clive* Ch 12.

circumstances of the case including any matrimonial misconduct.[1] It was therefore absurd to have complex rules as to *entitlement* to seek aliment when the amount, *if any*, awarded was entirely at the discretion of the courts.

The nature and extent of the obligation

The law of aliment was radically reformed by the Family Law (Scotland) Act 1985.[2] By s 1(1) it is declared that an obligation of aliment shall be owed by a) a husband to his wife and b) a wife to her husband.[3] The obligations are clearly mutual and the sex discrimination inherent in the common law is removed. Husband and wife include the parties to a polygamous marriage.[4]

A spouse's duty to aliment is 'to provide such support as is reasonable in the circumstances', having regard to the matters which a court is required or entitled to consider in determining the amount of aliment awarded.[5] The effect of this provision is that the complex rules on when a spouse was entitled to seek aliment are swept away: instead, a spouse will always have a prima facie right to aliment from the other, but the extent of the defender's duty to aliment will depend on the same factors as govern quantification of an award.

The factors which must be considered are set out in s 4(1). They are:
'a) the needs and resources of the parties;[6]
b) the earning capacities of the parties;[7]
c) generally, all the circumstances of the case.'

Section 4(3)(a)

In relation to s 4(1)(c), s 4(3)(a) provides that the court '*may*, if it thinks fit, take account of any support, financial or otherwise, given by the defender to any person whom he maintains as a dependant in his household, whether or not the defender owes an obligation of aliment to that person'. The effect of this provision can be illustrated by the following example: H leaves W, who is unemployed, and sets up home

---

1 *Lambert v Lambert* 1982 SLT 144 (A case concerned with s 5(2) in the context of divorce but the principle was applicable in relation to aliment).
2 References in this section are to the 1985 Act unless otherwise stated.
3 Obligations of aliment exist between parents and children: these are discussed *infra* Ch 9.
4 Section 1(5).
5 Section 1(2).
6 'Needs' means present and foreseeable needs; 'resources' means present and foreseeable resources: s 27.
7 The court is concerned with earning *capacity*, not merely a party's likely future earnings: consequently a claimant cannot elect to be unemployed.

with his mistress, M. H supports M financially. In an action for aliment brought by W against H, the court *may* take into account the fact that H is supporting M. If it does, there will be less resources available for W and consequently a smaller amount of aliment will be awarded.

Section 4(3)(a) reverses the previous rule under which financial or other support *in fact* made by a defender to a third party was *not* taken into account, unless he was under a legal obligation to aliment that person, for example, his child.[1] It is submitted that the courts should be prepared to exercise their discretion under s 4(3)(a), particularly where the defender is a low wage earner. If H, in the example, was earning very little, then if the fact that he was supporting M was taken into account, W would probably receive no aliment at all. This is a sensible result in the circumstances for it allows W to have full recourse to income support and other benefits. If it were not taken into account, the amount of aliment awarded would be small: even if H paid it regularly, W would be no better off financially, since the aliment would merely reduce the amount payable in income support.

Where either spouse is being financially or otherwise supported by a third party, this will be a relevant factor under s 4(1)(c) as it is clearly one of the circumstances of the case. For example, in an action for aliment by a wife against her husband, the court was entitled to take into account the fact that the husband's cohabitee was contributing to their joint outlays: but the joint incomes of the husband and cohabitee could not simply be aggregated as that would subject the cohabitee to an obligation of aliment to the wife, which the cohabitee did not owe.[2]

Section 4(3)(b)

In relation to s 4(1)(c), s 4(3)(b) provides that the court 'shall not take account of any conduct of a party unless it would be manifestly inequitable to leave it out of account'. The effect of this provision is that a spouse has a prima facie right to aliment from the other, even although the pursuer has committed adultery,[3] has behaved in an intolerable way, or refuses to adhere. Moreover, in assessing the amount of aliment such conduct is to be ignored by the court, unless it would be 'manifestly inequitable to leave it out of account'.[4] It is submitted that

---

1 *Henry v Henry* 1972 SLT (Notes) 26. Moreover, a pursuer's entitlement to supplementary benefit was ignored, with the result that defenders could be ordered to pay awards of aliment which they could not afford while continuing to support the third party: *McAuley v McAuley* 1968 SLT (Sh Ct) 81; *McCarrol v McCarrol* 1966 SLT (Sh Ct) 45.
2 *Munro v Munro* 1986 SLT 72; *Firth v Firth* 1990 GWD 5–266.
3 Discussed in the context of divorce, *infra* Ch 6.
4 Section 4(3)(b).

it should only be in very extreme circumstances that the pursuer's conduct should be taken into account to reduce the amount of aliment which would otherwise be awarded.[1] When a marriage is breaking down, there is usually fault on both sides: certainly, it is most unjust to penalise a spouse financially for conduct, for example, adultery, which is a symptom not a cause of matrimonial breakdown. Nor does this raise injustice to the defender. The purpose of aliment is to oblige the spouses to maintain each other *during the marriage*: the obligation to aliment ends in divorce. Consequently, if the defender feels aggrieved at being obliged to aliment a pursuer who has committed adultery or other matrimonial misconduct, his remedy is to sue for divorce.[2] On divorce, the obligation to aliment ceases and, instead, financial provision can be ordered which will hopefully result in a financial clean break between the spouses.[3] And it is thought this approach is consonant with current public policy which is to encourage marriages which have irretrievably broken down, as evidenced inter alia by matrimonial misconduct, to be decently buried.

Defences

Section 2(8) provides a general defence to a claim for aliment[4] if the defender makes an offer to receive the pursuer into the defender's household and to fulfil the obligation of aliment, *provided* it is reasonable to expect the pursuer to accept the offer. In considering whether it is reasonable for the pursuer to accept the defender's offer, s 2(9) enjoins the court to look at all the relevant circumstances including conduct and any decree, for example, an interdict against violence,[5] which has been obtained. So, for example, if W has been the victim of H's domestic violence, she will obtain aliment even though she is unwilling to adhere and despite the fact that H makes her an offer to return to his household: as a result of H's conduct, the offer is not one which it would be reasonable to expect W, the victim of his violence, to accept. Even if she had committed adultery, it is thought that H would not have a defence if he had been violent towards her; because of the violence, it is still not reasonable to expect W to return. Moreover, her

---

1 One example might be where the pursuer's conduct had reduced the defender's resources: for example, by injuring the defender so that his earning capacity was impaired. Another is illustrated by the facts of *Kyte v Kyte* [1987] 3 WLR 1114 where the wife had actively encouraged her husband's attempts at suicide!
2 See *infra* Ch 6.
3 See *infra* Ch 7.
4 Except where the claim is brought by or on behalf of a child under the age of 16: see *infra* Ch 9.
5 Discussed *infra* Ch 5.

adultery will not lead to any reduction in the amount of aliment awarded as it is thought that adultery per se is not conduct which it would be manifestly inequitable to leave out of account.[1]

Where a couple have agreed to separate, s 2(9) provides that the mere fact that they have agreed to live apart does not of itself establish that it is unreasonable to expect the pursuer to accept the defender's offer. Thus, if a couple agree to part and W later seeks aliment, if H makes her an offer to return to his household, this may constitute a s 2(8) defence because it is not unreasonable to expect the pursuer to accept such an offer merely because they have earlier agreed to part. Of course, other circumstances, for example, H's drinking or adultery or violence while they lived together, may make it unreasonable to expect W to accept H's offer.

Aliment where the parties are living together

At common law, a spouse who was being inadequately maintained had to leave the matrimonial home before an action for aliment could be brought.[2] Section 2(6) provides that an action for aliment is competent notwithstanding that the pursuer is living in the same household as the defender. Thus, for example, a wife can sue her husband for an adequate housekeeping allowance. But it is a defence to an action in these circumstances if the defender can show that he is fulfilling his obligation to aliment the pursuer and intends to continue doing so.[3]

The nature of an award

On granting a decree of aliment s 3(1) provides that the court may, if it thinks fit,

a) order the making of a periodical payment, whether for a definite or an indefinite period or until the happening of a specified event: but the court cannot substitute a lump sum for a periodical payment;[4]

b) order the making of alimentary payments of an occasional or special nature, for example, hospital expenses: these will usually be small amounts;

c) backdate awards to the date of bringing the action or, on special cause shown, even earlier;

---

1 Section 4(3)(b), discussed *supra* pp 49, 50.
2 *M'Donald v M'Donald* (1875) 2 R 705.
3 Section 2(7).
4 Section 3(2).

d) award less than the amount claimed even if the claim is undisputed.[1]

The prohibition of lump sum payments and the continued insistence that the award take the form of a periodical payment reflects the fact that aliment is an obligation which arises from, and continues throughout, marriage. As we shall see,[2] on divorce it is envisaged that financial provision will generally take the form of capital ie lump sum payments, to encourage a financial clean break between the parties.

A decree of aliment can, on an application by either party, be varied or recalled if there has been a material change of circumstances since the date of decree.[3] Thus, for example, if the value of the original award has been undermined by inflation, the decree may be varied upwards; conversely, if the defender has been made redundant since the date of the original award the decree can be varied downwards, or indeed, recalled. In an action for variation, the court has the same powers, for example, to backdate awards as in an original application for aliment.[4] The Act is retrospective and its powers in relation to variation apply to awards made before its date of commencement.[5]

Procedural matters

A spouse may bring a claim for aliment *simpliciter* in the Court of Session or the sheriff court.[6] In practice a claim for aliment is often brought along with other proceedings, for example, separation. In addition, in an action for aliment or in an action for divorce, separation, declarator of marriage or declarator of nullity of marriage, the court can order interim aliment until the final disposal of the action.[7] When decree of divorce has been granted, but a claim for financial provision is still pending, an award of interim aliment remains competent[8]. While technically an action for interim aliment is not an action of aliment within the meaning of the 1985 Act,[9] it has been held that it should be treated as such and therefore the court has the same powers

---

1 This overrules *Terry v Murray* 1947 SC 10, where it was held that the court was bound to grant decree for the amount claimed in an undefended action for aliment.
2 *Infra* Ch 7.
3 Section 5(1).
4 Section 5(2) impliedly incorporating s 3: see *Hannah v Hannah* 1988 SLT 82.
5 1 September 1986; see *Matheson v Matheson* 1988 SLT 238; *Nixon v Nixon* 1987 SLT 602.
6 Section 2(1). Thus the anachronistic common law distinction between interim and permanent aliment is abolished.
7 Section 6(1).
8 *Neill v Neill* 1987 SLT (Sh Ct) 143.
9 Section 2(2) and (3).

to vary an award of interim aliment as an award of aliment.[1] The factors in s 4 have also been held to be relevant to a claim for interim aliment.[2]

As interim aliment is awarded to a party to the proceedings, it does not matter that the proceedings finally establish that, for example, because the marriage was void, the parties did not owe an obligation to aliment each other because they were never spouses. A pursuer in an action of declarator of nullity can apply for interim aliment although denying the existence of the marriage.[3]

The relationship between aliment and income support

It will be clear that the guidelines in s 4 are sufficiently wide to allow a court considerable discretion in assessing the amount of aliment. However, apart from the prima facie exclusion of matrimonial conduct and the fact that the defender's financial or other support to a third party may be taken into account, there are few guidelines on how the court should exercise its discretion. Wealthy couples should be able to negotiate an appropriate figure with the advice of their lawyers. But where the couple is in the lower income bracket, there may not be enough money to aliment the family adequately when the marriage breaks down, particularly if the wage earner has become involved with another family. Consider the following example.

EXAMPLE

H, who is a small wage earner, deserts W who is unemployed in order to live with his mistress, M. H supports M financially and does not provide aliment for W. What can W do?
  (i) At common law, W could pledge her husband's credit for necessaries – if she could obtain food and clothing on credit. This right was distinct from her *praepositura* and has not been abolished.[4] The third party who supplied W with the necessary support can recover from H, provided H was liable to aliment her. H's liability is based on principles of recompense.[5]

---

1 *Donaldson v Donaldson* 1988 SLT 243.
2 *McGeachie v McGeachie* 1989 SCLR 99: for the s 4 factors, see *supra* pp 48 ff. An appeal from an award of interim aliment is possible: *MacInnes v MacInnes* 1990 GWD 13–690.
3 Section 17(2).
4 On the *praepositura*, see *supra* p 43. It is thought that the right has not been affected by the repeal of s 3(2) of the Married Women's Property (Scotland) Act 1920.
5 See *Clive* pp 276–78.

(ii) W could bring an action for aliment against H. However, if the court exercised its discretion and took into account the fact that he was supporting M, W would receive little, if any, aliment.[1] If this factor were ignored, it could cause hardship to M, who is unable to obtain income support because of the cohabitation rule.[2]

(iii) In practice W would apply for income support. There is no longer an obligation on a spouse to seek a decree of aliment before applying for income support. As we have seen, in financial terms, W is no worse off: indeed, she could be better off, than if an award of aliment had been obtained from H.[3] At the very least, she receives regular income and there is no problem of enforcement of a decree of aliment against H.[4]

By s 26(3) of the Social Security Act 1986 a man is liable to maintain his wife and children up to the age of 16[5] and a woman is liable to maintain her husband and children up to that age. Where the DSS pays income support to or on behalf of a person who is not being alimented by a liable relative, it can take proceedings against the liable relative to make a contribution towards the amount of support paid.[6] The sheriff, having regard to all the circumstances, including the defender's resources, can order the defender to pay such sum, weekly or otherwise, to the DSS, as may be appropriate.[7] Thus in the above example, the DSS could take proceedings against H (the liable relative) who has failed to aliment W (the dependant) for a contribution towards the amount of income support W has received.[8]

But, in practice, the DSS will only take proceedings against a liable relative, if his resources are in excess of the following: the income support, including any premiums and housing costs, which he could

1 Section 4(3)(a) discussed *supra* p 48. However, if W's entitlement to income support continues to be ignored as a resource, W would obtain *some* aliment: but this would simply reduce her income support and leave her no better off financially.
2 *Supra* p 46.
3 *Supra* p 49.
4 On enforcement of decrees, see *Clive* pp 202–207.
5 Section 20(11) of the Social Security Act 1986: The fact that the children are illegitimate is irrelevant: s 20(5).
6 Section 24 of the Social Security Act 1986.
7 The sheriff's discretion is very wide: he can, for example, order the liable relative to pay only a small fraction of the income support paid out: *Secretary of State for Social Services v McMillan* 1987 SLT 52.
8 The liable relative may have a defence if there was in the circumstances no duty to aliment the dependant: see *National Assistance Board v Wilkinson* [1952] 2 All ER 255, [1952] 2 QB 648, DC; *Clive* pp 390–391.

claim, plus a quarter of his net earnings.[1] If H is on a low wage, it is unlikely that he would have income in excess of the formula and the DSS would therefore not approach him for a contribution. Approximately, only eleven per cent of the money paid out in income support is recovered from liable relatives.

The DSS formula leaves the liable relative with an income which is in excess of subsistence level ie the income support rate for a single person. It was a serious criticism of the position before the Family Law (Scotland) Act 1985 that courts could make awards of aliment which, if paid, would leave the defender with resources below subsistence level.[2] This was because the pursuer's entitlement to income support and the fact that the defender was supporting a third party he was not obliged to aliment, were ignored. If the courts exercise their discretion under s 4(3)(a)[3] and take the fact of third party support into account, then this will be a major step in rationalising the law of aliment and income support.

It should be noticed that for the purposes of the Social Security Act 1986, neither a man nor a woman is a liable relative in respect of a former spouse. However, after a divorce parents remain liable relatives in respect of their children.[4]

SUCCESSION

Introduction

As submitted at the outset, in modern family law it is important for a person to have been married. This is particularly true in relation to succession where Scots law gives the surviving spouse certain rights to succeed to a proportion of the deceased spouse's estate which cannot be defeated by testamentary deed. In this section it is proposed to give

---

1 The formula was first published in the *Report of the Committee on One-Parent Families* (the Finer Report) (Cmnd 5629) (1974) para 4.188. It has subsequently been modified: it is not clear whether the DSS will continue to apply the formula in the future.
2 See, for example, *Henry v Henry* 1972 SLT (Notes) 26.
3 *Supra* p 48.
4 The aliment of children is discussed *infra* Ch 9. The government proposes to introduce measures to ensure that parents, in particular fathers, fulfil their obligations to aliment their children after the family has become dysfunctional.

an outline of these rights:[1] as they are closely integrated to similar rights enjoyed by the deceased's children it is convenient to discuss these at this stage.

Legal rights

Since the Succession (Scotland) Act 1964,[2] a surviving husband is entitled to his *jus relicti* out of his deceased wife's estate; a surviving wife is entitled to her *jus relictae* out of her deceased husband's estate; and children[3] are entitled to *legitim* out of their deceased parent's estate. Since they are identical it is proposed to call the *jus relicti* and the *jus relictae* by the composite term 'relict's right'.[4]

The relict's right is to a third of the deceased's free moveable estate, if the deceased is survived by children or to a half of the deceased's free moveable estate, if there are no surviving children. *Legitim* is the right to a third of the deceased parent's free moveable estate if survived by a spouse or to a half of the deceased's free moveable estate if there is no surviving spouse. Moveable estate consists of money, shares, pictures, cars etc, but excludes heritable property (heritage), of which the most important property is likely to be the matrimonial or family home. Thus, for example, if H dies survived by W and children, W is entitled to a third of his free moveable estate as her *jus relictae*, the children are entitled to a third of his free moveable estate as *legitim* and the deceased can only effectively test on the remaining third. But if the estate includes heritable property, for example, the matrimonial home, H is free to dispose of the property as he wishes by testamentary deed, as legal rights are not exigible out of heritage. So H could, by will, leave his house to his mistress, M.

Legal rights may be discharged in the lifetime of the spouses or parents. Similarly, legal rights may be renounced after a spouse's or parent's death, expressly, or impliedly by acceptance of testamentary provisions which were intended by the deceased to be in satisfaction of

---

1 For a full treatment, see *Clive* Ch 29.
2 References in this section are to the 1964 Act unless otherwise stated.
3 Scots law makes no distinction between legitimate and illegitimate children in this context: para 7(2) of Sch 1 to the Law Reform (Parent and Child) (Scotland) Act 1986, discussed *infra* Ch 8.
4 This is the term used by *Clive*.

legal rights.[1] If, however, the surviving spouse or children elect to take legal rights, they will forfeit any testamentary provisions in testamentary deeds executed after 1964, unless forfeiture is expressly excluded.[2]

Prior rights

Where a spouse dies intestate,[3] ie without a will, the surviving *spouse* enjoys substantial prior rights out of the intestate estate.

By s 8, the surviving spouse is entitled to the dwelling house in which he or she was ordinarily resident at the date of the death of the intestate.[4] If the house is worth more than £65,000, the surviving spouse is entitled to a sum of £65,000 instead.[5] In addition, the surviving spouse is entitled to the furniture and plenishings of a dwelling house[6] in which he or she was ordinarily resident at the date of the death of the intestate. However, if the value of the furniture or plenishings exceeds £12,000, the surviving spouse is entitled to such parts of them as he or she may choose, to a value not exceeding £12,000.[7]

By s 9, the surviving spouse is entitled to financial provision out of the intestate's estate. If the intestate is survived by issue,[8] however remote, the surviving spouse is entitled to £21,000: in other cases, the surviving spouse is entitled to £35,000.[9] Where the net intestate estate is less than £21,000 or £35,000, as the case may be, the surviving spouse is entitled to the whole of the intestate estate. Where it is more, the surviving spouse's financial provision is borne by the heritable and

---

1 By s 13 (as amended by the Law Reform (Miscellaneous Provisions) (Scotland) Act 1968 Sch 1), acceptance of a provision in a post–1964 testamentary disposition is, in the absence of express provision to the contary, deemed to be an implied renunciation of legal rights in so far as they would conflict with the settlement. This is, however, a complex area of the law of succession, and the reader is referred to *Clive* pp 690–694.

2 Section 13: for deeds executed pre-1964, see *Clive* pp 695–696.

3 For these purposes intestacy includes partial intestacy.

4 If more than one house qualifies, the surviving spouse has 6 months to elect which house is to be subject to prior rights.

5 Section 8(1) as amended. The current amount was set by the Prior Rights of Surviving Spouses (Scotland) Order 1988 (SI 1988/633).

6 It does not matter if the dwelling house did not form part of the deceased's intestate estate.

7 SI 1988/633 increasing the limit from £10,000 set by SI 1981/806.

8 There is now no distinction between legitimate and illegitimate issue: Sch 2 to the Law Reform (Parent and Child) (Scotland) Act 1986 amending s 36(1) of the 1964 Act.

9 The current sums were set by SI 1988/633.

moveable parts of the estate in proportion to the respective amounts of those parts.[1]

After satisfaction of these prior rights, the spouse is entitled to claim legal rights from the remaining free moveable estate.[2] Only then is the remaining intestate estate distributed to the deceased's heirs.[3]

It will be obvious, that a surviving spouse's prior rights will exhaust the value of most estates. Consequently, the surviving spouse may well be better off if the deceased dies intestate rather than leave a testamentary deed bequeathing all the estate to the surviving spouse. For in this latter case, any surviving children will be entitled to claim *legitim*: but on an intestacy, children can only succeed to the intestate estate after satisfaction of the surviving spouse's prior rights.

Conclusion

As a result of the system of prior rights, a surviving spouse is generously treated on an intestacy. Where the deceased has left a will, the system of legal rights affords some degree of protection for the deceased's surviving spouse and family. However, there is nothing to stop the deceased from defeating claims to legal rights by converting all the property into heritage and disposing of it by testamentary deed to whomsoever he or she chooses. Moreover, the same result can be achieved if the deceased has transferred his or her moveable property to a third party during his or her lifetime. The inter vivos transfer must be genuine: a simulate or sham transaction will not suffice.[4]

It should be noted, however, that, unlike English law, marriage does not have the effect of revoking prior testamentary writings. It is a question of construction whether a legacy to the deceased 'wife' or 'husband' means the deceased's spouse at the time the will was executed or the person who was the deceased's spouse at the date of death.[5]

In the present writer's view, there is force in the argument that at present the deceased's family may be over protected. While protection for a spouse is perhaps justified, it is difficult to see why *adult* children

---

1 Section 9(3).
2 Discussed *supra* p 56.
3 These will in the first place be the deceased's children and their issue. No distinction is now made between legitimate and illegitimate issue: Sch 2 to the Law Reform (Parent and Child) (Scotland) Act 1986 amending s 36(1) of the 1964 Act. For a full list of heirs see s 2: on representation see s 5.
4 See *Clive* pp 697–699.
5 See *Clive* p 700.

should be entitled to *legitim*, when they may have had no interest in their parent's welfare before his or her death. Nevertheless, the Scottish Law Commission has recommended further strengthening of the protection of the deceased's family by *inter alia* allowing the relict's right (legal share) to be exigible out of both moveable and heritable property.[1] On intestacy, if there is no issue, the surviving spouse should succeed to the whole estate: if there is no surviving spouse, the issue should succeed to the whole estate.[2] If there is both a surviving spouse and issue, the surviving spouse is to be entitled to £100,000 or the whole estate if less: if the estate is in excess of £100,000, the excess should be divided equally between the issue and the surviving spouse.[3] If legal share is claimed, the person will forfeit all rights under the law of intestate succession or all testamentary provisions from the deceased.[4]

1 *Report on Succession* SLC No 124, paras 3.15–3.16. For the proportions of the legal shares, see paras 3.18–3.29.
2 Ibid, paras 2.3 and 2.4.
3 Ibid, para 2.7.
4 Ibid, paras 3.45–3.48.

4 The legal consequences of marriage II: moveable property

INTRODUCTION

Until the Married Women's Property (Scotland) Act 1881[1] as a general rule all moveable property – money, shares, furniture etc – owned by a wife or subsequently acquired by her during marriage, for example, by legacy, passed to her husband as a result of his *jus mariti*. The husband could do anything he wished with the property. There were limited exceptions to this rule such as alimentary provisions in favour of the wife under a marriage contract and the wife's *paraphernalia*, ie her dresses and jewellery, including their receptacles. The 1881 Act abolished the *jus mariti*.[2] Where a wife owned heritable property, for example, land or a house, it remained hers, but the property was administered by her husband as a result of his *jus administrationis*.[3] The *jus administrationis* was abolished by the Married Women's Property (Scotland) Act 1920.[4]

As a result of the Acts of 1881 and 1920, Scots law accepted that marriage should have no effect on the property rights of spouses during marriage and that for this purpose they should be treated as strangers. In relation to the property of spouses, Scots law is a separate property system. This is enshrined in s 24 of the Family Law (Scotland) Act 1985 which provides that:

'. . . marriage shall not of itself affect—
(a) the respective rights of the parties to the marriage in relation to their property'.

Scots law therefore proceeds on the basis that prima facie the ordinary rules of property apply to spouses, as though they were unmarried. The separate property system thus achieves legal equality between the

---

1 For the history of the law, see *Clive* pp 295–299.
2 Section 1(1).
3 Until 1881, income arising from her lands, for example, rents, belonged to the husband by virtue of his *ius mariti* as the rents were, of course, moveable property.
4 Section 1.

spouses in respect of their property. But, in practice, this can lead to injustice, as it is still expected in our society that women should bear the major burden of child rearing and consequently, wives often do not have the same opportunity as their husbands to acquire property during the marriage.[1] Moreover, the separate property system ignores the fact that when spouses acquire property, they do not regard themselves as strangers. Often they will pool their resources to purchase a matrimonial home and other domestic property. Further, property, for example, a car, is often bought not for the use and enjoyment of the purchasing spouse but for the use and enjoyment of the family. In relation to such property, the application of the ordinary rules of the law of property is difficult and likely to lead to unrealistic results.

It has now been recognised in Scotland, that the property rules relating to spouses – and to a lesser extent cohabitees – cannot ignore the 'family' element in their property transactions. Consequently, special property rules have been introduced which are specifically applicable to spouses and do not treat them as strangers.

Thus while the basic property regime for spouses in Scots law is still that of a separate property system, there are now some special property rules which recognise that the parties are married and these are designed to take into account the 'family' element in the spouses' property dealings. These rules have, to some extent, alleviated the injustices which in practice arise from the strict application of the separate property system.

The law as it relates to moveable property is examined in this chapter: the law in relation to the matrimonial home is considered in Chapter 5.

WEDDING PRESENTS

The ownership of a wedding present depends on the intention of the donor. Did the donor intend the gift to be owned jointly by the spouses or only by one of the spouses? There is no difficulty if there is direct evidence of the donor's intention. But problems can arise if such evidence is not available.

In *McDonald v McDonald*[2] the sheriff took the view that 'the practical rule which is normally applied is to regard as the owner of the present the spouse from whose friends or relatives the gift was

---

1 A wife can now obtain compensation for economic disadvantages suffered by her as a result of marriage in the form of financial provision on divorce: see *infra* Ch 7.
2 1953 SLT (Sh Ct) 36.

received'.[1] But merely because a gift was intended to be *used* jointly by the spouses, for example, an electric toaster or bathroom scales, it does not follow that the donor intended that the present should be *owned* jointly by them.[2] Sometimes, however, the donor's intention can be inferred from the nature of the gift: thus, for example, a necklace can be presumed to be a gift to the wife and a set of guns can be presumed to be a gift to the husband. Although Clive has suggested[3] that in the absence of evidence of the donor's intention joint ownership of a wedding present should be presumed, it is doubtful whether this is in fact the current law of Scotland.

GIFTS BETWEEN SPOUSES

The ordinary law of donation applies in relation to the transfer of corporeal moveable property between spouses. Accordingly, the presumption *against* donation is prima facie applicable.[4] But as gifts between spouses are not uncommon, the presumption is not difficult to rebut.[5] Thus, for example, if H transfers a dress to W, while the onus is on W to show that H intended to make a gift of the dress to her, the presumption can easily be rebutted if W brings evidence that the transfer took place on her birthday or on their wedding anniversary or at Christmas. In addition to rebutting the presumption against donation, the transferee must establish that the property has been delivered to him or her, before the ownership of the property passes to the donee. This can give rise to difficulties where the property is already in the matrimonial home before the gift is made.[6]

The common law rule that gifts between spouses were revocable during the donor's lifetime has been abolished.[7]

---

1 1953 SLT (Sh Ct) 36.
2 *Traill v Traill* 1925 SLT (Sh Ct) 54.
3 *Clive* p 305.
4 *Jamieson v M'Leod* (1880) 7 R 1131; *Smith v Smith's Trustees* (1884) 12 R 186; *Beveridge v Beveridge* 1925 SLT 234 at 236.
5 There is no presumption against donation in transfers of property between parent and child: Stair I 8.2.
6 See generally *Clive* pp 305–307.
7 Section 5 of the Married Women's Property (Scotland) Act 1920. The gift may, however, be struck down as a gratuitous alienation under s 34 of the Bankruptcy (Scotland) Act 1985, if the donor becomes bankrupt.

CORPOREAL MOVEABLES BOUGHT BY THE SPOUSES

It is a cardinal principle of a system of separate property that the spouse who buys or otherwise acquires corporeal moveable property, for example, a motor car, prima facie owns it: so if H buys a motor car, he is the owner. Where both spouses contribute to the purchase price, they own the property jointly in proportion to their contributions to the price. But in the absence of evidence of joint contribution to the price, the common law did not assume joint ownership merely because the property was used by both spouses and the family.

Apart from the problems of proving which of the spouses paid for the property, perhaps many years after the date of its purchase, the separate property system could give rise to injustices in the following situations:

a) Where W gives up her job for several years to look after the children of the family she will lose the opportunity to earn and acquire property. The common law gave her no proprietary interest in the property acquired by H during that period.

b) Where both spouses are working and they agree that, for example, H's earnings should be used to run the household while W used her earnings to purchase antiques or lay down vintage claret, the common law gave H no proprietary interest in the property purchased by W.

As the Lord Justice General (Normand) observed in *Harper v Adair*, [1] when a spouse buys corporeal moveables out of his or her own funds, the presumption is that they are the property of the purchasing spouse. Only if the other spouse can discharge the formidable burden of proof and show that the purchasing spouse intended the property to be owned – as opposed to used or enjoyed – jointly, can he or she claim an interest in the moveables. As Lord Keith said in *Preston v Preston*:[2]

> 'Husband and wife in many cases may both be wage earners contributing to the common expenses of the house. Each will retain property in such part of their respective earnings as is not contributed to the common purse, but there is no reason why a wife's contributions, or the fact that her earnings may save her husband some expenditure on her personal needs, should give her a claim on any part of the earnings of her husband – [and therefore any property acquired by him out of his earnings] – and I should be sorry to lend any support to such a view, which would

1 1945 JC 21 at 28.
2 1950 SC 253 at 261.

militate against the independence of wives which it has been the aim of modern legislation to secure'.

Nevertheless, the injustices of the application of the system of separate property in practice are obvious, and Parliament has intervened to alleviate the position to some extent.

Household goods

Section 25(1) of the Family Law (Scotland) Act 1985[1] provides that 'if any question arises (whether during or after a marriage) as to the respective rights of ownership of the parties to a marriage in any household goods obtained in prospect of or during the marriage other than by gift or succession from a third party, it shall be presumed, unless the contrary is proved, that each has a right to an equal share in the goods in question'.

Household goods are defined[2] as 'any goods (including decorative or ornamental goods) kept or used at any time during the marriage in any matrimonial home[3] for the joint domestic purposes of the parties to the marriage'. However, (a) money or securities, (b) any motor car, caravan or other road vehicle[4] and (c) any domestic animal, are expressly excluded.[5]

Consider the following examples:
1. If H buys antique paintings *before* the marriage, the presumption of equal shares does not apply as the property was acquired before marriage. But if before marriage, H buys a Chinese carpet with the intention that it is to be used in the matrimonial home after marriage, the presumption of equal shares will apply as the goods were bought in prospect of marriage.
2. If W inherits a grandfather clock during the marriage the presumption of equal shares will not apply as property acquired by gift or succession from a third party is excluded.
3. If H wins £10,000 on the football pools during the marriage and invests £5,000 in a building society and uses the remainder to buy antiques which are kept in the matrimonial home, the presumption of equal shares does not apply to the money deposited with the

---

1 Section 25 is based on the Scottish Law Commission's Report on *Matrimonial Property:* SLC No 86. References in this section are to the 1985 Act unless otherwise stated.
2 Section 25(3).
3 This has the same meaning as 'matrimonial home' in s 22 of the Matrimonial Homes (Family Protection) (Scotland) Act 1981: see *infra* Ch 5.
4 For example, a bicycle!
5 Section 25(3)(a), (b) and (c).

building society, as money and securities are expressly excluded, but it will apply to the antiques as these are household goods.
4. If W buys a motor car during the marriage which is used by H for work and leisure purposes, the presumption of equal shares does not apply, as road vehicles are expressly excluded.

It must be stressed that s 25 only gives rise to a presumption of equal shares in household goods: it is therefore open to the purchasing spouse if he or she alleges that the goods were not intended to be owned jointly, to bring evidence to rebut the presumption and establish that they were to be owned outright by the purchasing spouse. However, s 25(2) provides that the presumption of equal shares will not be rebutted merely by the fact that 'while the parties were married *and living together* the goods in question were purchased from a third party by either party alone or by both in unequal shares'. Consider the following examples:
1. During the marriage and while the spouses were living together, H buys a silver tea pot from a dealer. Prima facie the tea pot is household goods and the presumption of equal shares applies. The mere fact that H bought the tea pot from a third party using his own money, is not in itself sufficient to rebut the presumption. Consequently the tea pot is owned jointly by H and W.
2. During the marriage and while the spouses were living together, H buys a silver tea pot from a dealer. Prima facie the tea pot is household goods and the presumption of equal shares applies. But if H could show that *before* the marriage he had collected silver, not with the prospect of marriage, this fact combined with the fact that he bought the tea pot from a third party using his own money, could be sufficient to rebut the presumption and establish that the tea pot was intended for his collection, to be owned along with the rest of the silver, outright by H.[1]
3. During the marriage but when the spouses were not living together, H buys a silver tea pot from a dealer. Prima facie the tea pot is household goods and the presumption of equal shares applies. But as the tea pot was bought when the couple were not living together, s 25(2) does not apply and the fact that H bought the tea pot from a third party using his own money may in itself be sufficient to rebut the presumption of equal shares and consequently establish that the tea pot is owned outright by H.

---

1 If the tea pot was kept in a display cabinet and never used, arguably it is not household goods as it has not been kept or used for *joint domestic purposes*: see *infra* p 66.

There may be difficulties in the interrelationship between s 25 and the law of gifts between spouses.[1] If H purchases a painting during the marriage, prima facie s 25 applies as the painting comes under household goods and therefore there is a presumption of equal shares. If H transfers the painting to W on her birthday, W may be able to rebut the presumption *against* donation and establish that H intended the painting to be an outright gift to her. It is submitted that, if W can do so, she would thereby rebut the presumption of equal shares in household goods in s 25.

The examples given are perhaps esoteric and the theoretical difficulties in s 25 must not be thought to undermine its evident utility. In the vast majority of cases the presumption will not be capable of being rebutted and consequently spouses will be taken to have equal shares in the normal contents of the matrimonial home, *viz* consumer durables, for example, furniture, carpets, televisions, fridges, cookers and kitchen utensils. Moreover, the definition of household goods[2] demands that not only must the goods be kept or used in the matrimonial home but also that they must be kept or used 'for joint domestic purposes'. Thus corporeal moveables used exclusively for a spouse's business, for example, a word processor, or hobby, for example, golf clubs, will be excluded. But difficulties arise where property is bought both as a collector's item and for use by the spouses, as in the example of the silver tea pot: such property could be defined as household goods so giving rise to the problems outlined above.[3]

More difficult to justify, perhaps, is the exclusion of motor cars, caravans or other vehicles, as these are often bought as a result of a couple pooling their resources: the application of the separate property system may give a result which is entirely fortuitous. The exclusion of family pets is, on the other hand, quite understandable.

Furniture and plenishings in the matrimonial home

The Matrimonial Homes (Family Protection) (Scotland) Act 1981 contains provisions which enable a spouse – and in certain circumstances a cohabitee – to continue living in a matrimonial home although the marriage or relationship is breaking down.[4] It was appreciated by Parliament that these rights would be of limited value if the spouse who owned the furniture and plenishings of the home could

---

1 *Supra* p 62.
2 Section 25(3).
3 *Supra* p 65.
4 The 1981 Act is discussed *infra* Ch 5. References in this section are to the 1981 Act unless otherwise stated.

sell them, leaving the house empty. Accordingly, a spouse or cohabitee who has a right to occupy the matrimonial home[1] can apply under s 3(2) of the Act for an order granting the applicant the possession or use in the matrimonial home of any of its furniture and plenishings owned by the other.[2] 'Furniture and plenishings' means any article situated in the matrimonial home which is owned or hired by either spouse[3] and 'is reasonably necessary to enable the home to be used as a family residence'.[4] In the present writer's view a s 3(2) order is not available when the spouses own the property jointly. But here a joint owner can apply for an interdict to stop the other joint owner preventing the applicant from using or possessing the property.[5]

The court[6] must first make an order declaring that the applicant has occupancy rights in respect of the matrimonial home.[7]

Under s 3(2), the court can then make such an order as appears just and reasonable having regard to all the circumstances of the case including inter alia:

a) the conduct of the spouses;
b) the needs and financial resources of the spouses;
c) the needs of any children of the family;
d) the extent, if any, to which any item of furniture and plenishings is used in connection with a trade, business or profession of either spouse.[8]

An interim order can be made, provided the non-applicant has been afforded an opportunity of being heard or represented before the court.[9] But the court cannot make an order if the effect of the order would be to exclude the non-applicant spouse from the matrimonial home: for example, an order for the sole and exclusive possession or use of the fitted carpets throughout the home.

---

1 See *infra* Ch 5. For definition of matrimonial home, see *ibid*, s 22.
2 Section 3(2).
3 Or is being acquired by either spouse under a hire-purchase agreement or conditional sale agreement.
4 Section 22: vehicles, caravans or houseboats are expressly excluded. For the definition of matrimonial home, see *infra*.
5 Section 3(2) was, of course, enacted before s 25 of the Family Law (Scotland) Act 1985, discussed *supra* pp 64 ff. Since the presumption of joint ownership will usually apply, the scope of s 3(2) is greatly reduced. Ironically, it can be argued that the remedy of a non-owning spouse under s 3(2) is more sophisticated that that of a joint owner at common law. However, it is possible that s 3(2) may be capable of being interpreted as including household goods owned jointly by the defender and the applicant: *sed quaere*.
6 The Court of Session or the sheriff court: s 22.
7 Section 3(1): see *Welsh v Welsh* 1987 SLT (Sh Ct) 30.
8 Section 3(3).
9 Section 3(4); *Welsh v Welsh* 1987 SLT (Sh Ct) 30.

Where the furniture or plenishings are being paid up under a hire purchase or a conditional sale agreement, an order does not prejudice the rights of the hirer or creditor to recover the property for non-performance of any obligations under the agreements.[1] But the spouse in whose favour the order is made is entitled to make any payments under the agreements in lieu of the debtor.[2] Similarly, he or she can carry out any essential repairs to the furniture and plenishings.[3] On the application of either spouse, the court can apportion any such expenditure between the spouses.[4]

The effect of a s 3(2) order is therefore to override the property rights of a spouse in relation to the furniture and plenishings of the matrimonial home, to the extent that the applicant is entitled to the use and possession of the relevant property for the duration of the order. It must be stressed that s 3(2) only regulates the possession and use of the property. Its ownership will, of course, be determined by reference to s 25 of the Family Law (Scotland) Act 1985[5] and the common law rules. Moreover, the definition of furniture and plenishings in the 1981 Act is narrower than that of household goods for the purposes of s 25, since it is only furniture and plenishings which are *reasonably necessary* to enable the home to be used as a family residence which can be the subject of a s 3(2) order.[6] The following examples illustrate the inter-relationship between the two provisions.

1. H buys a bed during the marriage. The presumption of equal shares applies and is not rebutted. H and W therefore own the bed jointly. Although a bed is an article reasonably necessary to enable the home to be used as a family residence, W cannot apply for a s 3(2) order for the use and possession of the bed because s 3(2) only applies where the furniture and plenishings are owned solely by one of the spouses. However, at common law, W as joint owner would be entitled to an interdict preventing H from disposing of the bed.[7]

2. During the marriage, H inherits a dining room suite from his grandmother. The presumption of equal shares does not apply[8] and

---

1 Section 3(2).
2 Sections 2(5)(a) and 3(2).
3 Ibid.
4 Section 2(5)(b).
5 Discussed *supra* p 64.
6 Section 22.
7 Since the bed is common property and H and W each own a one half *pro indiviso* share of its value, an action for division and sale is competent to enable H to realise his share. This is discussed in the context of heritage, *infra* Ch 5. Theoretically, H could attempt to sell his pro indiviso share of the bed, if anyone would like to buy half a bed!
8 Household goods inherited from third parties are expressly excluded by s 25(1) of the 1985 Act.

the suite is owned outright by H. But if they are the only table and chairs in the house, W can apply for a s 3(2) order for their use and possession as they are articles reasonably necessary to enable the home to be used as a family residence.
3. H inherits an oil painting during the marriage. The presumption of equal shares does not apply. H therefore owns the painting outright. But as the painting is not reasonably necessary to enable the home to be used as a family residence, W will be unable to obtain a s 3(2) order for the use and possession of the painting.

Again it should be emphasised that these theoretical difficulties should not be allowed to detract from the evident utility of s 3(2). It is further recognition that the incidents of ownership of property may have to be overridden in the interests of the family for whose benefit the property was acquired. In particular, it should be noticed that the needs of the children of the family will be an important factor in determining whether or not a s 3(2) order should be made.[1]

MONEY AND SECURITIES

As we have seen[2] money and securities are expressly excluded from the presumption of equal shares in household goods.[3] The ownership of money or securities will therefore be determined by the ordinary property rules, ie in accordance with the separate property system. Thus, for example, if H deposits £5,000 in a building society account in his name, the money in the account prima facie belongs to him. It is however, open to W to claim, for example, that the money was transferred by her to H to invest and consequently belongs to her. She will have the benefit of the presumption against donation[4] and she is not restricted in the type of evidence she can bring to substantiate her claim[5].

Problems have arisen in relation to joint bank accounts. When an account is opened in joint names of the spouses, this may, depending on the terms of the agreement with the bank, oblige the bank to honour cheques drawn by either spouse or, in the case of a deposit account, to pay money over to either of the spouses when called upon to do so. The fact that the account is in joint names does not determine the ownership of the money in it. Where one spouse has been the sole

1 Section 3(3).
2 *Supra* p 64.
3 Section 25(3)(a) of the Family Law (Scotland) Act 1985.
4 Discussed *supra* p 62.
5 *Smith v Smith* 1933 SC 701.

contributor of the funds in the account, it will be presumed, in the absence of evidence of donation, that the account was opened for administrative convenience only and the money in the account belongs to the contributing spouse. Where *both* spouses contributed to the fund, it will be readily inferred that they intended the account to be used as a common purse and that the money in the account is owned jointly.[1]

Where a spouse draws on a joint account to buy property prima facie the property belongs to that spouse outright – even although the account was opened for administrative purposes only.[2] However, where the spouse purchases household goods, the presumption of equal shares will apply by virtue of s 25 of the Family Law (Scotland) Act 1985.[3]

Similar principles will apply to money invested in a building society.

SAVINGS FROM HOUSEKEEPING

One of the harshest consequences of the system of separate property was where, for example, a husband provided a wife with a housekeeping allowance and the wife, being thrifty, was able to save some of the money. Because the husband had intended the money to be used to run the home, donation could not be inferred. Consequently, the husband was the owner of the savings made by the wife.[4] The Married Woman's Property Act 1964 attempted to alleviate the position. It provided that savings made by a wife from a housekeeping allowance made to her by her husband, should be presumed to be owned jointly by the spouses in the absence of an agreement to the contrary. The 1964 Act was defective in that it was not applicable to savings made by a husband from a housekeeping allowance paid to him by his wife: in these circumstances, any savings would still be owned by the wife. This discriminatory element has now been removed. Section 26 of the Family Law (Scotland) Act 1985 provides:

> 'If any question arises (whether during or after a marriage) as to the right of either party to a marriage to money derived from any allowance made by either party for their joint household expenses or for similar purposes, or to any property acquired out

---

1 Ie the court will infer donation to the extent necessary to give each spouse a half share of the money in the account.
2 Unless there is evidence that the property was bought as a joint investment.
3 Discussed *supra* p 64.
4 *Smith v Smith* 1933 SC 701; *Preston v Preston* 1950 SC 253. This did not apply to savings from aliment paid by a husband when the couple were separated.

of such money, the money or property shall, in the absence of any agreement between them to the contrary, be treated as belonging to each party in equal shares'.

It will be clear that s 26 applies both to allowances made by a husband to his wife and a wife to her husband. The allowances must be for 'their joint household expenses or for similar purposes'. It is not thought that money given to a spouse for payment of mortgage instalments would be included within the definition.[1] Money or property 'derived from the allowance' has been given a wide meaning. In *Pyatt v Pyatt*[2] Lord Fraser held that the prize money won by a wife on Littlewoods Football Pools was 'derived from' the allowance when the wife had taken the stake money from her housekeeping. The winnings had resulted both from the allowance which had provided the stake money and the wife's luck. As the stake money had been essential, the prize money had been derived from the allowance and consequently the husband was entitled to half the winnings.

The application of s 26 can lead to some odd results. Consider the following example. W gives H a housekeeping allowance. H uses some of the allowance to bet on a horse. H wins £1,000. He puts £500 in a building society account and buys a second hand caravan with the rest of the money. Following *Pyatt v Pyatt*[3] W is entitled to half the £500 in the building society account ie £250 and is joint owner of the caravan.[4] W is not entitled to choose the full £500 in the account in lieu of her half share of the caravan.[5]

MARRIED WOMEN'S POLICIES OF ASSURANCE (SCOTLAND) ACT 1880

Where A takes out an insurance policy for the benefit of B, B has no rights in the policy until it is delivered to B or the rights under the policy have been intimated to B. There is an exception to this principle, where a husband or wife takes out a life policy on his or her life, for the benefit of the other spouse (or children): in these circumstances, the policy is deemed to be held by the insured in trust for the

---

1 *Tymoszczuk v Tymoszczuk* (1964) 108 Sol Jo 676 (interpreting the similar phrase in the 1964 Act); but cf *Re John's Assignment Trusts, Niven v Niven* [1970] 2 All ER 210, n, [1970] 1 WLR 955.
2 1966 SLT (Notes) 73.
3 Ibid.
4 Section 25 of the Family Law (Scotland) Act 1985 is inapplicable, as caravans are expressly excluded from the definition of household goods: s 25(3)(b), see *supra*.
5 Moreover, if H used the £1,000 together with £1,000 of his own savings in order to buy a pony, W would own a quarter of the pony! Domestic animals are also excluded from s 25: s 25(3)(c).

beneficiaries who take an immediate right without the necessity of delivery or intimation of the policy to them.[1]

---

1 Married Women's Policies of Assurance (Scotland) Act 1880, s 2 as amended by the Married Women's Policies of Assurance (Scotland) (Amendment) Act 1980: see *Clive* pp 326–322.

5 The legal consequences of marriage III: the matrimonial home

INTRODUCTION

The most important heritable property which spouses are likely to possess is their matrimonial home. Increasingly, a married couple is likely to live in accommodation which is owned by one or both of the spouses.[1] In Scots law, title to heritable property is held on feudal tenure. When property is sold, the deeds must be recorded in the Register of Sasines or the interest registered in the Land Register of Scotland. Until recording or registration, the buyer does not have a real right in the property, ie he is not the owner with a proprietary interest which is good against the world: as against the seller, however, the buyer will have a personal right to sue him for breach of contract, if he disposes of the property to a third party before recording or registration. Many couples will be unable to purchase a matrimonial home outright and will have to borrow the necessary sum from a bank or building society (the heritable creditor). Until the loan is repaid, the bank or building society will have a heritable security (a mortgage) over the house: this enables the heritable creditor to sell the house if the loan (and interest thereon) is not repaid. This form of heritable security is known as a standard security, which is itself recorded in the Register of Sasines or registered in the Land Register of Scotland.

Many couples, of course, cannot afford to buy their home. Instead, they will simply rent accommodation. Since 1974, a lease of residential property cannot be granted for more than 20 years.[2] Accordingly, most leases are not for long periods but are terminable by notice, stipulated in the lease. However, tenants enjoy a considerable measure of secur-

---

1 In their survey, *Family Property in Scotland* (HMSO 1981), Manners and Rauta found that 37% of all matrimonial homes in Scotland were owner-occupied: ibid Table 2.1. In 57% of these, title was taken in the joint names of the spouses: ibid Table 2.4. Among homes purchased after 1977, the proportion where the title was taken in joint names rose to 78%. It is thought that the proportion of matrimonial homes where title is taken in joint names will continue to rise. See Scottish Law Commission, *Report on Matrimonial Property* (SLC No 86).
2 Land Tenure Reform (Scotland) Act 1974, s 8.

ity of tenure, in both the public and private housing sector, as a result of legislation.[1] The person who has security of tenure is the tenant. Joint tenancies are possible, but it is more usual for the tenancy to be in the name of one of the spouses, usually the husband.

It will be obvious that where, for example, property is owned by a husband or a tenancy has been taken in his name, his wife may experience difficulties in relation to her continued occupation of the matrimonial home if their marriage begins to break down. As a result of the Matrimonial Homes (Family Protection) (Scotland) Act 1981,[2] (the 1981 Act) the rights of a spouse to occupy the matrimonial home have been greatly improved: these rights will be discussed, at some length, in this chapter. However, before doing so, consideration must be given to the operation of the system of separate property on the question of the ownership of the matrimonial home.

THE OWNERSHIP OF THE MATRIMONIAL HOME

Title in the name of one of the spouses

When a person purchases heritable property, title to which is taken in that person's name, it is a cardinal principle of the Scots law of property that that person is the owner of the property. Thus, for example, if H buys a house, title to which is taken in H's name, he is the owner of the house. This is an inevitable consequence of a system of separate property. The fact that the house is to be used as the matrimonial home is irrelevant to the question of its ownership.

When a house is purchased solely from the funds of one of the spouses, then the application of the separate property principle is justified. But, in practice, it is more likely that a house will be purchased through the means of a mortgage. A couple will often agree to pool their resources in order to acquire their matrimonial home. For example, a wife may make a direct financial contribution to the downpayment or the mortgage instalments. Alternatively, the spouses may agree that while the husband's earnings are used to pay the instalments, the wife's earnings will be used for household expenses: in these circumstances, the wife will have made an indirect contribution to the acquisition of the matrimonial home. Yet, if the title has been taken in the husband's name, he will be the sole owner of the house, even although it could not have been purchased without the wife's

---

1 See in particular the Rent (Scotland) Act 1984, the Housing (Scotland) Act 1987, and the Housing (Scotland) Act 1988. Discussion of these statutes is outwith the scope of the present book.
2 Throughout this chapter, references are to the 1981 Act unless otherwise stated.

direct or indirect financial assistance. The injustice of the application of the separate property principle in these circumstances is readily apparent.

In England, a wife who has made a direct or indirect financial contribution towards the acquisition of the matrimonial home may obtain an interest in the property because a court can in these circumstances infer that the husband was holding the property for the benefit of his wife on an implied, constructive or resulting trust. The extent of the wife's interest in the house will be proportional to the size of her contribution.[1] However, a solution upon these lines is not open in Scots law, as a result of the Blank Bonds and Trusts Act 1696.[2] When A voluntarily transfers property to B which B holds under a deed which gives him an ex facie valid irredeemable title to the property, ie B appears from the deed to be the owner of the property, the deed is regarded as a deed of trust: if A later claims that he has an interest in the property because B is holding the property as trustee for the benefit of A, under the 1696 Act proof of the trust is limited to B's, ie the alleged trustee's, writ or oath.[3]

It has been held that the Blank Bonds and Trusts Act 1696 applies to disputes between husband and wife.[4] The implications of this are considered in the following examples.

EXAMPLE 1

H transfers £30,000 to W to buy property, title to which, for tax reasons, is to be taken in W's name. As W has an ex facie valid irredeemable title, the 1696 Act is applicable if H later claims that it is his property which W is holding on trust for his benefit. Consequently proof of trust will be restricted to W's, ie the alleged trustee's, writ or oath. If, however, H had told W to buy the property for him as his agent and she, contrary to his mandate, takes the title in her name, proof of the alleged agency and W's subsequent fraud is not restricted to W's writ or oath. Before the 1696 Act applies, W must have obtained the title to the property with H's consent.

1 On these developments see, generally Cretney, *Principles of Family Law* (4th edn, 1984) at Ch 21.
2 Blank Bonds and Trusts Act 1696 (c 25).
3 Ie the trust must be evidenced by the alleged trustee's acknowledgement in writing or on oath that he is holding the property in trust for the transferor. Where the alleged trustee has been put on oath and denies the existence of the trust, the trust will not be established even if the alleged trustee has perjured himself.
4 *Weissenbruch v Weissenbruch* 1961 SC 340.

EXAMPLE 2

Suppose a house cost £3,000 in 1960. W voluntarily transferred £1,500 to H which he used to purchase the house as the matrimonial home. With the agreement of W, title to the property is taken in H's name. The house is now worth £50,000. If W claims she owns half the house, she will be met by the 1696 Act and proof of trust will be restricted to H's, ie the alleged trustee's, writ or oath, as she is alleging that he is holding the property on trust for her to the extent of one half of its value. Unless she can establish the trust by such evidence, she will fail in her attempt to claim half the value of the property.[1]

W can, of course, attempt to recover the £1,500 which she transferred to H but even if she is successful she will not receive any share of the increased value of the house. Even in recovering the £1,500, W may experience difficulties. While the presumption against donation will operate in her favour,[2] in Scots law proof of a debt is restricted to the creditor's ie H's writ or oath!

EXAMPLE 3

Suppose a house cost £3,000 in 1960. W voluntarily transferred £1,500 to H who told her that he would purchase the house and that the title would be taken in joint names. The title is taken in H's name only. In these circumstances, H is guilty of fraud and W can bring an action of reduction of the deed or sue H in delict: the 1696 Act does not apply as there was fraud in the constitution of the title. Proof of fraud is therefore not restricted to H's writ or oath.[3] If the house is now worth £50,000, W will be entitled to £25,000.

If, on the other hand, W transferred £1,500 in the erroneous belief that title would be taken in joint names and H was not guilty of fraud when title was taken in H's name only, then W can only recover the £1,500 on general principles of recompense because the 1696 Act will apply as the title was not vitiated by fraud. Similarly, if in the erroneous belief that title was taken in

---

1 See, for example, *Adam v Adam* 1962 SLT 332, where W provided the whole purchase price of a public house, title to which was taken in H's name as he was to be licensee. W failed to establish any interest in the property as a result of the 1696 Act, as she could not adduce evidence by H's writ or oath that he was holding the property in trust for her benefit.
2 See *supra* Ch 4.
3 Ie evidence is *prout de jure: Marshall v Lyall and Marshall* (1859) 21 D 514.

joint names W expended money on improving the property, she will obtain recompense to the extent of the value of the improvement.[1]

EXAMPLE 4

H and W agree that H will put a downpayment on the purchase of a house and will pay the mortgage instalments. In order to enable him to do so, W agrees that she will use her earnings to pay the costs of the household. Title to the property is taken in H's name, and he grants the standard security. Although W has made an indirect contribution to the acquisition of the matrimonial home, she is unable to acquire an interest in the property as she will be met by the 1696 Act. In the absence of fraud or error, she will also be unable to obtain any compensation for her indirect financial contributions.

The only way in which the wives in these examples would be able to obtain a share in the value of the matrimonial home commensurate with their direct or indirect financial contributions to its acquisition, would be to establish an agreement between the spouses as to the true beneficial ownership of the property. While such an agreement is not an *obligatio literis*, ie does not have to be constituted in writing,[2] it is thought that such an agreement will not be readily inferred. Even if such an agreement existed it would only be binding between the spouses, and would not prevent the spouse with legal title selling the property to a third party, who is entitled to rely on the title as it appears in the Register of Sasines or the Land Register of Scotland.

As we shall see,[3] on divorce a spouse will prima facie receive half the value of, inter alia, the matrimonial home. But as Clive has observed, 'property questions between spouses do not arise only on divorce'.[4]

Title in the name of both of the spouses

As we have seen, spouses are increasingly taking title to the matrimonial home in joint names.[5] While this will alleviate many of the

---

1 Contrast *Newton v Newton* 1923 SC 15 (H met by 1696 Act when argued W holding the matrimonial home in trust for him) with *Newton v Newton* 1925 SC 715 (when H successfully claimed recompense for the vaue of improvements made in the belief that the house was his).
2 *Denvir v Denvir* 1969 SLT 301 at 303.
3 *Supra* Ch 7.
4 *Clive* p 319.
5 *Supra* p 73.

problems discussed in the previous section, to take title in both names raises its own difficulties.

Where title to a house is taken in joint names, the property is regarded as common property. This means that while the property is possessed undivided, each of the spouses has his or her own separate title to half of the property, ie each spouse owns a one half *pro indiviso* share of the value of the property. Accordingly, each is entitled during his or her lifetime to dispose of their share, by selling or donating it to a third party, against the wishes of the co-owning spouse[1]. Similarly, each is free to dispose of his or her share by will.

Complications have arisen from the conveyancing practice of taking the title in the names of husband and wife *and the survivor*. This is known as a special destination. On the death of, for example, the husband, his share of the property will automatically pass to his wife, the survivor. This has the advantage that the wife will receive the deceased husband's *pro indiviso* share free from all her husband's debts.[2] But there are difficulties. While the spouses remain free to dispose of their share during their lifetime,[3] a special destination may prevent a spouse disposing of his or her share by will. Where both spouses have contributed to the purchase of the property, the courts will readily infer from a special destination to the survivor that there is a contractual relationship between the parties, and neither can revoke the arrangement by testamentary deed.[4] Where only one of the parties has purchased a house, this principle does not apply to the spouse who bought the property and he or she remains free to dispose of his or her *pro indiviso* share by will – but not, of course, the other spouse's share. Moreover, since the latter has in effect received his or her share as a gift, the court will readily imply that the donee took the gift under the condition that the donor should obtain that share if the donor is the survivor, and consequently the donee cannot dispose of his or her share by will. But, even in these circumstances, the donee is free to dispose of his or her share during his or her lifetime.[5] In spite of its advantages, because of these difficulties the use of special destinations to husband and wife and survivor should be discouraged.

1 But see *McLeod v Cedar Holdings Ltd* 1989 SLT 620 where H took out a further heritable security over property owned by H and W. H had forged W's signature. The Inner House granted W reduction in respect of her *pro indiviso* share.
2 Unless, of course, the creditors have a heritable security over the husband's share: see *Barclay's Bank v McGreish* 1983 SLT 344, criticised by Morton, 1984 SLT (News) 133.
3 *Steele v Caldwell* 1979 SLT 228.
4 *Perrett's Trustees v Perrett* 1909 SC 522.
5 *Hay's Trustee v Hay's Trustees* 1951 SC 329.

THE OCCUPATION OF THE MATRIMONIAL HOME

In the last section, we discussed the question of the ownership of the matrimonial home. In this section we shall consider the different but related question of the occupation of the matrimonial home. There are two situations: a) where one spouse has the legal title to the property or is the tenant and the other spouse has no proprietary interest in the property and b) where both spouses have an interest in the property.

Where one spouse has legal title or is the tenant

At common law, the legal owner or the tenant had the right of exclusive possession of his or her property. Thus, if, for example, H owned the matrimonial home, he could tell W to leave: if W refused, H could obtain an interdict preventing her access to the house. While H remained under a duty to aliment W, this did not oblige him to continue to allow W to occupy the matrimonial home.

In *MacLure v MacLure*,[1] a husband who was the tenant of a hotel which was used both as a business and as the matrimonial home, was granted an interdict to exclude his admittedly drunken wife from the premises, on condition that he continued to pay her a reasonable amount of aliment. This was followed in *Millar v Millar*.[2] There a wife who had let property to her husband was held entitled to give him notice to quit the premises. It was irrelevant that the wife who owned the property had deserted her husband and that it was used as the matrimonial home.

The common law rule that a spouse who owned or was the tenant of a matrimonial home was entitled to order the non-owning spouse to leave has been radically altered as a result of the Matrimonial Homes (Family Protection) (Scotland) Act 1981.[3]

The nature of the statutory rights

By s 1(1) where one spouse, 'the entitled spouse', is the owner or tenant of the matrimonial home[4] and the other spouse, 'the non-

---

1 1911 SC 200.
2 1940 SC 56.
3 For an excellent commentary on the Act, see Nichols and Meston *The Matrimonial Homes (Family Protection) (Scotland) Act 1981* (2nd edn, 1986). On the operation of the Act in practice, see Jackson, Robertson and Robson *The Operation of the Matrimonial Homes (Family Protection) (Scotland) Act 1981* (Scottish Home and Health Department, 1988).
4 Or is permitted by a third party to occupy the home: s 1(1).

entitled spouse' is not the owner or tenant,[1] then the non-entitled spouse has the following statutory rights—
a) if in occupation to continue to occupy the matrimonial home;
b) if not in occupation to enter into and occupy the matrimonial home.[2]
These statutory rights of a non-entitled spouse to occupy the matrimonial home expressly include the right to do so 'together with any child of the family'.[3]

The effect of this provision is to give the non-entitled spouse a positive right to occupy the matrimonial home together with any child of the family. 'Matrimonial home' has a wide meaning. It includes any house, caravan, houseboat or other structure which has been provided as or become a *family* residence.[4] Although the term 'family residence' is used, it is clear that it is not limited to a family where there are children. It is enough that a house has been acquired with the intention that it should be used as a family home; the couple do not need to have lived there.[5] If there are two or more family residences, for example, a town house and a country cottage, the non-entitled spouse will have a statutory right to occupy both (or more) houses. On the other hand, if one spouse has acquired a house in which he or she lives separately from the other spouse this will not constitute a matrimonial home, even if children of the family also reside there.[6] A child of the family includes any child or grandchild of either spouse or any person brought up or accepted by either spouse as if he or she was a child of that spouse: the age of the child is irrelevant.[7] Thus, for example, a severely handicapped adult son or daughter of either spouse will be a child of the family for the purposes of the 1981 Act.

The statutory rights arise as soon as the spouses marry and the entitled spouse acquires a matrimonial home. The rights continue

1 Or is not permitted by a third party to occupy the home: s 1(1).
2 Section 1(1) as amended by s 13(2) of the Law Reform (Miscellaneous Provisions) (Scotland) Act 1985.
3 Section 1(1A), added by s 13(3) of the Law Reform (Miscellaneous Provisions) (Scotland) Act 1985: the original statutory right could be frustrated if the entitled spouse allowed the non-entitled spouse to occupy the home but not to allow the children to remain there.
4 Section 22: any garden or outbuildings, for example, a garage are included.
5 *O'Neil v O'Neil* 1987 SLT (Sh Ct) 26.
6 Section 22, as amended by s 13(10) of the Law Reform (Miscellaneous Provisions) (Scotland) Act 1985. Similarly, where one spouse provides the other with a house where the other spouse lives separately it has been held that this is not a matrimonial home within the meaning of the 1985 Act: *McRobbie v McRobbie* 1983 (unreported) OH.
7 Section 22.

throughout the marriage even if the couple separate. However, they cease when the marriage ends in death or divorce.[1] Most importantly, the rights of the non-entitled spouse are not defeated if during the marriage, the matrimonial home is sold or otherwise disposed of to a third party.[2]

Upkeep and maintenance of the matrimonial home

For the purposes of securing the statutory rights of occupation, a non-entitled spouse has the right, without the consent of the entitled spouse, inter alia to pay any rent, mortgage instalments etc instead of the entitled spouse; to carry out essential repairs; to carry out non-essential repairs approved by a court as appropriate for the reasonable enjoyment of the occupancy rights; and to take any other steps necessary to ensure the occupancy of the matrimonial home.[3] The court has the power to apportion such expenditure between the spouses.[4]

Regulatory orders

By s 3 the court has the power to regulate the spouses' occupancy of the matrimonial home. An order may be sought by either the entitled or non-entitled spouse. The court can make orders declaring or enforcing the applicant's rights of occupation, restricting the non-applicant's occupancy rights and regulating the occupancy rights of both spouses. While the court is obliged to declare that the applicant has occupancy rights when it is satisfied that the property constitutes a matrimonial home,[5] its exercise of its other powers under s 3 is discretionary. By s 3(3) the court is obliged to make such an order as appears—

> 'just and reasonable having regard to all the circumstances of the case including—
> a) the conduct of the spouses in relation to each other and otherwise;
> b) the respective needs and financial resources of the spouses;
> c) the needs of any child of the family;

---

1 Where on divorce, the court makes an incidental order entitling the applicant spouse to continue to occupy the matrimonial home after the divorce, certain of the rights in s 2 to take steps in relation to the upkeep of the home and its contents, will continue: s 14(5) of the Family Law (Scotland) Act 1985. On financial provision, see *infra* Ch 7. Nevertheless it is common and accepted practice to incorporate craves for relief under the 1981 Act in divorce proceedings: *Nelson v Nelson* 1988 (Sh Ct) 26.
2 Discussed in detail *infra* p 86.
3 Section 2(1). The court is the Court of Session or the sheriff court.
4 Section 2(2).
5 Section 3(3). Indeed, it would appear that declarator is essential before other relief can be given under s 3: *Welsh v Welsh* 1987 SLT (Sh Ct) 30.

d) the extent (if any) to which—
  (i) the matrimonial home . . . is used in connection with a trade, business or profession of either spouse; and
e) whether the entitled spouse offers or has offered to make available to the non-entitled spouse any suitable alternative accommodation.'

Interim orders are possible if considered necessary or expedient[1] and compensation is available for loss or impairment of occupancy rights.[2] However, a court cannot make an order under s 3(3) if its effect would be to exclude the entitled spouse from the matrimonial home. While the power to grant declarator of a non-entitled spouse's statutory rights is important, in practice little use has been made of the court's powers to make regulatory orders under s 3(3).

Exclusion orders

By s 4 of the Act, the court has, however, the power to exclude either of the spouses from the matrimonial home. The order may be sought by either the entitled or non-entitled spouse.[3] By s 4(2) the court—

> '*shall* make an exclusion order if it appears to the court that the making of an order is *necessary* for the protection of the applicant or any child of the family from any *conduct* or threatened or reasonably apprehended conduct of the non-applicant spouse which is or would be injurious to the physical or mental health of the applicant or child'.[4]

In spite of the mandatory wording of s 4(2), by s 4(3)(a) the court shall not make an exclusion order if it would be unjustified or unreasonable having regard to all the circumstances of the case including the factors specified in s 3(3).[5] Interim exclusion orders are available[6] but the necessity criterion must still be satisfied.[7]

The construction of s 4 has caused the Scottish courts much difficulty. At first there was a reluctance to grant an interim order when the

---

1 Section 3(4): the non-applicant spouse must have been afforded an opportunity of being heard or represented in court.
2 Section 3(7).
3 See, for example, *Brown v Brown* 1985 SLT 376 where the applicant was the entitled spouse.
4 Italics added.
5 *Supra* pp 81, 82. Exclusion orders are also not available if the matrimonial home is part of an agricultural tenancy or has been let as an incident of employment: s 4(3)(b).
6 Section 4(6): the non-applicant spouse must be afforded an opportunity of being heard or represented before the court.
7 *Bell v Bell* 1983 SLT 224; *Smith v Smith* 1983 SLT 275; *Ward v Ward* 1983 SLT 472.

court was proceeding on affidavit evidence. In *Bell v Bell*,[1] and *Smith v Smith*,[2] the Inner House of the Court of Session held that the necessity criterion in s 4(2) was a 'high and severe' test. The judges indicated that it would be unlikely to be satisfied unless the applicant was living in the matrimonial home at the time of the application. This caused considerable apprehension until the Lord Justice Clerk (Wheatley) attempted to remove such fears in *Colagiacomo v Colagiacomo*:[3]

> 'If there is any misconception that following *Bell v Bell* an interim exclusion order will only be granted if the parties are both occupying the matrimonial home, the sooner that misconception is removed the better. The fact that only one of the parties is occupying the matrimonial home is a factor to be taken into account but is not per se to be regarded as a conclusive one'.[4]

While exclusion orders have been granted in later cases where the applicant has left the matrimonial home,[5] s 4(1) now expressly provides that an application for an exclusion order can be made, 'whether or not that spouse [the applicant] is in occupation at the time of the application'.[6]

In *Bell v Bell*[7] and *Smith v Smith*[8] the judges also indicated that an exclusion order should not be made if a matrimonial interdict, prohibiting the molestation of the applicant, would be sufficient protection.[9] This could lead to a 'Catch 22' situation: a wife, for example, could not be granted an interim exclusion order unless she had applied for a non-molestation interdict, but if she obtained such an interdict, an exclusion order would not be granted without evidence that the husband had been in breach of the interdict.[10] However, in *Brown v Brown*,[11] Lord Dunpark held that a matrimonial interdict was not a pre-requisite for an exclusion order although in considering whether it would be unjustified or unreasonable to make the order,[12] the sheriff or Lord Ordinary must consider inter alia whether a matrimonial interdict would suffice. Moreover, when granting a s 4 order, the judge

---

1 1983 SLT 224.
2 1983 SLT 275.
3 1983 SLT 559.
4 Ibid at 562.
5 See, for example, *Ward v Ward* 1983 SLT 472; *Brown v Brown* 1985 SLT 376.
6 Section 13(5) of the Law Reform (Miscellaneous Provisions) (Scotland) Act 1985.
7 1983 SLT 224.
8 1983 SLT 275.
9 Matrimonial interdicts are granted under s 14 of the Act: discussed *infra* pp 93 ff.
10 As happened in *Smith v Smith* 1983 SLT 275.
11 1985 SLT 376.
12 Section 4(3).

should state the reasons why an interdict did not afford sufficient protection.[1] On the facts of *Brown*, for example, an interdict was not enough as the husband was only violent when he was drunk and this conduct would not be affected by the existence of an interdict.[2]

Lastly, there are dicta in *Bell v Bell*[3] to support the contention that an interim exclusion order should only be made if the court was satisfied that the applicant would be in danger of 'serious injury or irreparable damage' if the order was not granted. However, in *McCafferty v McCafferty*[4] the Inner House of the Court of Session held that these dicta were an unnecessary gloss on the necessity test which stipulates that it is sufficient that the non-applicant's conduct or threatened or reasonably apprehended conduct 'is or would be injurious to the physical or mental health of the applicant or child'.

In spite of these developments, it has never been doubted that the criterion for an exclusion order is not easy to satisfy. The applicant must satisfy the court that the order is *necessary* for the protection of the applicant or any child of the family because the non-applicant's *conduct* (or threatened or reasonably apprehended conduct) is or would be injurious to the physical or mental health of the applicant or child[5]. The fact that on a balance of convenience test, it is desirable that the applicant and the child of the family should have exclusive occupation of the matrimonial home will not suffice.[6] While s 4(2) expressly includes harm to the applicant's or child's mental as well as physical health,[7] this must be occasioned by the non-applicant's *conduct* and not merely be the result of the breakdown of the marriage.[8]

Finally, it should always be remembered, that even if the necessity test is satisfied, the court can refuse an exclusion order if in all the circumstances of the case, including the factors listed in s 3(3), it would

1 *McCafferty v McCafferty* 1986 SLT 650.
2 See also, for example, *Oliver v Oliver* 1988 GWD 26–1110.
3 1983 SLT 224 per Lord Robertson at 231 and Lord Grieve at 232.
4 1986 SLT 650 per Lord Justice Clerk (Ross) at 652, Lord Robertson at 654 and Lord Dunpark at 655.
5 *Barbour v Barbour* 1990 GWD 3–135: it did not appear that the exclusion order was necessary to protect anyone. *Cf Raeburn v Raeburn* 1990 GWD 8–424.
6 *Smith v Smith* 1983 SLT 275. In *Hampsey v Hampsey* 1988 GWD 24–1035, the Sheriff Principal (Caplan) held that a sheriff has 'no power to grant an exclusion order simply because the best interests of the child required it'.
7 *McCafferty v McCafferty* 1986 SLT 650.
8 *Matheson v Matheson* 1986 SLT (Sh Ct) 2.

be unjustified or unreasonable to do so[1]. But as Lord Dunpark observed in *Brown v Brown*,[2] the Inner House of the Court of Session

> 'had difficulty in envisaging circumstances in which an order which is necessary for the protection of the spouse may be "unjustified or unreasonable" . . .'.

Nevertheless the court has suspended the operation of an exclusion order for three months in order to enable the defender to find alternative accommodation: this is difficult to accept given that the exclusion order was *ex hypothesi* 'necessary'[3]. In *McCafferty v McCafferty*,[4] Lord Dunpark said that in an application for an exclusion order the court should ask four questions:

> '(1) What is the nature and quality of the alleged conduct?
> (2) Is the court satisfied that the conduct is likely to be repeated if cohabitation continues?
> (3) Has the conduct been or, if repeated, would it be injurious to the physical or mental health of the applicant or to any child of the family?
> (4) If so, is the order sought necessary for the future protection of the physical or mental health of the applicant or child?'[5]

The necessity for an exclusion order will only be established if the court is satisfied that a matrimonial interdict will not afford sufficient protection, but as we have seen,[6] a matrimonial interdict is not a pre-requisite for an exclusion order.

It will be clear that the success of an application for an exclusion order will greatly depend on the readiness of the judge at first instance, the Lord Ordinary or the sheriff, to find the necessity test satisfied. This is important, for an appellate court will not interfere with a judge's discretion unless 'no reasonable Lord Ordinary [or sheriff] could have reached the decision, and that he was completely wrong.'[7]

---

1 It is ironic that the needs of the children is one of the s 3(3) factors and is, therefore, only relevant when considering whether it would be unjustified or unreasonable to make an exclusion order!
2 1985 SLT 376 at 378.
3 *Mather v Mather* 1987 SLT 565.
4 1986 SLT 650.
5 Ibid at 656.
6 *Supra* p 83.
7 *McCafferty v McCafferty* 1986 SLT 650 per Lord Robertson at 655. In *Brown v Brown* 1985 SLT 376, Lord Dunpark held that an appellate court could only interfere if the judge at first instance did not apply the proper test or the decision was wholly unwarranted on the facts.

Whatever the difficulties inherent in the legislation and experienced in practice, it cannot be doubted that the protection afforded by s 4 is an important step forward in the protection of wives and children in Scotland who are the victims of domestic violence. The necessity criterion can be criticised as too narrow, but it will clearly cover at least the most blatant forms of domestic violence. However, there is much in the contention that where a marriage is breaking down, the needs of any children of the family should be paramount and that the courts should have the power to exclude a spouse from the matrimonial home when, giving paramount consideration to the welfare of the children of the failing marriage, on the balance of convenience it is desirable that the spouse with the custody of the children should have exclusive occupation of the matrimonial home. At present, this remains the most important gap in the protection provided by s 4.

Statutory rights and third parties

A non-entitled spouse's statutory right of occupation is not prejudiced as the result of the entitled spouse's dealings with the property.[1] Dealings include the sale or lease of the matrimonial home or grant of a heritable security over it.[2] Thus, for example, while the entitled spouse may still sell the matrimonial home, the purchaser will take the property subject to the non-entitled spouse's statutory rights of occupation. Moreover, by s 6(1)(b) the purchaser is not entitled to occupy the matrimonial home or any part of it while the non-entitled spouse continues to enjoy statutory rights of occupation in relation to that property. While this provision is laudable in so far as it protects the non-entitled spouse's statutory rights vis à vis third parties, it clearly

---

1 Section 6(1)(a). This protection does not apply where the entitled spouse occupies the home by permission of a third party or shares the occupation of the home with a third party: s 6(2)(a) and (b).
2 Dealing does not include the compulsory acquisition of the property or the transfer of property by operation of law, for example, bankruptcy. By s 41 of the Bankruptcy (Scotland) Act 1985, the sequestration can be recalled if the petition for sequestration was wholly or mainly to defeat the occupancy rights of the non-entitled spouse. Moreover, by s 40 of the Bankruptcy (Scotland) Act 1985, a debtor's spouse or ex-spouse are protected in their occupation of the family home, in that the consent of the debtor's spouse is required before the sale of the debtor's interest in the property. Further, an application by the permanent trustee to obtain the relevant consent can be refused by the court or an order postponed for a period of up to twelve months in the interests of inter alia the debtor's spouse or children of the family. If the debtor lives in the family home with a child of the family, but separated from the other spouse, it is the debtor's consent which is relevant: thus the interests of the children of the family will be safeguarded. On the application of s 40, see *Salman's Trustee v Salman* 1989 SLT (Sh Ct).

causes conveyancing difficulties as the statutory rights are not recorded in the Register of Sasines or registered in the Land Register of
Scotland. Thus, a third party could buy a house in good faith and in
reliance upon the Registers, only to find that he cannot occupy his
property because it is a matrimonial home in which the non-entitled
spouse of the seller has statutory rights of occupation.

The 1981 Act provides various solutions to this problem. A non-
entitled spouse can renounce in writing the statutory rights in relation
to a particular matrimonial home, provided that, at the time it was
made, the non-entitled spouse swore or affirmed before a notary
public that the renunciation was made freely and without coercion of
any kind.[1] Where such a renunciation is made, the property is no
longer subject to statutory rights of occupancy.[2]

Similarly, occupancy rights are not effective against a third party if
the non-entitled spouse has consented to the dealing.[3] When a non-
entitled spouse refuses to consent to the dealing, the court has power
to dispense with the consent on the ground, inter alia, that it is being
unreasonably withheld.[4] A non-entitled spouse will be taken to have
withheld consent unreasonably if (i) the entitled spouse had been led
to believe that the consent would be forthcoming and there has been
no change of circumstances which would prejudice the non-entitled
spouse or (ii) the entitled spouse having taken all reasonable steps, has
been unable to obtain an answer to a request for consent.[5] In all other
cases, the onus rests on the entitled spouse to show that the non-
entitled spouse has unreasonably withheld consent to the dealing.
Before the court can consider this issue, the proposed dealing must
have reached a stage of negotiations where price and other conditions
have been discussed: it is not enough that the entitled spouse proposes
to put the property up for sale.[6] In determining whether the consent is
being unreasonably withheld the court will consider all the circum-

---

1 Sections 1(5) and (6). It is not necessary that the non-entitled spouse comes to
  Scotland to swear or affirm provided it is done before a person authorised to administer oaths or receive affirmations under the law of the country where the non-entitled
  spouse swears or affirms.
2 Section 6(3)(a)(ii).
3 Section 6(3)(a)(i).
4 Section 7(1). The other grounds for dispensation are that the non-entitled spouse is
  unable to consent because of physical or mental disability; or cannot be found after
  reasonable steps have been taken to trace him; or is a minor.
5 Section 7(2).
6 *Fyfe v Fyfe* 1987 SLT (Sh Ct) 38. This effectively prevents the entitled spouse from
  selling the property on the open market without the non-entitled spouse's consent.

stances of the case, including the factors listed in s 3(3).[1] In *O'Neil v O'Neil*[2] where the non-entitled spouse had no intention of living in the house but was merely withholding consent as a bargaining lever in relation to a financial settlement on divorce, the court indicated that her consent was being withheld unreasonably.[3] If the court dispenses with the non-entitled spouse's consent to the dealing, the third party is not affected by the statutory rights.

There are also exceptions when the entitled spouse entered into a binding obligation in respect of the dealing before the marriage[4] or commencement of the Act.[5] If the entitled spouse has permanently ceased to be entitled to occupy the matrimonial home, for example by selling it to a third party, the non-entitled spouse's statutory rights cease to be exercisable against a third party if the non-entitled spouse has, at any time thereafter, not occupied the property for a continuous period of five years.[6] For example, H is the entitled spouse who sells the matrimonial home to X in 1983 and W leaves the matrimonial home in January 1985: then provided W does not occupy the matrimonial home for any period during the next five years, her statutory rights of occupation will not be enforceable against X after January 1990.

However, in practice the most important exception is to be found in s 6(3)(e).[7] This provides that the non-entitled spouse's rights are not enforceable against a third party where—

> 'the dealing comprises a sale to a third party who has acted in good faith, if there is produced to the third party by the seller—
> (i) an affidavit sworn or affirmed by the seller declaring that the subjects of sale are not or were not at the time of the dealing a matrimonial home in relation to which a spouse of the seller has or had occupancy rights; or

---

1 Section 7(3). For the s 3(3) factors, see *supra* pp 81, 82.
2 1987 SLT (Sh Ct) 26. The house was only a matrimonial home because the husband had hoped that his wife would live there: see *supra* p 80.
3 The court will proceed as expeditiously as possible, but there must be evidence to justify dispensing with consent: see *Longmuir v Longmuir* 1985 SLT (Sh Ct) 33.
4 Section 6(3)(c).
5 Section 6(3)(d).
6 Section 6(3)(f), added by s 13(6)(c) of the Law Reform (Miscellaneous Provisions) (Scotland) Act 1985.
7 As amended by s 13(6)(b) of the Law Reform (Miscellaneous Provisions) (Scotland) Act 1985; and para 31(1) of Sch 8 to, and Sch 9 to, the Law Reform (Miscellaneous Provisions) (Scotland) Act 1990.

(ii) a renunciation of occupancy rights or consent to the dealing which bears to have been properly made or given by the non-entitled spouse.'[1]

Provided the third party is in good faith, then if such an affidavit is sworn or affirmed, he will take the property free from the occupancy rights of the seller's non-entitled spouse. In these circumstances the non-entitled spouse will have recourse against the entitled spouse for compensation for loss of occupancy rights as a result of the entitled spouse's fraud.[2] The provision is so worded that it enables a seller who is not married to swear or affirm that the property is not a matrimonial home but also enables a seller who is married and whose spouse does have statutory rights in relation to the matrimonial home to swear or affirm when the property which is subject to the dealing is not *in fact* a matrimonial home. A similar affidavit is used to protect the rights of a heritable creditor[3] in respect of a matrimonial home which is subject to a mortgage, being prejudiced by a non-entitled spouse's statutory rights of occupation.[4]

Where a dealing has occurred and the third party has taken the property subject to the non-entitled spouse's statutory rights, the third party can apply to a court for an order dispensing with the consent of the non-entitled spouse to the dealing, if, inter alia, the consent was unreasonably withheld.[5] If successful, the third party will then take the property free from the non-entitled spouse's statutory rights.

Since the 1981 Act came into effect, in spite of initial conveyancing difficulties, these provisions have been the cause of little, if any, litigation. In particular, where a third party has relied on a s 6(3)(e) affidavit, there has been no reported case in which a non-entitled spouse has claimed that occupation rights are nevertheless enforceable against the third party because of an absence of good faith. Nevertheless, these provisions remain controversial among conveyancers and

1 The time of the dealing in the case of a sale of the property is the date of delivery of the deed transferring title to the property: s 6(3)(c) as amended by s 13(6)(b)(iv) of the Law Reform (Miscellaneous Provisions) (Scotland) Act 1985.
2 Section 3(7).
3 For example, a bank or building society.
4 Sections 8(1) and (2) (as amended by ss 13(7) and (8) of the Law Reform (Miscellaneous Provisions) (Scotland) Act 1985; and para 31(2) of Sch 8 to, and Sch 9 to, the Law Reform (Miscellaneous Provisions) (Scotland) Act 1990).
5 Section 7.

the Scottish Law Commission is considering further proposals for reform.[1]

Where both spouses have legal title or are joint tenants

The statutory rights of occupation of the matrimonial home are only available to a non-entitled spouse, ie a spouse who has no proprietary interest in the property. Where a spouse has a proprietary interest in the matrimonial home, at common law, he or she is entitled to occupy it. However, the 1981 Act contains important provisions which strengthen the position of a spouse who has a joint legal title and it is these provisions which will be discussed in this section.

Although it was contrary to principle that a co-owner or co-tenant could be ejected by the other from the common property, there was a suggestion in *Price v Watson*[2] that this was possible. Section 4(7) of the 1981 Act has clarified the position: it provides that where both spouses are entitled, or permitted by a third party, to occupy a matrimonial home, it shall be incompetent for one spouse to bring an action of ejection from the matrimonial home against the other spouse. Moreover, while at common law either co-owner could carry out necessary repairs and pay essential outgoings, there was no power to carry out non-essential repairs. The 1981 Act gives co-owners the power to do so and allows a court to apportion the expenditure between them.[3]

As we have seen,[4] where the spouses are common owners of the matrimonial home, each spouse is free to sell his or her own half *pro indiviso* share of the property without the agreement of the other. This could lead to problems where the purchaser insisted on occupying the property. Section 9(1) of the 1981 Act provides that the right to occupy the matrimonial home enjoyed by a co-owning spouse is not to be prejudiced by reason only of any dealing of the other spouse in respect of the property and that a third party shall not by reason only of such a dealing be entitled to occupy the matrimonial home or any part of it. The effect of this provision is that while a co-owning spouse is still entitled to sell his or her half *pro indiviso* share, the purchaser of his interest is unable to occupy the matrimonial home while the other co-owning spouse continues to reside there.[5]

---

1 These are discussed in *Family Law: Pre-consolidation Reforms* SLC Discussion Paper No 85, paras 6.1–6.29. In the present writer's view only the minor modifications suggested in paras 6.19–6.25 are either necessary or desirable.
2 1951 SC 359.
3 Sections 2(4)(a) and (b) and (6).
4 *Supra* p 78.
5 When a co-owning spouse becomes bankrupt, the provisions of s 41 of the Bankruptcy (Scotland) Act 1985, are applicable to protect the occupancy rights of the other co-owning spouse and children of the family: see *supra* p 86 note 2.

It was an axiomatic principle of the common law that where property was held in common, either of the co-owners was entitled to obtain a decree of division and sale to realise his or her share of the value of the property. The court had no discretion to refuse the decree. Thus, for example, in *Dickson v Dickson*,[1] the Lord Ordinary (Kincraig) held that a husband was entitled to a decree of division and sale in respect of property he owned in common with his wife: it was irrelevant that she would not agree to the sale as she wished to use the house as a home for herself and her children of the family. Thus by applying for a decree of division and sale, a spouse could frustrate the underlying purpose of owning a matrimonial home, ie to provide a home for the co-owning spouse and their family. Section 19 provides a partial solution to this problem. Where a matrimonial home is owned in common by a married couple, if one of the spouses brings an action for the division and sale of the property, the court has a discretion, after having regard to all the circumstances of the case, to refuse or postpone the granting of the decree or only to grant the decree subject to conditions. The court is expressly directed to consider the factors listed in s 3(3)[2] and whether the spouse bringing the action has offered to make suitable alternative accommodation available to the other spouse.[3] It is not clear where the onus lies in s 19 applications. In *Hall v Hall*[4] the Sheriff Principal (Caplan), arguing by analogy with dispensation of consent under s 7,[5] held that the onus lay on the spouse seeking the sale to show that the sale is reasonable. On the other hand, in *Berry v Berry*,[6] Lord Sutherland held that as a co-owner has a *prima facie* right to an action of division and sale, the onus lay on the defender to show why it was unreasonable for the sale to go ahead. In practice, however, the court will not allow a sale to go ahead when the continued occupation of the matrimonial home is clearly in the interests of the defender and the

---

1 1982 SLT 128.
2 *Supra* pp 81, 82.
3 Section 19(a) and (b). The offer must be of specific alternative accomodation; a general offer to help a co-owning spouse find somewhere to live is not enough. See *Hall v Hall* 1987 SLT (Sh Ct) 15.
4 Ibid.
5 Discussed *supra* p 87.
6 1988 SC LR 296. The sale was ordered in this case. The most appropriate method of sale is by private treaty in open market: *Berry v Berry No 2* 1989 SLT 292. Where a spouse refused to pay a capital sum payment as financial provision on divorce, he was forced to sell his *pro indiviso* share of the former matrimonial home to his co-owning former spouse: *Scrimgeour v Scrimgeour* 1988 SLT 590. This was an exceptional case.

family. The needs of children are important.[1] In *Crow v Crow*,[2] Lord Wylie held that s 19 had made very material inroads into the rights of *pro indiviso* proprietors who were married. In particular, he stressed that the needs of the family were crucial. Accordingly, he had no hesitation in postponing the grant of a decree of division and sale beyond a date when the marriage would be terminated by divorce.[3] So, for example, if H applied for an action of division and sale, the court can now delay granting decree until any children of the marriage reach the age of 18, even although the couple may divorce before the youngest child has reached that age.

It is important to note that s 19 is only applicable when the co-owners are spouses. If, after divorce, an ex-spouse applies for an action of division and sale, he or she must be granted decree. Moreover, if during the marriage, a spouse sells his or her half *pro indiviso* share to a third party, the third party is entitled to a decree of division and sale as s 19 only applies when both spouses are common owners of the property.[4]

Where both spouses are joint owners of the matrimonial home, ie entitled spouses, the court has the same powers under s 3 to make regulatory orders in respect of its occupation as it has when there is an entitled and non-entitled spouse.[5] Similarly, the court may make an exclusion order under s 4 where both spouses are entitled, in exactly the same way as in the case of an entitled and non-entitled spouse.[6] The availability of exclusion orders as an important step towards the protection of wives and children from domestic violence cannot be overestimated.

TENANCIES

By s 13(1) of the 1981 Act, a non-entitled spouse can apply to a court for an order transferring the tenancy of the matrimonial home from the entitled to the non-entitled spouse subject to the non-entitled spouse paying just and reasonable compensation to the entitled spouse.

---

1 Significantly, in *Berry v Berry* the couple had no children: but a home was not required for the children in *Hall v Hall*, yet the sale was refused: for criticism, see Thomson 1987 SLG 96.
2 1986 SLT 270.
3 Indeed a divorce action was pending in this case.
4 However, this 'dodge' may be caught by s 9(1)(a) which provides that the co-owning spouse's rights 'in that home' are not to be prejudiced by any dealing of the other spouse.
5 *Supra* p 81.
6 *Supra* p 82.

Notice must be given to the landlord who has to be given an opportunity to be heard in the proceedings. In considering whether the tenancy should be transferred the court is directed to consider the factors in s 3(3)[1] and whether the non-entitled spouse is suitable to become a tenant and to perform the obligations in the lease. There are exceptions where the matrimonial home is, for example, part of an agricultural holding or a croft.[2] An order granting an application under s 13(1) can be made on granting a decree of divorce or declarator of nullity of marriage.[3]

Where both spouses are joint or common tenants there is a similar right to apply to a court for an order vesting the tenancy in the applicant's name solely, provided that the applicant pays just and reasonable compensation to the other spouse.[4]

Where an entitled spouse is the tenant of a matrimonial home, the non-entitled spouse retains possession of the tenancy, and therefore the protection of the Rent (Scotland) Act 1984, if the entitled spouse leaves the home.[5]

MATRIMONIAL INTERDICTS

A spouse's right to occupy the matrimonial home can, of course, be undermined as a result of the other spouse's violent behaviour. Since this is so, it is thought to be convenient to discuss the law relating to matrimonial interdicts in this section.

In the leading case of *Tattersall v Tattersall*, the Lord President (Emslie) opined[6] that 'interdict in the law of Scotland is designed only to prevent the apprehended commission of a wrong'. Interdict is granted at common law to protect proprietary rights. Thus in *MacLure v MacLure*,[7] for example, a husband who owned a hotel which was also used as the matrimonial home obtained an interdict against his wife who had no interest in the property from entering the hotel. However, interdict is also granted to protect the integrity of the person and

1 *Supra* pp 81, 82. Thus in *McGowan v McGowan* 1986 SLT 112, Lord Kincraig ordered the transfer of a tenancy in H's name to his W. H had been violent during the marriage and had had an adulterous affair. W was living with the son of the marriage in overcrowded conditions with her married daughter. Lord Kincraig thought it would be a 'travesty of justice' if H was allowed to retain occupation of the matrimonial home.
2 For a full list, see ss 13(7) and (8).
3 Section 13(2) as amended by para 11 of Sch 1 to the Family Law (Scotland) Act 1985.
4 Section 13(9).
5 Section 2(8), reversing the decision in *Temple v Mitchell* 1956 SC 267.
6 1983 SLT 506 at 509.
7 1911 SC 200: discussed *supra* p 79.

therefore one spouse can obtain interdict against molestation by the other.[1] However, it is a fundmental principle of Scots law that an interdict must be granted in sufficiently precise terms to leave the defender in no doubt as to what he or she can or cannot do and that the conduct prohibited should be no wider than is necessary to curb the defender's illegal actions. Thus in *Murdoch v Murdoch*[2] an interim interdict preventing a husband from telephoning his wife or calling at her house was incompetent by reason of being too wide.

The major drawback of an interdict at common law was the question of enforcement. Where there was an alleged breach of interdict, a petition and complaint had to be brought with the concurrence of the Lord Advocate or procurator fiscal, to establish to the courts that breach of interdict had taken place.[3] The action was a civil one and the police had no power to arrest a person merely because he or she was in breach of interdict, though they could, of course, intervene if a crime or offence, for example, an assault, had occurred.

The 1981 Act introduces a system of matrimonial interdicts to which the court must, in certain circumstances, attach a power of arrest. Where a power of arrest is attached to an interdict, a police constable may arrest the defender without warrant if he has reasonable cause to suspect that he or she is in breach of an interdict.

Section 14(1) of the 1981 Act provides that it shall not be incompetent for a court to entertain an application by a spouse for a matrimonial interdict by reason only that the spouses are living together as man and wife. This clarifies the doubt which had existed at common law about the competency of an application for interdict when the spouses are living together.[4]

By section 14(2) a matrimonial interdict means an interdict, including an interim interdict, which—

'a) restrains or prohibits any conduct of one spouse towards the other spouse or a child of the family, or
b) prohibits a spouse from entering or remaining in a matrimonial home or in a specified area in the vicinity of the matrimonial home.'

There is little difficulty in relation to s 14(2)(a) interdicts, ie non-molestation interdicts. It appears that the criteria in *Murdoch v*

---

1 This was certainly the case if the spouses were living apart: it was uncertain whether interdict was available when they were cohabiting: but see now s 14, discussed *infra*.
2 1973 SLT (Notes) 13.
3 *Gribben v Gribben* 1976 SLT 266.
4 See *supra* note 1.

Murdoch[1] are still followed and that the interdict must specify the conduct prohibited which should be no wider than necessary to prevent the illegal act, ie the molestation of the other spouse or a child of the family.

More difficulties have been experienced in relation to s 14(2)(b) interdicts, which have the effect of banning the defender from the matrimonial home. Where an entitled spouse seeks a s 14(2)(b) interdict to exclude a non-entitled spouse from the home, the interdict is being used to protect the applicant's proprietary rights. In *Tattersall v Tattersall*[2] the Inner House of the Court of Session held that it was not competent for a non-entitled spouse who has no proprietary rights to seek a s 14(2)(b) interdict to exclude the entitled spouse from enjoying the incidents of ownership of his or her property. Instead, the non-entitled spouse must seek enforcement of his or her *statutory* rights to occupy the matrimonial home, and resort must be made to a s 4 exclusion order, when interdicts preventing the entitled spouse from entering or remaining in the matrimonial home can also be granted.[3] Where both spouses are entitled, since an action of ejection is no longer competent,[4] it is thought that neither spouse can obtain an interdict under s 14(2)(b) excluding the other from the matrimonial home in which he or she has a one half *pro indiviso* share: once again resort must be made to a s 4 exclusion order.

Thus the effect of *Tattersall v Tattersall*[5] is that a s 14(2)(b) interdict can only be granted to an entitled spouse against a non-entitled spouse. Otherwise an exclusion order must be sought under s 4. The important distinction between the two remedies is that a s 14(2)(b) interdict can be granted when, on the balance of convenience, it is just to do so while a s 4 exclusion order cannot be made unless the court is satisfied it is *necessary* to do so.[6]

Where a s 14(2)(b) interdict has been granted to an entitled spouse and consequently the non-entitled spouse has been excluded from the matrimonial home, it will, of course, be open to the non-entitled spouse to obtain declarator of his or her statutory rights of occupation and seek a s 3 regulatory order to re-enter the home and, if necessary, a s 4 exclusion order.

1 1973 SLT (Notes) 13.
2 1983 SLT 506.
3 Sections 4(4)(a) and (5)(a).
4 Section 4(7), *supra* p 90.
5 1983 SLT 506.
6 See *supra* p 82.

Where a matrimonial interdict is made which is ancillary to an exclusion order under s 4,[1] s 15(1)(a) provides that the court *must* attach a power of arrest to such an interdict, if this is requested by the applicant. In relation to any other matrimonial interdict, for example, a non-molestation interdict under s 14(2)(a),[2] the court has a discretion by s 15(1)(b) to refuse a request to attach a power of arrest where 'it appears to the court that in all the circumstances of the case the power is unnecessary'. It will be noticed, therefore, that a court has no discretion to refuse to attach a power of arrest when the interdict is ancillary to an exclusion order and a power of arrest is requested by the applicant.

When a power of arrest is attached to a matrimonial interdict, a police constable may arrest the non-applicant spouse without a warrant, if the policeman has reasonable cause for suspecting that the defender is in breach of the interdict.[3]

In spite of the theoretical difficulties surrounding s 14(2)(b), nevertheless it is thought that the introduction of matrimonial interdicts, with powers of arrest, marks an important advance in Scots law for the protection of a spouse or child of the family from domestic violence. It should be stressed that before making an exclusion order under s 4, the court must have determined that a non-molestation interdict under s 14(2)(a) would not be sufficient to protect the applicant spouse or the children of the family, and that an exclusion order is therefore necessary for their protection.

COHABITEES

Couples who are unmarried may also experience difficulties in relation to the occupation of their 'family' accommodation when their relationships begin to break down. The 1981 Act takes the important step of providing some relief to an unmarried cohabiting couple in this situation. A cohabiting couple for the purpose of the Act is defined as a man and a woman who are living with each other as if they were man and wife.[4] In determining whether a couple are cohabiting the court

---

1 Including an interim order. Interdicts prohibiting the non-applicant spouse from entering or remaining in the matrimonial home, can be granted as ancillary to an exclusion order, ss 4(4) and (5). These are matrimonial interdicts for the purpose of s 15.
2 Or an 'exclusion' interdict under s 14(2)(b).
3 Section 15(3). For full discussion of the procedure, see *Clive* Appendix pp 731–734. Minor amendments to s 15(2) and (4) were made by s 64 of the Law Reform (Miscellaneous Provisions) (Scotland) Act 1990.
4 Section 18(1). Homosexual couples are therefore excluded.

must consider all the circumstances of the case including the length of their relationship and whether they have any children.[1] Section 18(1) provides that where there is a cohabiting couple and one partner is entitled to occupy a house and the other is non-entitled, the non-entitled partner may apply to a court for the grant of occupancy rights in relation to the house in which they are cohabiting.[2] Occupancy rights can be granted for a period not exceeding six months,[3] though the initial period can be extended for further periods of up to six months with no overall limit. A non-entitled partner's rights of occupation are the same as those of a non-entitled spouse.[4] When an order granting occupancy rights is in force or both partners are entitled to occupy the property, certain provisions of the 1981 Act apply to the couple:[5] in particular, regulatory and exclusion orders are available under ss 3 and 4 as are the provisions relating to matrimonial interdicts.[6] However the non-entitled partner's occupancy rights are not protected from dealings by the entitled partner with third parties, nor is there any restriction on the grant of a decree in an action of division and sale where the property is owned in common.

It must be stressed that when one cohabiting partner is non-entitled, the protection afforded by these provisions of the 1981 Act does not apply unless and until there has been a successful application by the non-entitled partner for occupancy rights. Thus, for example, in *Clarke v Hatten*,[7] an entitled partner was unable to use the 1981 Act to obtain *inter alia* a matrimonial interdict, as the non-entitled partner, whose violence she had fled, had not applied for occupancy rights.[8] A non-entitled spouse, on the other hand, has statutory rights of occupation of the matrimonial home as a result of simply being married. Although the protection afforded a spouse is also more extensive, nevertheless the 1981 Act is at least a first step towards the recognition by Scots law that the needs of an unmarried couple when their relationship is deteriorating are similar to those of spouses whose marriage is

1 Section 18(2).
2 Indeed, a person has been held not to be 'homeless' for the purposes of the Housing (Scotland) Act 1987 because of the right to apply for occupancy rights under s 18: see *McAlinden v Bearsden and Milngavie District Council* 1986 SLT 191.
3 Section 18(1) as amended by s 13(9)(a) of the Law Reform (Miscellaneous Provisions) (Scotland) Act 1985.
4 Section 18(6) as amended by s 13(9)(b) of the Law Reform (Miscellaneous Provisions) (Scotland) Act 1985.
5 Section 18(3).
6 A tenancy transfer order under s 13 is also available.
7 1987 SCLR 527.
8 It would have been different if both partners were entitled as s 18(3) would operate.

breaking down, and that legal remedies should be available to persons in this situation regardless of their marital status.[1]

1 For proposals for further extension of co-habitees' rights, see *The Effects of Cohabitation in Private Law* SLC Discussion Paper No 86, paras 7.2–7.10

6 Divorce

INTRODUCTION

Divorce on the ground of adultery has been recognised at common law since the Reformation and divorce for desertion was introduced by statute in 1573.[1] Until the Divorce (Scotland) Act 1938, these remained the only two grounds of divorce. The 1938 Act introduced further grounds: cruelty, incurable insanity, sodomy and bestiality.[2] With the exception of incurable insanity, the grounds of divorce were fault-based and divorce was perceived as a punishment for the defender's matrimonial offence. Divorce for incurable insanity was manifestly a non-fault ground and to this can be traced the idea that divorce should be regarded as a remedy to enable a spouse to escape from a dead marriage. This view of divorce gradually became more prevalent. For example, as the result of judicial and statutory developments,[3] any requirement of moral fault on the part of a defender was whittled away from the concept of cruelty, so that the pursuer could obtain a divorce whenever the defender's conduct was detrimental to the pursuer's health.

By the 1970s the movement for the reform of divorce law on the basis of a 'non-fault' ground of irretrievable breakdown of marriage had built up considerable momentum.[4] The Law Commission took the view that a system based on the matrimonial offence did not achieve the objectives of a good divorce law which were—

'(i) to buttress, rather than to undermine, the stability of marriage; and
(ii) where, regrettably, a marriage has irretrievably broken down, to enable the empty legal shell to be destroyed with

---

1 Act 1573, c 55.
2 The Act also enabled a marriage to be dissolved on the ground of the presumed death of one of the spouses: see *supra* p 29, note 2.
3 Most importantly s 5 of the Divorce (Scotland) Act 1964.
4 See, for example, *Putting Assunder: A Divorce Law for Contemporary Society*, Society for Propagation of Christian Knowledge, 1966.

the maximum fairness, and the minimum bitterness, distress and humiliation.'[1]

However, the Law Commission considered that it was impracticable to make irretrievable breakdown of marriage the sole ground of divorce. How was breakdown to be established without some form of inquisitorial procedure alien to an adversarial system of adjudication? Would not this involve a new system of courts or tribunals manned by social workers rather than lawyers? Was not the equation of matrimony with a commercial partnership too revolutionary a concept for contemporary British society? The Scottish Law Commission recommended merely the addition of new separation grounds to the existing grounds of divorce but considered that the legal effect of the grounds was that they established that a marriage had in fact broken down.[2]

In England, a compromise was reached between the concept of non-fault divorce based on irretrievable breakdown and the existing matrimonial offences in the Divorce Reform Act 1969, now consolidated in the Matrimonial Causes Act 1973. While irretrievable breakdown was to be the sole ground of divorce it could only be established by proof of at least one of five guideline facts, which included modified versions of the previous matrimonial offences and two new facts based on separation.[3] The Divorce (Scotland) Act 1976 follows a similar compromise.[4]

IRRETRIEVABLE BREAKDOWN OF MARRIAGE

If a system of divorce is based on the sole ground of irretrievable breakdown of marriage as opposed to the concept of matrimonial offence, two consequences should follow. First, a pursuer should be entitled to a divorce whenever the marriage has in fact broken down irretrievably. It is irrelevant that the defender's conduct was morally blameless. Moreover, and more importantly, it is irrelevant that the pursuer's conduct could be perceived to be a contribution to the failure of the marriage. If, for example, a pursuer has committed adultery, this should not be held against him or her: the adultery is merely a symptom of the breakdown.

---

1 *Reform of the Grounds of Divorce: The Field of Choice*, Cmnd 3123 para 15.
2 *Divorce: The Grounds Considered* (1967) (Cmnd 3256).
3 Section 1 of the Matrimonial Causes Act 1973.
4 For an excellent commentary on the Act, see Clive *The Divorce (Scotland) Act 1976*, (1976).

Second, even though the defender's conduct amounted to what had formerly been a matrimonial offence, for example, adultery, the pursuer should not be entitled to a divorce unless the marriage has in fact broken down. There should therefore be built into the system provisions for establishing whether or not reconciliation is possible and to encourage reconciliation where this possibility exists.

As a result of the fact that the current Scottish divorce law is a compromise between the concept of irretrievable breakdown and matrimonial offences, the full implications of a non-fault theory of divorce have been ignored. Section 1(1) of the Divorce (Scotland) Act 1976[1] provides that irretrievable breakdown of marriage is the sole ground of divorce in Scots law 'if, but only if, it is established in accordance with the following provisions of the Act'. Section 1(2) provides that irretrievable breakdown will be established on proof of a) the defender's adultery, b) the defender's behaviour, c) the defender's desertion for two years, d) the non-cohabitation of the parties for two years and their consent, or e) the non-cohabitation of the parties for five years. Thus, a pursuer will be unable to obtain a divorce unless he can prove one of the facts or guidelines in s 1(2), even though the marriage has in fact irretrievably broken down. Conversely, a pursuer will be entitled to a divorce if one of the facts or guidelines is established, even although the marriage has not in fact irretrievably broken down. In other words, proof of a s 1(2) fact or guideline is both a necessary and sufficient condition of establishing irretrievable breakdown within the meaning of the Act. Irretrievable breakdown in the context of Scottish divorce law is simply an artificial legal construct enabling a party who can prove one or more of the facts and guidelines in s 1(2) to obtain a divorce.[2] The concept of matrimonial fault has therefore not been eroded from the Scots law of divorce. Moreover, because the Act is not concerned with whether a marriage has *in fact* broken down irretrievably, it is significant that it contains no provisions for compulsory attempts at reconciliation nor is there any obligation on solicitors to discuss with clients the possibility of reconciliation.[3] If, however, it appears to the court that there is a reasonable prospect of reconciliation, the court can continue the

1 References in this chapter are to the 1976 Act unless otherwise stated.
2 The phrase could as well be 'abracadabra', see WA Wilson, 1976 SLT (News) 27.
3 Cf s 6 of the Matrimonial Causes Act 1973. However a Court of Session Practice Note of 11 March 1977 enjoins practitioners to encourage clients to seek marriage counselling if the clients might benefit. There are also provisions in the Court of Session and sheriff court rules under which parties can be advised to attempt conciliation in respect of the custody of any children of the marriage. Rules 170B(15) and 260D(10) (Court of Session): Rule 132F (Sheriff Court).

action for an attempt to be made,[1] but in practice it is unlikely that reconciliation is possible once the action has begun.

The result of the reforms introduced by the 1976 Act has been simply to widen the grounds of divorce. In these circumstances, it is hypocritical to regard irretrievable breakdown as the sole ground of divorce: the provisions of s 1(2) constitute grounds for divorce in Scots law, not simply facts or guidelines to determine whether a marriage has in fact irretrievably broken down.

THE GROUNDS OF DIVORCE

Adultery

By s 1(2)(a) irretrievable breakdown of marriage is established if 'since the date of the marriage the defender has committed adultery'.

Adultery has been defined as voluntary sexual intercourse between a married person and a person of the opposite sex, not being the married partner. The sexual intercourse must be voluntary; thus a woman who is the victim of a rape is not guilty of adultery.[2]

The physical requirements of adultery were discussed by Lord Wheatley in *MacLennnan v MacLennan*.[3] The pursuer sought a divorce on the ground of his wife's adultery. She had gone to the United States and returned with a child which the pursuer could not have fathered. Her defence was that she had conceived the child as a result of artificial insemmination from a donor (AID). While Lord Wheatley regarded the wife's conception of a child by AID without her husband's consent as 'a grave and heinous breach of the contract of marriage', it did not amount to adultery. Adultery involved a mutual surrender of the sexual and reproductive organs and some degree of penetration of the woman's vagina was necessary: in Lord Wheatley's words adultery necessitated 'physical contact with an alien and unlawful sexual organ, and without that element there cannot be what the law regards as adultery'.[4] He therefore dismissed the argument that adultery could be committed by a woman 'when alone in the privacy of her bedroom, she injects into her ovum by means of a syringe the seed of a man she does not know and has never seen'.[5]

---

1 Section 2(1).
2 The fact that a person believes in good faith that he or she is not married, does not prevent them from being guilty of adultery: *Sands v Sands* 1964 SLT 80.
3 1958 SC 105.
4 Ibid at 114.
5 Ibid at 114. AID without the husband's consent could give rise to a divorce based on s 1(2)(b), as would other forms of sexual gratification not involving sexual intercourse.

A defender's adultery is only relevant if it has occurred 'since the date of the marriage'. Thus, if a young man commits adultery with a married woman and subsequently marries, his spouse cannot rely upon his pre-marital adultery to found an action of divorce. A single isolated act of adultery will suffice.

The standard of proof is on the balance of probabilities.[1] Corroboration is not required[2] but the defender's adultery must be established by evidence emanating from a source other than a party to the marriage.[3] Where the defender has been found guilty of rape or incest by a United Kingdom court evidence of his conviction can be used to establish adultery, provided a third party identifies the defender as the person convicted.[4] Moreover a finding of adultery in earlier matrimonial proceedings is admissible in divorce proceedings to establish adultery, but, once again, a third party must identify the defender as the party in the earlier proceedings.[5]

In an action of divorce on the ground of adultery, the pursuer may be met by certain defences.

(i) *Lenocinium*

The common law defence of *lenocinium* was preserved by s 1(3) of the 1976 Act. The defence of *lenocinium* is difficult to define.[6] The essence of the defence is that the pursuer actively promoted the defender's adultery or was art and part in the offence. This would cover, for example, a husband who encouraged his wife to take up prostitution or a wife who suggested to her husband that they should join a 'spouse swapping' party. The defence can be illustrated by the leading case of *Gallacher v Gallacher*,[7] where a husband sent a letter to his wife entreating her to do something to enable him to divorce her. A few months later, the wife fell passionately in love with another man. In divorce proceedings based on adultery, the action failed on account of *lenocinium*. The court refused to accept the husband's contention that the adultery arose as a result of the wife's passion for her lover rather than his letter. As Lord Anderson said,[8]

---

1 Section 1(6).
2 Civil Evidence (Scotland) Act 1988, s 1(1). This is also the case for establishing the other grounds.
3 Ibid, s 8(1) and (3).
4 Section 10 of the Law Reform (Miscellaneous Provisions) (Scotland) Act 1968; *Andrews v Andrews* 1971 SLT (Notes) 44.
5 Section 11 of the Law Reform (Miscellaneous Provisions) (Scotland) Act 1968.
6 *Gallacher v Gallacher* 1928 SC 586 per Lord Justice Clerk (Alness) at 591.
7 1928 SC 586.
8 1928 SC 586 at 599.

'No woman invited by her husband to commit adultery would go into the street and offer herself to the first man she met. Affection for her lover must always be a cause, and it may be the main cause of her lapse from virtue'.

However, the husband's letter had been the reason why she had even contemplated adultery. Lord Ormidale took the view[1] that—

'Passion no doubt was a factor before she finally fell, but I have no doubt that but for the letter and invitation of her husband, she would have resisted and not responded to the advances [of her lover]'.

Thus the pursuer's conduct does not have to be *the* cause *(causa causans)* of the adultery: it is sufficient if it is a cause *(conditio sine qua non)*.

Six years later, Gallacher again attempted to obtain a divorce.[2] This time he was successful. The wife had continued to live with her lover but the court held that her continuing adulterous relationship was no longer caused by the pursuer's letter. Lord Hunter[3] maintained that the husband's act of connivance six years before could not be regarded as a perpetual licence to the wife to commit adultery for the rest of her lifetime: on the facts, the defender no longer required his encouragement. Consequently, the defence of *lenocinium* failed as the wife could no longer show that her husband's letter was a cause of her continuing her adulterous affair.

It is important to stress that before *lenocinium* can be established, the pursuer must actively encourage the defender's adultery. Thus in *Thomson v Thomson*,[4] the pursuer thought that his wife was having an affair. When she asked him for money to visit friends, he suspected she was going to meet her lover. Nevertheless he gave her the money she requested but had her followed by inquiry agents. They discovered her committing adultery in Gateshead. The wife's defence of *lenocinium* failed on the ground that since she believed she had succeeded in keeping the knowledge of her affair from her husband, he could not have been actively encouraging her to commit adultery when he gave her the money she requested – albeit that he suspected how she would

1 Ibid at 595.
2 1934 SC 339.
3 Ibid at 346.
4 1908 SC 179.

in fact use it. Similarly, it is not *lenocinium* to hire inquiry agents to watch a spouse suspected of adultery.[1]

(ii) *Condonation*

By s 1(3) of the 1976 Act, the defender's adultery will not be a ground of divorce if it has been 'condoned by the pursuer's cohabitation with the defender in the knowledge or belief that the defender has committed the adultery'. Section 13(2) provides that for the purposes of the Act 'the parties to a marriage shall be held to cohabit with one another only when they are in fact living together as man and wife'. Thus the parties must in fact live together as husband and wife before the defence is operative:verbal forgiveness[2] or an isolated act of sexual intercourse will not suffice. But s 1(3) must be read with s 2(2) of the Act. Section 2(2) provides that adultery will not be condoned unless the pursuer has continued or resumed cohabitation with the defender at any time after the end of a period of three months from the date on which cohabitation was continued or resumed. Some examples will illustrate how this section operates: in all cases it is assumed that the pursuer knows or believes the defender has committed adultery.

1. If the pursuer continues to cohabit with the defender for less than three months, adultery is not condoned.
2. If the pursuer continues to cohabit with the defender for more than three months, adultery is condoned.
3. If the pursuer continues to cohabit with the defender for less than three months but then resumes cohabitation, the adultery will be condoned if cohabitation takes place at any time after a three month period beginning from the date when he knew or believed the defender was committing adultery and continued to cohabit.

    For example:
    a) P learns of D's adultery on 31 January. P continues to cohabit with D for a week. If P resumes cohabitation, for however short a period after 30 April, the adultery will be condoned, as the resumption of cohabitation took place outside the three month period beginning on 31 January.
    b) P learns of D's adultery on 31 January. P continues to cohabit with D for a week. If P resumes cohabitation on 1 April, the adultery will not be condoned if P leaves before 1 May. But if the cohabitation continues beyond or is resumed after 30 April,

---

1 For proposals that *lenocinium* should be replaced by a defence of actively promoting or encouraging adultery, see *Family Law: Pro-consolidation Reforms* SLC Discussion Paper No 85, paras 8.2–8.4.
2 This was the position at common law: *Annan v Annan* 1948 SC 532.

the adultery will be condoned, as cohabitation has taken place outside the three month period beginning on 31 January.

4. If P ceases cohabitation with D but resumes cohabitation for less than three months, the adultery will not be condoned.

5. If P ceases cohabitation with D but resumes cohabitation for more than three months the adultery will be condoned.

6. If P ceases cohabitation with D but resumes cohabitation for less than three months, the adultery will be condoned if cohabitation takes place at any time after a three month period from the date of the initial resumption. For example:

a) P learns of D's adultery. He ceases to cohabit for a year. P resumes cohabitation on 31 January. P continues to cohabit with D for a week. If P resumes cohabitation, for however short a period after 30 April, the adultery will be condoned, as cohabitation has taken place outwith the three month period beginning on 31 January when cohabitation was first resumed.

b) P learns of D's adultery. He ceases to cohabit for a year. P resumes cohabitation on 31 January. P continues to cohabit with D for a week. If P resumes cohabitation on 1 April, the adultery will not be condoned if he leaves before 1 May. But if cohabitation continues beyond or is resumed after 30 April, the adultery will be condoned, as cohabitation has taken place outwith the three month period beginning on 31 January.

It is thought that s 1(3) only operates as a defence in relation to the adultery on which the action is founded. Thus if the pursuer cohabited in the knowledge or belief that the defender committed adultery with A, it would not operate as a bar to an action based on the defender's adultery with B. Similarly, if the pursuer knew or believed that the defender has committed specific acts of adultery, s 1(3) would not operate in relation to other acts of adultery which subsequently came to the pursuer's knowledge.

(iii) *Collusion*

If the parties *agree* to put up a false case or keep back a relevant defence, this will operate as an absolute bar to a divorce if discovered before decree is granted: if discovered after decree has been granted, the decree can be reduced.[1] Collusion will be a bar to a divorce based on any of the five grounds.[2]

---

1 *Walker v Walker* 1911 SC 163.
2 See generally *Clive* pp 480–481. For proposals that collusion should cease to be a bar, see *Family Law: Pre-consolidation Reforms* SLC Discussion Paper No 85, paras 8.5–8.8.

Behaviour

By s 1(2)(b) irretrievable breakdown of marriage is established if—

'since the date of the marriage the defender has at any time behaved (whether or not as a result of mental abnormality and whether such behaviour has been active or passive) in such a way that the pursuer cannot reasonably be expected to cohabit with the defender'.

The defender's conduct must have occurred after the date of the marriage: a spouse's behaviour before the marriage is irrelevant. Thus, for example, a husband cannot use s 1(2)(b) to obtain a divorce on the ground that he was induced to marry the defender as a result of her fraudulent misrepresentation that she was pregnant by him: the wife's behaviour, ie the lie, took place *before* the date of the marriage.[1] Similarly, a wife who discovers that her husband had committed a heinous offence before the marriage, cannot rely on this offence to obtain a divorce.[2]

Before s 1(2)(b) is applicable, the defender must have behaved. What does behaviour mean in this context? A mere physical condition does not per se constitute behaviour. Thus if a defender is incontinent, that in itself does not amount to behaviour. But if an incontinent spouse refused to wear protective underwear, the refusal to do so would constitute behaviour. However, it is settled that symptoms of an illness can in certain circumstances amount to behaviour. If, for example, a spouse became violent as a result of an illness, the violence would clearly constitute behaviour. But it can be difficult to determine when the symptom of an illness is merely a physical condition and when it amounts to behaviour. Thus, a husband's sleepiness and general lack of interest in his family caused by schizophrenia has been held to amount to behaviour[3] and bad personal hygiene as a result of disseminated sclerosis has not.[4]

A solution to this problem may be found in that the 1976 Act includes behaviour 'whether such behaviour has been active or passive'. In *Thurlow v Thurlow*[5] it has been accepted in England that where as a result of a debilitating illness a spouse is unable to fulfil the obligations of marriage, this failure can constitute behaviour for the purposes of divorce. As the 1976 has expressly enacted that behaviour

---

1 On fraudulent misrepresentation, see *supra* p 32.
2 Cf *Hastings v Hastings* 1941 SLT 323.
3 *Fullarton v Fullarton* 1976 SLT 8.
4 *Grant v Grant* 1974 SLT (Notes) 54.
5 [1975] 2 All ER 979, [1976] Fam 32.

may be passive,[1] it is thought that the principle in *Thurlow* has been transplanted into Scots law. Thus if an illness prevents a spouse from fulfilling the obligations of married life, this passive negative behaviour – as opposed to the illness – can amount to grounds for divorce.[2]

The fact that a defender's behaviour is caused by mental illness is irrelevant: s 1(2)(b) expressly states that conduct will constitute behaviour 'whether or not as a result of mental illness'.[3]

The pursuer must establish that the defender behaved 'in such a way that the pursuer cannot reasonably be expected to cohabit with the defender'. The test is a compromise between a subjective and objective test. The criterion is whether the particular pursuer can, at the time of the action, reasonably be expected to cohabit with the defender. Thus a highly sensitive spouse may not reasonably be expected to put up with conduct which a spouse of ordinary fortitude could withstand.[4] But because of the phrase 'reasonably be expected', utterly trivial conduct (for example, snoring)[5] or socially useful conduct (membership of a lifeboat or mountain rescue team) will not constitute grounds for divorce, however sensitive the pursuer may be.

The range of behaviour which could satisfy s 1(2)(b) is as wide as human conduct. It includes both physical[6] and verbal assaults. Moreover, as Lord Davidson explained in *Hastie v Hastie*,[7]

'. . . conduct on the part of a defender, by word or act, may be of such a nature that even if there is no risk of a repetition it is so destructive of a marriage relationship as to make it unreasonable to expect the pursuer to cohabit with the defender'.

1 There is no express reference to passive behaviour in s 1(2)(b) of the Matrimonial Causes Act 1973.

2 If this thesis be accepted doubt must be cast on such pre-1976 cases as *H v H* 1968 SLT 40, where a wife's frigidity which was caused by neurotic depression was held not to constitute cruelty. However, the frigidity would now amount to passive behaviour and the fact that it was a symptom of an illness is irrelevant.

3 In so doing the 1976 Act follows the policy of s 5 of the Divorce (Scotland) Act 1964; *Williams v Williams* [1963] 2 All ER 994, [1964] AC 698, HL.

4 See, for example, *Livingstone-Stallard v Livingstone-Stallard* [1974] 3 All ER 766, [1974] Fam 47; *O'Neill v O'Neill* [1975] 3 All ER 289, [1975] 1 WLR 1118, CA. In *Meikle v Meikle* 1987 GWD 26–1005, a wife who came from a town background and went to live on her husband's hill farm obtained a divorce on the grounds that her husband spent too much time at work and she was disillusioned with life in the country.

5 Assuming, of course, that snoring constitutes behaviour.

6 The assault need not be directed at the pursuer: *AB v CB* 1959 SC 27.

7 1985 SLT 146 at 148: wife's false accusation that husband was engaging in an incestuous association. See also *MacLeod v MacLeod* 1990 GWD 14–767: husband's unfounded suspicions of wife's adultery. A husband's boast that he was having an affair has been held to constitute unreasonable behaviour even although the wife could not establish adultery: *Stewart v Stewart* 1987 SLT (Sh Ct) 48.

In relation to sexual behaviour, this would include, for example, excessive demands for sexual intercourse, wilful and unjustified refusal of sexual intercourse,[1] non-adulterous sexual relations with a third party and homosexual activities.[2] Excessive drunkenness[3] or other abuse of drugs would also suffice.

The mere fact that the pursuer has continued to cohabit with the defender after the alleged behaviour took place does not per se prevent the pursuer relying upon it for the purpose of s 1(2)(b). A woman who has been the victim of violence may continue to live with her husband after the assaults through fear or because she has simply nowhere else to go.[4] But where the alleged behaviour is objectively trivial, the longer the pursuer remains with the defender, the more difficult it will be to establish that the pursuer cannot reasonably be expected to cohabit with the defender as a result of that conduct.[5] The pursuer's conduct after separation, for example forming a new relationship, may be used as evidence to establish that the pursuer cannot reasonably be expected to live with the defender.[6]

The standard of proof is on the balance of probabilities.[7] Corroboration is not required. By s 3(1) of the 1976 Act, if a decree of separation[8] has previously been granted in respect of the same or substantially the same facts, an extract of the decree may be regarded as sufficient proof of these facts in an action for divorce on the ground, inter alia, of behaviour, but the court must still receive further evidence from the pursuer of what has occurred between the parties since the date of the decree.[9] Finally, where the behaviour relied upon led to a criminal conviction of the defender by a United Kingdom court, s 10 of the Law Reform (Miscellaneous Provisions) (Scotland) Act 1968 is applicable.[10]

There are no specific defences in relation to s 1(2)(b) but collusion will constitute an absolute bar.[11]

---

1 In *Mason v Mason, Times* 5 December 1980, CA, a wife's limitation of sexual intercourse to once a week was held in England not to be such that her husband could no longer reasonably be expected to cohabit.
2 *White v White* 1966 SC 187.
3 *Campbell v Campbell* 1973 SLT (Notes) 82.
4 See, for example, *Britton v Britton* 1973 SLT (Notes) 12; *Bradley v Bradley* [1973] 3 All ER 750, [1973] 1 WLR 1291, CA.
5 Section 1(6).
6 *Findlay v Findlay* 1988 GWD 24–1034.
7 Section 1(6).
8 See *infra* p 117.
9 This will usually simply be that the parties have neither lived together or had sexual relations since the date of the decree of separation.
10 Discussed in the context of adultery, *supra* p 103.
11 Collusion is discussed in the context of adultery, *supra* p 106.

Desertion

By s 1(2)(c) irretrievable breakdown of marriage is established if—

> 'the defender has wilfully and without reasonable cause deserted the pursuer; and during a continuous period of two years immediately succeeding the defender's desertion—
>   (i) there has been no cohabitation between the parties, and
>   (ii) the pursuer has not refused a genuine and reasonable offer by the defender to adhere'.

This ground falls into two parts. First, the defender must have deserted the pursuer. Second, this initial desertion must be followed by two years non-cohabitation during which the pursuer has not refused a genuine and reasonable offer to adhere.

The initial desertion

First, the defender must have *wilfully* deserted the pursuer ie the defender must intend to leave the pursuer and end their married life. As it must be wilful, there is no desertion if the defender is mentally ill and incapable of forming the necessary intention. Nor is there desertion if the defender is separated from the pursuer against his will, for example, as a result of imprisonment.

Second, in order to amount to desertion, the pursuer must be willing to adhere at the date on which the defender leaves. Thus if a couple agree to separate, this is not desertion, as neither was willing to adhere when they parted.[1] It must be stressed that the pursuer's willingness to adhere is only required to establish initial desertion: there is no need for the pursuer to continue to be willing to adhere beyond the initial period of the separation.

Third, there must be withdrawal of cohabitation. The fact that sexual relations have ceased between the couples is not sufficient.[2] But it is possible that if the couple live in separate households, ie no longer cohabit, the factual element of desertion will be satisfied even although they are living under the same roof.[3]

---

1 If, for example, the wife later wished to resume cohabitation, then, if, when she calls him to adhere, he unreasonably refuses, desertion by the husband begins at that date. It is thus necessary for the wife to communicate to her husband her change of mind. But where, for example, a couple are temporarily living apart, both being willing to adhere, then if the wife decides that she is never going to return to her husband, desertion begins at that date and there is no need for the wife to communicate this fact to her husband.
2 *Lennie v Lennie* 1950 SC (HL) 1.
3 Ibid at 5 and 16.

Fourth, the defender's desertion must be without reasonable cause. This could include, for example, the pursuer's adultery or behaviour which would justify a divorce under s 1(2)(b).[1] The reasonable cause must be known[2] to the defender at the date when he or she left.

Two years' non-cohabitation

Once the initial period of desertion is established, the pursuer is entitled to a divorce if 'during a continuous period of two years immediately succeeding the defender's desertion' the parties have not cohabited and the pursuer has not refused a genuine and reasonable offer by the defender to adhere.

The parties will be held to cohabit only when 'they are in fact living together as man and wife'.[3] The fact that the couple have had sexual intercourse during the two year period does not constitute cohabitation.[4] The parties must resume life together as husband and wife.[5]

Resumption of cohabitation before two years have elapsed from the date of the initial desertion may not operate to prevent the pursuer obtaining a divorce. By s 2(4) of the 1976 Act it is provided that in considering whether the two year period has been continuous, no account shall be taken of any period or periods not exceeding six months in all: but no such period or periods count as part of the period of non-cohabitation. In other words, period(s) of cohabitation which amount to less than six months do not break the continuity of the period of non-cohabitation but they do not count towards it.

EXAMPLE 1

D deserts P on 1 January 1988. The couple resume cohabitation on 1 January 1989. They separate on 1 April 1989. The action for

---

1 Behaviour before the marriage could perhaps constitute just cause for separation, although it would not constitute grounds for divorce or separation under s 1(2)(b): *Hastings v Hastings* 1941 SLT 323. See *supra* p 107.
2 Cf *Wilkinson v Wilkinson* 1943 SC (HL) 61 (pursuer's adultery unknown to defender is reasonable cause). But at that time the pursuer had to be willing to adhere throughout the desertion period and could not call upon the defender to adhere if the pursuer had been guilty of a matrimonial offence, albeit unknown to the defender at the date when he left. The *Wilkinson* principle was reversed in relation to adultery by s 5(1) of the Divorce (Scotland) Act 1964. It is thought that it does not apply to other grounds of reasonable cause in the context of the 1976 Act: for full discussion, see *Clive* pp 460–463.
3 Section 13(2).
4 *Edmond v Edmond* 1971 SLT (Notes) 8.
5 The absence of sexual intercourse probably does not prevent a couple from being regarded as living together as man and wife.

divorce can be brought after 1 April 1990. The three months period of cohabitation between 1 January 1989 and 1 April 1989 does not break the continuity of the two years non-cohabitation but does not count towards it.

EXAMPLE 2

D deserts P on 1 January 1988. The couple resume cohabitation on 1 November 1989. They separate on 30 June 1990. A divorce action cannot be brought on the ground of D's desertion on 1 January 1988. The period of cohabitation between 1 November 1989 and 30 June 1990 is greater than six months. The continuity of the non-cohabitation after the desertion has been broken and it is therefore impossible to establish that they have not cohabited for a *continuous* period of two years immediately succeeding the initial desertion on 1 January 1988. If P was deserted by D on 30 June 1990, a divorce action could be brought after 30 June 1992.

During the two year period of non-cohabitation after the initial desertion, the couple's intentions are irrelevant. Thus, provided that the pursuer was willing to adhere when the defender left, it does not matter that a week later the pursuer was unwilling to have the defender back. The only factor which would prevent a divorce in these circumstances would be if the pursuer during the two years non-cohabitation refused a genuine and reasonable offer by the defender to return.[1] If such an offer was made *after* the two year period had expired, the pursuer can refuse to accept it and still sue for divorce on the ground of desertion.

The standard of proof is on the balance of probabilities.[2] Corroboration is not required. The pursuer may be able to use s 3 of the 1976 Act if a decree of separation has previously been granted on the ground of desertion.[3]

It should be emphasised that provided there is initial desertion and the couple have not cohabited for the immediately succeeding two years, the pursuer may seek a divorce at any time after the two year period has elapsed. This illustrates how desertion is still conceived as a matrimonial offence. However, there is a defence if after the expiry of the two year period of non-cohabitation the pursuer resumes cohabitation and cohabits with the defender at any time after the end of three

1 Whether the offer is genuine and reasonable is a question of fact in the particular case.
2 Section 1(6).
3 Discussed in relation to behaviour, *supra* p 109.

months from the date when cohabitation was first resumed.[1] This defence operates in a similar way to condonation of adultery.[2] Collusion will operate as an absolute bar.[3]

Non-cohabitation for two years

By s 1(2)(d) irretrievable breakdown of marriage is established if—

'there has been no cohabitation between the parties at any time during a continuous period of two years after the date of the marriage and immediately preceding the bringing of the action and the defender consents to the granting of the decree'.

First, there must be no cohabitation between the parties for the requisite period. Section 13(2) provides that 'the parties to a marriage shall be held to cohabit with one another only when they are in fact living together as husband and wife'. Interpreted literally, a couple who are not *in fact* living together as husband and wife are not cohabiting for the purpose of s 1(2)(d). The reason why they are not in fact living together is irrelevant. Thus, for example, if a couple are not living together because the husband is in prison or in hospital or working abroad, they are not cohabiting within the meaning of the 1976 Act.

It is hoped that Scottish courts will not follow the interpretation of the parallel English provisions[4] laid down by the Court of Appeal in *Santos v Santos*.[5] There it was held that a couple are not to be treated as living apart for the purpose of divorce merely because they are physically separated: in addition, it is necessary that one of them had formed the intention that the marriage had broken down and no longer wished to continue with their married life. This requirement of a mental element is an unwarranted gloss on the wording of the English legislation. *A fortiori* it should not be followed in Scotland. There is no ambiguity in the wording of s 13(2) and, construed literally, there is no need for a mental element: physical separation will suffice.

Conversely, a couple may not be cohabiting within the meaning of s 13(2) even although they live in close physical proximity. They will only be treated as cohabiting if they are in fact living together *as husband and wife*. The absence of sexual relations will be an important factor in determining whether they are living in that capacity – but absence of sexual relations per se will probably not be enough. But if

1 Section 2(3).
2 Discussed *supra* p 105.
3 Discussed in the context of adultery, *supra* p 106.
4 Section 1(6) of the Matrimonial Causes Act 1973.
5 [1972] 2 All ER 246, [1972] Fam 247, CA.

sexual relations have ceased, or the spouses provide no services for each other or if they have no joint social life, then it is possible to argue that they are not living together as husband and wife even although they occupy the same house. In these circumstances, it is hoped that Scottish courts would take the approach of the Court of Appeal in *Fuller v Fuller*.[1] After their marriage had deteriorated H left the matrimonial home. W and their former lodger became lovers. When H fell ill W took pity on H and allowed him to return. While W looked after his domestic needs, she and her lover continued to live together in the matrimonial home. The Court held that the spouses had been living apart: for while they lived in the same house – indeed in the same household – they were not living together *in the capacity* of husband and wife. If similar circumstances arose in Scotland, it is submitted that the spouses should be treated as not cohabiting as they were not in fact living together as husband and wife, but rather as patient and nurse.

The non-cohabitation must be for a continuous period of at least two years after the date of the marriage and immediately preceding the bringing of the action. As in the case of desertion, by s 2(4) resumption of cohabitation for a period or periods not exceeding six months in all does not break the continuity of the period of non-cohabitation but does not count towards it.[2]

Finally, the defender must positively consent to the granting of the decree. Consent can be withdrawn at any time before decree. Moreover in *Boyle v Boyle*[3] Lord Maxwell held[4] that 'it is perfectly open to a defender to withhold consent for any reason he thinks fit or for no reason'. Thus the defender's consent can be used as a bargaining counter between the parties in reaching agreement over ancillary matters like financial provision on divorce.

The standard of proof is on the balance of probabilities.[5] Corroboration is not required, and the divorce can proceed as a simplified divorce application.[6] The pursuer may be able to rely on s 3 of the 1976 Act if a decree of separation has previously been granted on the ground of non-cohabitation.[7]

1 [1973] 2 All ER 650, [1973] 1 WLR 730, CA.
2 Section 2(4) is discussed in the context of desertion *supra* pp 111, 112.
3 1977 SLT (Notes) 69.
4 Ibid at 69.
5 Section 1(6).
6 Section 2 of the Divorce Jurisdiction, Court Fees and Legal Aid (Scotland) Act 1983; Evidence in Undefended Divorce Actions (Scotland) Act Order 1983 (SI 1983/949). Simplified divorce procedure is discussed *infra* p 118.
7 Discussed in relation to behaviour, *supra* p 109.

Non-cohabitation for five years

By s 1(2)(e) irretrievable breakdown of marriage is established if 'there has been no cohabitation between the parties at any time during a continuous period of five years after the date of the marriage and immediately preceding the bringing of the action'.

In relation to the meaning of non-cohabitation and continuity of a non-cohabitation, including the application of s 2(4), this ground raises precisely the same legal issues as those in s 1(2)(d).[1] The difference is, of course, that the period of non-cohabitation is five years and the consent of the defender is not necessary. Accordingly, a defender who has not been guilty of a matrimonial offence can be divorced against his or her will. The rationale of this ground, however, is that since the parties have not cohabited for five years, the marriage has in fact broken down irretrievably and consequently should be legally brought to an end.

The defender is able to apply for financial provision on divorce.[2] But, in addition, in order to avoid excessive financial hardship to a defender, s 1(5) provides that a court is not bound to grant decree by reason of s 1(2)(e), 'if in the opinion of the court *the grant of decree* would result in grave financial hardship to the defender'. Several points should be noticed:

1. The defence is only available where the grave financial hardship arises from the grant of the divorce, not the breakdown of the marriage. Most marriage breakdowns will result in some financial hardship for the spouse but s 1(5) only applies if the *divorce* will cause grave financial hardship to the defender. This immediately limits the scope of the defence.

2. The divorce must result in *grave* financial hardship. Obviously, s 1(5) will not be available to wealthy spouses who will be able to afford to make generous financial provision on divorce. But very poor couples will also be excluded. For example, in *Boyd v Boyd*[3] H left W in 1959 after twenty years of marriage. During the next twenty years H paid W aliment of only £4.50 a week. On divorce, H could only offer W a periodical allowance of £5.00 a week. As 1(5) defence failed on the ground that as a result of the breakdown of the marriage, W had suffered financial hardship but this would not be increased if she were divorced: indeed she would be 50p a week better off.

It is to be hoped that for the purpose of s 1(5), the Scottish courts

1 Discussed *supra* pp 113, 114.
2 Discussed *infra* Ch 7.
3 1978 SLT (Notes) 55.

will follow the decision of the Court of Appeal in *Reiterbund v Reiterbund*[1] where it was held that in considering whether or not a spouse would suffer grave financial hardship on divorce, the defender's entitlement to income support if the divorce was granted, should be taken into account. Where the spouses are poor, the defender may be no worse off when aliment ceases on divorce because he or she may be entitled to as much or more in the form of income support and other benefits.

In practice, therefore, s 1(5) will only be available to middle class, middle-aged women, particularly, where their husbands are in pensionable employment and the pension is payable to their *widow* on death. The Act recognises this by specifically providing that hardship includes 'the loss of the chance of acquiring any benefit'. In *Nolan v Nolan*[2] the s 1(5) defence succeeded because the defender would lose the chance of obtaining the benefit of two-fifths of the husband's index-linked pension payable to his widow if the husband predeceased her. Lord Cowie was not satisfied that the husband's offer to take out an insurance policy for his wife's benefit compensated sufficiently for the loss of her contingent right to his index-linked pension.[3] If, however, the husband had had sufficient resources to compensate the defender adequately, the defence would not have succeeded.

3. Unlike the parallel provision in England,[4] s 1(5) only operates if the divorce will result in grave *financial* hardship. Accordingly, there is no defence if other hardship will arise, for example, if divorce is contrary to the defender's religious beliefs or the defender will be ostracised by his or her community, if the divorce is granted.[5]

It is submitted that since the marriage has irretrievably broken down as a result of at least five years of non-cohabitation, the s 1(5) defence should be construed narrowly and only be applicable in exceptional cases of grave financial hardship arising from the divorce.[6]

---

1 [1975] 1 All ER 280, [1975] Fam 99, CA.

2 1979 SLT 293.

3 Since the portion of any rights in an occupational pension scheme acquired during the marriage must be shared fairly between the spouses on divorce, the scope of s 1(5) in this respect is even further reduced: s 10(5) of the Family Law (Scotland) Act 1985, discussed *infra* Ch 7.

4 Section 5 of the Matrimonial Causes Act 1973.

5 This aspect of the s 5 defence has rarely, if ever, succeeded in England: see, for example, *Rukat v Rukat* [1975] 1 All ER 343, [1975] Fam 63, CA.

6 Indeed the Scottish Law Commission has recommended that the s 1(5) defence be abolished: *Family Law: Pre-consolidation Reforms* SLC Discussion Paper No 85, paras 8.9–8.11.

The same rules as to standard of proof and collusion apply as in s 1(2)(d).[1] The divorce can proceed as a simplified divorce action.[2]

JUDICIAL SEPARATION

The grounds for judicial separation are exactly the same as the grounds for divorce and the same defences apply.[3] When a decree of separation is granted, the parties' obligation to adhere comes to an end. The marriage still subsists, however, and the spouses remain under their obligation to aliment each other[4] and their obligations of fidelity and tolerable behaviour continue. Thus, for example, a divorce can be sought on the ground of adultery committed after the decree of separation. If a decree of separation is obtained the same facts can be used as a ground for a subsequent divorce.[5] The Scottish Law Commission has recommended that judicial separation should be abolished.[6]

PROCEDURAL MATTERS

Jurisdiction

The Court of Session has jurisdiction to entertain an action of divorce if either of the parties to the marriage a) is domiciled in Scotland on the date when the action is begun or b) was habitually resident in Scotland throughout the period of one year ending with that date.[7] A sheriff court has jurisdiction if a) or b) is satisfied and either party to the marriage—

(i) was resident in the sheriffdom for a period of 40 days ending with that date, or
(ii) was resident in the sheriffdom for a period of not less than 40 days ending not more than 40 days before the said date, and has no known residence in Scotland at that date.[8]

---

1 Discussed *supra* p 113.
2 Simplified divorce procedure is discussed *infra* p 118.
3 Section 4.
4 Discussed *supra* pp 47 ff.
5 Section 3.
6 *Family Law: Pre-consolidation Reforms* SLC Discussion Paper No 85, paras 8.9–8.11.
7 Section 7 of the Domicile and Matrimonial Proceedings Act 1973.
8 Section 8(2) of the Domicile and Matrimonial Proceedings Act 1973 as amended by the Divorce Jurisdiction, Court Fees and Legal Aid (Scotland) Act 1983, Sch 1, para 18. The parties are not free to agree that a sheriff has jurisdiction where neither is resident in the sheriffdom, however convenient the forum: *Singh v Singh* 1988 SCLR 541.

There is no minimum period which must elapse before an action of divorce can be brought.

Proof

As a general principle, a divorce cannot be granted unless the ground of action has been proved, whether or not the action has been defended.[1] But where an action is undefended, proof is, unless the court otherwise directs, by way of affidavits instead of parole evidence. A simplified procedure – in effect a do-it-yourself divorce – is possible in relation to divorces based on s 1(2)(d) and (e). However its scope is severely restricted. An application can proceed if, and only if—

  (i) in relation to a divorce based on s 1(2)(d) the other spouse consents;

 (ii) there are no proceedings pending in any court which could have the effect of bringing the marriage to an end;

(iii) there are no children of the marriage under the age of sixteen;

(iv) neither party is seeking financial provision on divorce; and

 (v) neither party is suffering from a mental disorder.

The simplified procedure is an exception to the rule, that in divorce actions, the evidence from a source other than one or both of the spouses is required.

Conclusion

This Chapter has primarily been an attempt to outline the substantive Scots law of divorce. In theory, the right to a divorce is restrictive but, in practice, little difficulty is experienced in obtaining the necessary grounds. The vast majority of divorces are undefended[2] and there have been few reported decisions on the legal difficulties which the grounds in the 1976 Act raise. In short, it would appear that in relation to establishing a ground of divorce, as opposed to ancillary matters such as financial provision and the custody of children, the role of the court is largely administrative. But there must still be cases where a marriage has in fact irretrievably broken down, yet divorce is not possible because a s 1(2) ground cannot be established.

It is submitted that further reform of the Scots law of divorce is desirable. We should accept that in late twentieth century society, there is and will continue to be a high rate of matrimonial breakdown.[3] The primary concerns of a modern divorce law should be to attempt to

---

1 There is no need for corroboration but there must be evidence emanating from a source other than a party to the marriage: Civil Evidence (Scotland) Act 1988, ss 1(1), 8(1), (3).

2 Approx 90%.

3 At present, approximately one in four marriages end in divorce.

protect the children of the marriage as much as possible and to provide a fair system for the re-allocation of the family's income and capital. Accordingly there is force in the view that if the spouses are agreed on custody and financial provision, they should be able to divorce by consent provided the court approves of the settlement. If the couple are not agreed, then the court, on an application by one of the spouses, should allow the couple a period of say six months in which, with the assistance of their legal advisers, a settlement could be reached. If this is not achieved during that period, the court on the application of one of the parties should then make orders as to custody and financial provision and grant decree, without the necessity of any grounds for divorce.[1]

In its discussion paper, *The Ground for Divorce*,[2] the Scottish Law Commission put forward a radical proposal that divorce should be obtained by the lapse of a period after notice had been given, on the lines suggested in the preceding paragraph. However, in its final Report[3] this proposal was abandoned. Instead the Commission recommended that desertion be abolished as a ground of divorce and the periods of non-cohabitation for the purposes of s 1(2)(d) and (e) be reduced to one year and two years respectively.[4] It remains to be seen whether these reforms will be enacted.[5] However, it is hoped that the momentum for more radical change in the system of divorce has not been dissipated.

1 On steps towards a more rational system of divorce, see for example, Eekelaar *Family Law and Social Policy* (2nd edn, 1984) Ch 3.
2 SLC Discussion Paper No 76.
3 *Report on Reform of the Ground for Divorce* SLC No 116.
4 Paras 1.1–1.2 respectively.
5 These reforms were dropped from the Law Reform (Miscellaneous Provisions) (Scotland) Bill 1990 for political reasons.

7 Financial provision on divorce

INTRODUCTION

A major function of contemporary family law is to provide a system of rules whereby a couple's capital and income can be redistributed in a just way when their marriage ends in divorce. Before the enactment of the Family Law (Scotland) Act 1985, Scots law left this important matter largely to the discretion of the judges. Section 5(2) of the Divorce (Scotland) Act 1976 baldly stated that on an application for financial provision the court—

> 'shall make . . . such order, if any, as it thinks fit, having regard to the respective means of the parties to the marriage and to all the circumstances of the case, including any settlement or other arrangements made for financial provision for any child of the marriage'.

The 1976 Act provided no criteria on how the courts should exercise their discretion. As Clive observed, s 5 'provides absolutely no guidance as to the purpose of financial provision on divorce . . . Everything is left to the sense of "fitness" of a single judge. This is not good law. It is hardly law at all'.[1]

Yet certain principles were discernible amid the morass of decided cases. First, where the applicant was responsible for the breakdown of the marriage, any matrimonial misconduct was taken into account and could substantially reduce the financial provision which would otherwise have been awarded.[2] This principle was, of course, inconsistent with a law of divorce which was theoretically based on the non-fault ground of irretrievable breakdown of marriage. Second, the courts were anxious to reward through a generous capital payment, a spouse who had made a positive contribution to the acquisition of the couple's economic assets during the marriage.[3] Third, where a wife had not been responsible for the breakdown of the marriage, she could expect to receive a periodical allowance for an indefinite period after the

---

1 *Clive* p 511.
2 *Lambert v Lambert* 1982 SLT 144.
3 *Russell v Russell* 1977 SLT (Notes) 13; *Chalkley v Chalkley* 1984 SLT 281.

divorce and her earning potential – as opposed to any wages she actually earned – was ignored.[1] Finally, in cases of a short marriage, there was a tendency simply to divide the capital assets unless this was impossible because the assets were not in an easily realisable form or consisted of a matrimonial home which was still required for the children of the marriage.[2]

Moreover, a court's ability to achieve a just settlement was inhibited because it could only make awards of periodical allowances and capital sums. In particular, the court had limited power on divorce directly to regulate the occupancy and title of the matrimonial home. Resort had to be made to the artificial device of ordering a spouse to make a capital payment which the applicant could then use to buy out the payer's share of the property.[3] However, this was not always a practical solution. The payer might have been unable to raise the capital sum or the property, for example, a farm, might have been required for business purposes and its sale might therefore jeopardise the payer's ability to provide periodical allowances for the applicant and aliment for the children of the family.[4]

The law on financial provision was therefore unsatisfactory. The Scottish Law Commission considered the options for reform in a very full and detailed report[5] which led to the system of financial provision on divorce in the Family Law (Scotland) Act 1985.[6] Before considering this system in detail, several important issues must be discussed.

For many couples who divorce, there is little property or income to be redistributed.[7] In 1980, a capital sum was awarded in only six per cent of divorces granted and a periodical allowance was awarded to an ex-wife in only twenty-two per cent of divorces granted: the average

1 *Fergusson v Fergusson* 1977 SLT (Notes) 40: this was particularly so where there was a long marriage.
2 For full discussion, see Thomson 1985 SLT (News) 29.
3 See, for example, *Cowie v Cowie* 1977 SLT (Notes) 47.
4 See, for example, *Clark v Clark* 1978 SLT (Notes) 45; *Gray v Gray* 1979 SLT (Notes) 94.
5 *Report on Aliment and Financial Provision* (SLC No 67).
6 References in this chapter are to the 1985 Act unless otherwise stated. For a useful commentary see Nichols *The Family Law (Scotland) Act 1985* and Macdonald *A Guide to the Family Law (Scotland) Act 1985* (CCH). The 1985 Act came into force on 1 September 1986. On the effect of the Act on the practice of solicitors, see *The Impact of the Family Law (Scotland) Act 1985 on Solicitors' Divorce Practice* Scottish Office Central Research Unit Papers (November 1990).
7 See Doig *The Nature and Scale of Aliment and Financial Provision on Divorce* (Scottish Office, Central Research Unit, 1982); Manners and Rauta *Family Property in Scotland* (OPCS Social Survey Division, 1981).

capital sum was £4,500 and the average periodical allowance to an ex-wife was £18 per week. As Clive has observed,[1]

> 'it seems only realistic to recognize that in a large proportion of cases the law of financial provision on divorce is irrelevant to the actual financial position of divorced people. Any hope of improving the general condition of one-parent families cannot to any material extent depend on improvements in the law of financial provision on divorce.'

Nevertheless, where couples do have considerable assets, they are surely entitled to a rational system of redistribution of their property and income when their marriage ends in divorce.

A major difficulty in determining the criteria for financial provision on divorce is that any system must endeavour to accommodate the different kinds of marriages which end in divorce. These would include short childless marriages where both spouses work, medium range marriages where there are dependent children or long marriages where the wife has given up paid employment and has no prospect of such in the future. The Scottish Law Commission concluded that given the variety of marriages, there was no one principle which, if followed, would produce a satisfactory financial settlement in every case. For example, in a short childless marriage it is simply not fair – even if it were practicable – that a spouse should, as a result of financial provision, be placed in the same financial position he or she would have enjoyed if the marriage had not broken down. On the other hand, if a wife has given up her career in order to care for the children of the marriage and has, in effect, been an unpaid housekeeper for many years, why should she lose the expectation that her husband would maintain her in her old age, merely because the marriage has ended in divorce? Again, even after a short marriage, the financial needs of a wife who is unable to earn because she is caring for dependent children may not be met merely by the equal division of the spouses' capital assets.

In these circumstances the Scottish Law Commission took the view that it was necessary to provide a set of principles or objectives which were to be achieved by a system of financial provision on divorce but which, at the same time, would allow the courts to retain a considerable degree of discretion so that orders could be made which took account of the particular circumstances of the marriage in question.

---

1 *The financial consequences of divorce: reform from the Scottish perspective*, in *State, Law and the Family* (1984, ed Freeman) p 197.

Finally, it must be stressed at the outset that the provisions of the 1985 Act are only concerned with financial provision for *spouses*. As we shall see,[1] in Scots law children have an independent right to aliment from their parents or those who have accepted them as children of their family.[2] This right to aliment prima facie continues until the child reaches the age of eighteen.[3] A child's claim for aliment can be made, inter alia in proceedings for divorce.[4] Aliment for the children of the family will therefore be determined *before* the court considers financial provision for the spouses. In other words, it is only *after* aliment has been awarded for the children that the question of financial provision for the spouses will arise. In this way, Scots law gives primacy to the financial needs of the children of a family when a marriage ends in divorce. But aliment will take the form of a periodical allowance only: children are not entitled to substantial capital simply because their parents' marriage has ended in divorce.

THE NATURE OF THE ORDERS

By s 8(1) of the Family Law (Scotland) Act 1985, in a divorce action,[5] the court[6] has the power to make one or more of the following orders by way of financial provision for the applicant.

(i) *An order for the payment of a capital sum or the transfer of property*

The court has the power to make orders for the payment of a capital sum and/or a transfer of property.[7] Such an order can be made either at the date of divorce or within a period specified by the court.[8] Moreover, the court can stipulate that the order is to come into effect at a specified future date.[9] So where, for example, a couple's only substantial asset is the matrimonial home if this would have to be sold to raise

---

1 See *infra* pp 170 ff.
2 Section 1(1)(c) and (d).
3 Section 1(5)(a).
4 Section 2(2)(a).
5 The provisions on financial provision also apply in an action of declarator of nullity: s 17.
6 Ie the Court of Session or the sheriff court: s 27.
7 Section 8(1)(a) and (aa) as amended by para 34 of Sch 8 to, and Sch 9 to, the Law Reform (Miscellaneous Provisions) (Scotland) Act 1990.
8 Section 12(1)(a) and (b).
9 Section 12(2). See, for example, *Little v Little* 1990 SLT 230 approved by the Inner House 1990 SLT 785: in this case, the major assets – the defender's interest in a pension fund –was not in an easily realisable form, thus justifying the court to delay payment of one half the capital sum for six years.

the finance necessary for the payment of a capital sum, the court may delay the operation of such an order until a specified date, for instance, when the youngest child of the family has reached the age of eighteen and the property is no longer required as a matrimonial home.

The court can order that a capital sum be paid by instalments.[1] This is important where a couple's assets are not in an easily realisable form. If, for example, a wife was granted a capital sum of £20,000 but the husband's assets were tied up in a small business, the court could order that the £20,000 be paid in five annual instalments of £4,000. It will also be useful where a spouse has few capital assets but a high income. The advantages of an award of a capital sum by instalments over periodical allowances is that the total capital sum awarded cannot be varied[2] and it will not therefore be perceived by the payer as an indefinite financial burden.

By empowering the courts to make property transfer orders, s 8(1)(aa) removes one of the most glaring inadequacies of the previous law.[3] Apart from the power to order the transfer of the tenancy of a matrimonial home,[4] the courts were unable to make an out-and-out transfer of property from one spouse to another. Now a property transfer order can be made. So, for example, if the matrimonial home is owned by the husband, the court can order the transfer of the ownership of the property to the wife if the husband has no other means available to make the financial provision to which she is entitled in the circumstances of their marriage. It is now clear that orders for a property transfer and a capital sum payment can be made in the same action.[5]

(ii)   *Periodical allowances*

It is an axiomatic principle of the 1985 Act that before ordering a periodical allowance, the court must be satisfied that the payment of a capital sum or transfer of property order is inappropriate or insufficient in the circumstances. Moreover, a periodical allowance can only be made if it is justified by one of the principles in s 9(1)(c), (d) or

1 Section 12(3).
2 The date or method of payment of an order can be varied on a material change of circumstances: s 12(4).
3 *Supra* p 121.
4 Section 13 of the Matrimonial Homes (Family Protection) (Scotland) Act 1981: discussed *supra* p 92.
5 Section 8(1)(a) and (aa) as amended by para 34 of Sch 8, to, and Sch 9 to, the Law Reform (Miscellaneous Provisions) (Scotland) Act 1990. Before the 1990 Act, doubts had been raised whether an order for both a capital sum payment and a property transfer was competent: *Walker v Walker* 1990 SLT 229; cf *Little v Little* 1990 SLT 230. The Inner House indicated that such an order was competent: *Walker v Walker* 1990 GWD 34–1958.

(e).[1] Thus, the whole thrust of the Act is that the 'normal' orders for financial provision should take the form of capital sum payments or transfer of property orders rather than periodical allowances. This is to encourage 'a clean break' with the consequence that the spouses cease to be economically dependent on each other after the divorce. It is clear therefore why the court's power to order a capital sum to be paid by instalments is so important.

Accordingly, it should only be in exceptional circumstances that orders for periodical allowances should be made. The order can be for a definite or indefinite period or until the happening of a specified event.[2] If there has been a material change of circumstances, a periodical allowance can be varied or recalled and an order for a periodical allowance can be converted into the payment of a capital sum or property transfer of property.[3]

A periodical allowance ends with the death or remarriage of the payee,[4] but it continues if the payer dies, though his executor can apply to the court to recall the order.[5]

(iii) *Incidental orders*

In addition to making orders for capital sums, transfers of property and periodical allowances, the court has the power to make incidental orders. These are listed in s 14. These include an order for the sale of the couple's property,[6] the valuation of their property[7] and a declarator as to the ownership of any disputed property.[8] Most importantly, the court can make an order regulating the occupation of the matrimonial home and the use of its furniture and plenishings[9] including an order regulating liability as between the parties for outgoings in

---

1 Section 13(2). The principles are discussed in detail, *infra* pp 126 ff. See *Thirde v Thirde* 1987 SCLR 335. The pursuer's pleadings must refer to the principle(s) in s 9(1)(c)–(e) being relied upon and there must be averments and proof which make it clear why the payment of a capital sum or transfer order is inappropriate or insufficient. See also *Atkinson v Atkinson* 1988 SCLR 396; *Bell v Bell* 1988 SCLR 457.
2 Section 13(3).
3 Section 13(4). Any variation or recall can be backdated to the date of the application or, on cause shown, to an earlier date: s 13(4)(b). On variation, the periodical allowance can be made for a definite or indefinite period or until the happening of a specified event: s 13(5) impliedly incorporating *inter alia* s 13(2).
4 Section 13(7)(b).
5 Section 13(7)(a) and s 13(4). This was the position under the previous law: see *Sandison's Exrx v Sandison* 1984 SLT 111.
6 Section 14(2)(a).
7 Section 14(2)(b).
8 Section 14(2)(c).
9 Section 14(2)(d); see *Little v Little* 1989 SCLR 613, approved by the Inner House 1990 SLT 785.

respect of the home and its contents.[1] Under these provisions, the court can exclude one of the parties from the matrimonial home. While an order subsists as to the occupation of the matrimonial home and its contents, the occupant spouse retains[2] the powers of management conferred by the Matrimonial Homes (Family Protection) (Scotland) Act 1981.[3] However, the provisions of the 1981 Act protecting a spouse's occupancy rights against dealings with third parties[4] do not apply, but it has been suggested[5] that the court's power[6] to make any expedient ancillary order coupled with its common law powers, for example, interdict, may be sufficient to stop adverse dealings.

Other incidental orders include an order that security should be given for any financial provision[7] and an order as to the date from which any interest on any amount awarded should run.[8] Powers also exist for the payment or transfer of property to a trustee on behalf of a party to the marriage[9] and for setting aside or varying any term in an antenuptial or postnuptial marriage settlement.[10] Finally, the court can make any ancillary order which is expedient to give effect to the principles set out in s 9[11] or any order made under s 8(2).[12]

Armed with this plethora of powers, the court can make orders for financial provision which can be tailor made for the particular couple concerned.

THE PRINCIPLES

In an application for financial provision s 8(2) provides that the court shall make such order, if any, as is justified by the principles set out in s 9 and is reasonable having regard to the resources of the parties.[13] Resources include the couple's present and foreseeable resources. Thus, the court's discretion is limited in that the order must be justified by the s 9 principles, but the discretion is still wide as, even if justified by the principles, the order must still be reasonable in the light of the

---

1 Section 14(2)(e).
2 Section 14(5)(a).
3 Ie ss 2(1), (2), (5)(a) and (9) of the 1981 Act, discussed *supra* Ch 5.
4 Discussed *supra* p 86.
5 D I Nichols *The Family Law (Scotland) Act 1985*, 37/15.
6 Section 14(2)(k).
7 Section 14(2)(f).
8 Section 14(2)(j). See *McKeown v McKeown* 1988 SCLR 355.
9 Section 14(2)(g).
10 Section 14(2)(h).
11 Discussed *infra*.
12 Section 14(2)(k).
13 Section 8(2)(a) and (b).

couple's resources. This discretion can be used to reduce an award of financial provision which is otherwise due in the light of both the payer's and payee's resources at the date of the divorce:[1] it cannot be used to increase an award beyond that justified by the s 9 principles.[2] The s 9(1) principles will now be discussed.

Principle 9(1)(a): The net value of the matrimonial property should be shared fairly between the parties to the marriage

The first principle is s 9(1)(a). This provides that the net value of the matrimonial property should be shared fairly between the parties to the marriage. The net value of the matrimonial property is the value of the property at the relevant date, after deduction of any outstanding debts incurred by the parties either during the marriage or before the marriage, so far as they relate to matrimonial property.[3] So, for example, if the couple's only property is a house bought on a mortgage during the marriage, the net value of the property at the relevant date will be the value of the house after deducting the outstanding loan.

The relevant date is the date on which the parties cease to cohabit as husband and wife or the date of service of the summons in the action of divorce, if they continue living together.[4] Thus if a couple cease to cohabit in June 1985, that will be the relevant date for this purpose even although the action for divorce is not brought until several years later. This is, however, subject to s 10(7) which provides that no account is to be taken of any cessation of cohabitation where the parties resume cohabitation, ie when they in fact resume living together as man and wife.[5] But where the couple have ceased to cohabit for a continuous period of 90 days or more and then resume cohabitation for a period or periods of less than 90 days in all, the relevant date remains the date of the original cessation of cohabitation.[6]

The effect of this provision is clear. Where a couple have separated for a short period (less than 90 days) followed by an unsuccessful reconciliation, the initial period of separation is ignored and the rel-

---

1 *Buczynska v Buczynski:* 1989 SLT 558 (capital sum reduced because payee (wife) had resources which did not constitute matrimonial property).
2 *Latter v Latter* 1990 SLT 805.
3 Section 10(2)(a) and (b). 'Matrimonial property' is normally limited to property acquired during the marriage. Where a property transfer order is made, the payee may obtain an interest which is more valuable than the net value of the property at the relevant date, for example, because of the increase in value of the property between the relevant date and the date of divorce: *Little v Little* 1990 SLT 785.
4 Section 10(3).
5 Section 27(2).
6 Section 10(7).

evant date is the date when they finally ceased to cohabit. Conversely, where a couple have separated for a long period (90 days or more) followed by an unsuccessful reconciliation, the relevant date is the date of the initial separation, unless the period of conciliation was for 90 days or more when the relevant date becomes the date when they finally ceased to cohabit.

The following examples illustrate the complexities inherent in the section.

EXAMPLES

1. H and W cease to cohabit for more than 90 days and then resume cohabitation for more than 90 days. The relevant date is the date when they finally cease to cohabit.
2. H and W cease to cohabit for less than 90 days and then resume cohabitation for more than 90 days. The relevant date is the date when they finally cease to cohabit.
3. H and W cease to cohabit for less than 90 days and then resume cohabitation for less than 90 days. The relevant date is the date when they finally cease to cohabit.
4. H and W cease to cohabit for more than 90 days and then resume cohabitation for less than 90 days. The relevant date is the date of the original cessation of cohabitation.
5. H and W cease to cohabit for less than 90 days, then resume cohabitation for less than 90 days, cease to cohabit for less than 90 days and finally resume cohabitation for less than 90 days: even if the two periods of non-cohabitation together constitute 90 days or more, as they are not continuous, the relevant date is the date when the couple finally cease to cohabit.
6. H and W cease to cohabit for more than 90 days, then resume cohabitation for less than 90 days, cease to cohabit for more than 90 days and finally resume cohabitation for less than 90 days. If the periods of resumption of cohabitation are together less than 90 days the relevant date is the date of the original cessation of cohabitation. But if the periods of resumption of cohabitation are together more than 90 days, the relevant date becomes the date when the couple separated after the initial resumption of cohabitation. If, however, the second period of cohabitation lasts 90 days or more, the relevant date would then become the date when they finally ceased to cohabit.

Because a couple are deemed not to cohabit unless they are in fact living together as husband and wife,[1] the relevant date may occur before a couple finally separate where they were not in fact living together as husband and wife, albeit residing in the same house.[2] This is important as it will follow that the net value of their matrimonial property may be much less than the value of their property at the date they finally separated.

Matrimonial property is defined[3] as *all* the property belonging to the spouses or either of them at the relevant date which was acquired by the spouses(s)—

a) before the marriage for use by them as a family home or as furniture or plenishings for such a home, ie the matrimonial home and its contents;[4] or

b) during the marriage but before the relevant date.

However the following property is excluded:

a) property acquired before marriage, with the important exception of property acquired for use as the matrimonial home or its contents;

b) property acquired by a spouse *after* the relevant date; and

c) property acquired during the marriage from a third party by way of gift or succession.[5]

Most importantly, matrimonial property includes the portion of any rights or interests of either spouse under a life policy or occupational pension scheme which is referable to the period of marriage before the relevant date.[6]

In applying principle 9(1)(a) the first task is to identify the matrimonial property which should be shared fairly between the parties. In

---

1 Section 27(2).
2 *Buczynska v Buczynski:* 1989 SLT 558. For full discussion of the meaning of cohabitation see *supra* pp 113 ff. The statutory definition of cohabitation for the purpose of divorce is identical to that in s 27(2).
3 Section 10(4).
4 The house must have been acquired with the intention that it be used as a matrimonial home for the parties: *Maclellan v Maclellan* 1988 SCLR 399. While s 27(1) provides that matrimonial home has the same meaning in the 1985 Act as in the Matrimonial Homes (Family Protection) Act 1985, which includes property which has become a family home, this is irrelevant for this purpose as s 10(4) refers to property acquired as a *family*, not a matrimonial home. Cf *Buczynska v Buczynski:* 1989 SLT 558. For the definition of matrimonial home in the 1981 Act, see p 80 *supra*.
5 Section 10(4). On the difficulties which can arise on property acquired by gift, see *Latter v Latter* 1990 SLT 805.
6 Section 10(5). Actuarial evidence of the value of the interest should be obtained: on the difficulties, see *Muir v Muir* 1989 SCLR 445; *Little v Little* 1990 SLT 230. A redundancy payment paid after the relevant date has not been treated as analogous to an interest under a life policy or pension: *Tyrrell v Tyrrell* 1990 SLT 405.

Little v Little,[1] the Inner House held that there was no need for the court to calculate a single value of the total matrimonial property at the relevant date: moreover, the court could leave out certain items, for example, a couple's motor cars or personal possessions, if this would have no practical result on the claim for financial provision. In addition, it was held that the matrimonial home could be excluded if a property transfer order was desirable in the circumstances of the case.[2] It is submitted that the approach of the Inner House runs counter to the express language of s 10(4) which refers to *all* the couple's property at the relevant date and therefore a court should still proceed to calculate the total net value of their property at that date.

Consider the following example.

EXAMPLE

H bought a house for £5,000 shortly before he married W. H bought it intending that it should be used as their matrimonial home. H paid a downpayment of £500 and raised the rest of the price by a mortgage. Title to the house was taken in H's name. When H left W after 16 years of marriage, the house was worth £30,000 with an outstanding mortgage of £1,000.

During the marriage, H bought furniture, a car, and golf clubs, worth £8,000, £5,000 and £500 respectively at the time that H left W. During the marriage, W bought furs and jewellery worth £2,000 and £3,000 respectively at the time that H left W. She also inherited a diamond ring worth £5,000, at the time that H left W.

H had contributed to an occupational pension scheme which he joined four years before he married. The actuarial value of H's interest in the scheme when H left W was £60,000. He has shares which he bought before the marriage which were worth £30,000 when H left W. W's savings made from her earnings during the marriage were worth £5,000. After H left W, she won £2,500 on the football pools.

The relevant date is the date when the parties ceased to cohabit, ie when H left W.

---

1 1990 SLT 785. For full discussion, see J Thomson 1990 SLT (News) 313.
2 The court maintained that the court's discretion to depart from equal sharing in special circumstances under s 10(1) and (6) was wide enough to exclude certain items from being valued as matrimonial property. However, it is thought that the discretion only operates *after* all the couple's property at the relevant date has been valued: see *infra* pp 132 ff.

At that date, the net value of the matrimonial property consists of the following:

(i) the matrimonial home. While the property was acquired by H *before* marriage, it was acquired for use as a family home and therefore qualifies. Its net value at the relevant date was £30,000−£1,000 (outstanding mortgage)=£29,000.

(ii) H's furniture, car and golf clubs, ie property acquired by him during the marriage and before the relevant date=£8,000+£4,500+£500=£13,000.

(iii) W's furs and jewellery, ie property acquired by her during the marriage and before the relevant date but excluding the diamond ring which was acquired by way of succession from a third party=£2,000+£3,000=£5,000.

(iv) W's savings made during the marriage and before the relevant date=£5,000. But H's shares are excluded as he acquired them *before* marriage:[1] W's football pools winnings are excluded because she acquired them *after* the relevant date.

(v) the proportion of H's interest in the occupational pension scheme which is referable to the period of marriage before the relevant date. H has been in the scheme for twenty years, sixteen of which were during the marriage and before the relevant date. At the relevant date value of interest is £60,000. Therefore portion referable to period of marriage is

$$\frac{£60,000 \times 16}{20} = £48,000.$$

Thus the total value of the matrimonial property at the relevant date is £100,000.

By s 10(1) of the Act, fair sharing is prima facie equal sharing. Accordingly, in the example, H and W are prima facie entitled to £50,000. As W has already property valued at £10,000 *viz* £5,000 furs and jewellery and £5,000 savings, H must transfer to her either as a capital sum or an actual transfer of property, £40,000. In considering whether this should be done, the court must consider whether it is reasonable to do so, in the light of the couple's resources.[2] These will include the

---

1 It is not thought that any increase in the value of the shares during the marriage constitutes matrimonial property: cf the approach of Lord Marnoch in *Latter v Latter* 1990 SLT 805, criticised by Thomson 1990 SLG 51.
2 Section 8(2)(b).

non-matrimonial property belonging to the spouses *viz* H's shares worth £30,000 and W's diamond ring and football pools win which are worth £5,000 and £2,500 respectively, ie £7,500. In these circumstances, it is thought that it would prima facie be reasonable to order H to make a payment to W of £40,000 – to be paid in instalments if his capital is not easily realisable.

While fair sharing is prima facie equal sharing of the net value of all the matrimonial property, the court can depart from the principle if other proportions are justified by special circumstances. Some special circumstances are listed by way of illustration in s 10(6)(a)–(e) and will now be considered:

a) the terms of any agreement between the parties on the ownership or division of any of the matrimonial property. The most common example of such an agreement is a joint minute tendered to the court hearing the divorce but it could, of course, be an agreement made earlier in the marriage on how the matrimonial property should be divided on divorce.[1] While a gift made by one spouse to another is matrimonial property,[2] the couple might agree expressly or impliedly that gifts inter se should be excluded from the division of matrimonial property;

b) the source of the funds or assets used to acquire any of the matrimonial property where these funds or assets were not derived from the income or efforts of the parties during the marriage.

If, as in the example above, H used his own funds, ie £500 as the downpayment of the matrimonial home *before* the marriage, the court could depart from the principle that fair sharing is equal sharing, to compensate the husband. In the present writer's view, H should be given the proportion of the value of the house at the relevant date which corresponds to the proportion of the value of the property represented by his contribution at the date of its acquisition. Thus, H's £500 represented $^1/_{10}$th of the value of the property when it was bought: consequently, he should have $^1/_{10}$th of the net value of the property at the relevant date, ie $^1/_{10}$th of £29,000=£2,900. No account should be taken of the mortgage payments which were derived from H's income during the marriage. Thus the court could, if it wished, regard the value of the home for the purpose of fair sharing as £29,000−£2,900=£26,100.

While property acquired from a third party as a result of gift or inheritance is excluded from the definition of matrimonial prop-

---

1 If the agreement relates to heritable property, it must be in probative writing: *Mulhern v Mulhern* 1987 SLT (Sh Ct) 62.
2 Cf a gift of property made to a spouse by a third party.

erty, where a spouse uses funds acquired in this way to purchase property during the marriage, for example, a painting or a motor car, this will prima facie be matrimonial property which is subject to fair sharing. However, it is thought that in these circumstances the court should deviate from the principle that equality is fairness, to compensate the spouse concerned as the matrimonial property was not bought from funds deriving from the income or efforts of the parties during the marriage.[1] Similarly, the court would deviate if the matrimonial propety was damages awarded to a spouse during the marriage.[2]

c) any destruction, dissipation or alienation of property by either party.

This provision enables the court to deviate from the principle that fair sharing is equal sharing, when a spouse has destroyed, dissipated or alienated matrimonial property before or after the relevant date.

This provision is additional to the general protection in s 18 against transactions intended to defeat claims for, inter alia, financial provision on divorce.[3]

d) the nature of the matrimonial property, the use made of it (including use for business purposes or as a matrimonial home) and the extent to which it is reasonable to expect it to be realised or divided or used as security.

This is probably the most important of the special circumstances which may justify deviation from the principle that fair sharing is equal sharing. If, in the example above, H used the house for business purposes, it might be unreasonable to order H to sell the property in order to realise its value to make a capital payment to W. The court could, in those circumstances, allow H to retain the property and order him to pay whatever capital sum he could afford to W to compensate her so far as practicable for the loss of her prima facie entitlement to half the value of all the matrimonial property including the house. This capital sum need not be equivalent to half the net value of the matrimonial property, though in

1 Cf the approach taken by Lord Marnoch in *Latter v Latter* 1990 SLT 805 criticised by Thomson 1990 SLG 51. See also *Kerrigan v Kerrigan* 1988 SCLR 603.
2 *Petrie v Petrie* 1988 SCLR 390. The damages did not constitute matrimonial property in this case because the husband was injured before the marriage and the damages were not awarded until after the relevant date. While the matter is controversial, it is thought that damages will constitute matrimonial property if awarded during the marriage regardless of when the injuries were sustained. As an alternative to deviation, the court might exclude damages for pain and suffering and divide only the value of the damages relating to loss of earnings.
3 Section 18 is discussed *infra* p 146.

the circumstances of the example, it would still be substantial. H could be required to raise the capital by a second mortgage or the capital sum could be paid by instalments out of his income. Similarly, while a spouse's business assets acquired during the marriage constitute matrimonial property, the court may award less than half their net value as, clearly, they may not be easily realisable.[1]

On the other hand, if in the above example there were children of the family who required the house as a family home, the court could make an incidental order that the house should not be sold until the youngest child reached the age of eighteen or had finished a course in higher education. Alternatively, if W had custody of the children, the court could order that the house be transferred outright to W and her share of the rest of the matrimonial property proportionately reduced even if the reduction did not fully compensate H for the loss of half the value of all the matrimonial property.[2] However, if as in the circumstances of the example, the couple have substantial resources, so that there would be little difficulty in the custodial parent acquiring suitable alternative accommodation for the family, the court might well simply order the home to be sold and the proceeds divided equally between the spouses provided evidence was brought that it would not be contrary to the interests of the children to do so. If a spouse seeks the transfer of the matrimonial home, the court will more readily grant the order if the other spouse will thereby be relieved of liability for payment of mortgage instalments.[3]

Where the asset is an interest in a life policy or pension fund, the court may award less than half its value as it will often not be easily realisable.[4] If the matrimonial property includes damages, again there could be deviation on the grounds that they were intended to be used to support the spouse who was the victim of the injuries sustained.[5]

e) actual or prospective liability for any expenses of valuation or transfer of property in connection with the divorce.

---

1 *Morrison v Morrison* 1989 SCLR 574. Alternatively the capital sum could be ordered to be paid by instalments or payment delayed until a later date.
2 *Cooper v Cooper* 1989 SCLR 347 (wife obtained a property transfer of the matrimonial home even although it was the couple's major capital asset: however, the husband did not require accommodation as he was seriously ill).
3 Ibid.
4 *Muir v Muir* 1989 SCLR 445; *Carpenter v Carpenter* 1990 SCLR 206. Alternatively the capital sum could be ordered to be paid by instalments or payment delayed until a later date: *Little v Little* 1990 SLT 230 and 785.
5 *Petrie v Petrie* 1988 SCLR 427.

In applying the principle in s 9(1)(a), prima facie the conduct of either party to the marriage shall not be taken into account.[1] Thus if a marriage has irretrievably broken down as a result of a wife's adultery or a husband's behaviour, this is irrelevant and does not affect the prima facie principle that fair sharing of matrimonial property means equal sharing.[2] However, where a spouse's conduct has adversely affected the financial resources of the couple, for example by dissipation of assets or unreasonably refusing to find employment, the conduct will be relevant. Often, of course, such conduct may well have already been taken into account by virtue of s 10(6)(c), ie deviation from equality of sharing as a result of destruction, dissipation or alienation of property.[3] The reason why, as a general rule, matrimonial misconduct will not be relevant is that the principle in s 9(1)(a) is intended to recognise that a spouse deserves a fair share of the matrimonial property as a result of his or her contribution to the marriage and that responsibility for its breakdown should not undermine that entitlement unless the spouse's conduct has adversely affected the resources of the couple which are to be divided.

Principle 9(1)(b): Fair account should be taken of any economic advantage derived from either party from contributions by the other, and of any economic disadvantage suffered by either party in the interests of the other party or of the family

This principle is intended to compensate a spouse who has either (i) made a contribution to the economic advantage of the other, for example, by putting money into the other spouse's business or working in the business as an unpaid secretary, or (ii) has suffered an economic disadvantage in the interests of the other spouse or the family, for example, by a wife giving up a well paid job to bear and look after children. Where a spouse has suffered an economic disadvantage, there need not be a corresponding economic advantage to the other spouse: it is sufficient if the economic disadvantage was suffered in the interests of the other spouse or the family.[4] Economic advantage includes gains in capital, income and earning capacity and economic disadvantage is to be construed accordingly.[5] Contributions include indirect and non-financial contributions, for example, gardening or decorating the matrimonial home. A contribution made by a spouse in

---

1 Section 11(7).
2 Cf the position under the previous law, discussed *supra* p 120.
3 Discussed *supra*.
4 But cf approach of the sheriff in *Thomson v Thomson* 26 June 1990 (unreported) where it was held that before a disadvantage was relevant there had to be a corresponding advantage to the other spouse.
5 Section 9(2).

keeping the home and caring for the family is specifically recognised.[1] It is important to note that principle 9(1)(b) applies to economic advantages made, economic disadvantages suffered and contributions made by a party *before* the marriage took place.[2] Thus, for example, if W had worked before a couple married in order to support H when he was undergoing training for a profession, that contribution would be taken into account under s 9(1)(b) even though it was made before the parties married.

Claims under this principle are particularly difficult to quantify. By s 11(2), the court must consider whether the economic advantages or disadvantages sustained by either spouse have been balanced by the economic advantages or disadvantages sustained by the other: it is only when there is an economic imbalance in the applicant's favour that an award can be made. The onus rests on the applicant to show such an imbalance.[3] Moreover, the court will also have to determine whether or not any resulting imbalance has been or will be corrected by a sharing of the value of the matrimonial property under principle 9(1)(a) or otherwise.[4] As any awards under principle 9(1)(b) must take the form of capital sum payments or property transfer orders, it is thought that in practice principles 9(1)(a) and (b) will be considered together. Where items of matrimonial property have increased in value between the relevant date and the date of divorce, the courts have consistently refused to allow s 9(1)(b) to be used to give the applicant a share in the increase in value of the asset: this is because the increase is not a result of any economic contribution of the applicant during that period.[5]

Thus, for example, having determined that a wife should receive compensation under principle 9(1)(b) for her contributions to the family during the marriage, the court may decide that the most appropriate form it should take is an outright transfer of the matrimonial home to her, even though she would thereby receive more than half

1 Section 9(2).
2 Cf position in the previous law: see *Fraser v Fraser* 1976 SLT (Notes) 69. Contributions *after* the relevant date are also included.
3 *Petrie v Petrie* 1988 SCLR 190.
4 However, an award under s 9(1)(b) is intended to be *additional* to fair sharing of matrimonial property under s 9(1)(a): therefore it is thought that an imbalance will not have been corrected unless the payee had obtained more than half the net value of the matrimonial property under s 9(1)(a). This could arise, for example, if a wife had obtained the outright transfer of the matrimonial home under s 9(1)(a): see generally *Little v Little* 1990 SLT 230.
5 See *Carroll v Carroll* 1988 SCLR 104; *Phillip v Phillip* 1988 SCLR 427; *Muir v Muir* 1989 SCLR 445 (inflationary increase in the value of heritage); *Tyrrell v Tyrrell* 1990 SLT 406 (increase in the value of husband's interest in a pension scheme between the relevant date and the date of divorce).

the value of the matrimonial property to which she was prima facie entitled under principle 9(1)(a). As in principle 9(1)(a), in applying principle 9(1)(b) a spouse's matrimonial misconduct is irrelevant unless it has adversely affected the financial resources of the couple.

Principle 9(1)(b) was intended to recognise the economic contributions made by women who had followed the traditional child rearing and housekeeping role in marriage. The economic contribution so made and the economic disadvantages sustained in doing so, were to be compensated by an award under s 9(1)(b). Hitherto, this has not occurred in practice. There are two main reasons. First, as we have seen,[1] an applicant must show that there is an economic imbalance in her favour: unless an attempt is made realistically to assess the economic value of housekeeping and child care services, there is likely to be equilibrium given that she will usually have been alimented by her husband during the marriage.[2] Secondly, since only a capital sum or transfer of property orders are available under s 9(1)(b), the courts are reluctant to make an award if the husband has no capital assets. However, it is submitted that a capital sum payment is nevertheless appropriate in these circumstances – to be paid by instalments out of the husband's income. As we shall see,[3] the courts are acutely aware of the economic difficulties facing middle aged women who have followed this traditional role. Their solution has been to award periodical allowances under principle 9(1)(e). In the present writer's view, this is often a distortion of the function of the s 9(1)(e) principle. Instead, recourse should be made to principle 9(1)(b) which has been designed to compensate women in this situation. The under-utilisation of s 9(1)(b) is perhaps the most disappointing feature of the way in which the 1985 Act has been applied in practice.

Principle 9(1)(c): Any economic burden of caring, after divorce, for a child of the marriage under the age of sixteen years should be shared fairly between the parties

Where there are dependent children of a marriage[4] which ends in divorce, there cannot usually be a clean break as in most cases it will be in the children's best interests to retain contact with both parties.[5] As

---

1 *Supra* p 136.
2 In *McCormack v McCormack* 1987 GWD 9–287, Lord Davidson gave the wife a capital sum which was the equivalent of £125 a year for these services!
3 *Infra* pp 141 ff.
4 Children of a marriage include children who have been accepted by the parties as a child of the family: s 27.
5 On custody and access see *infra* Ch 11.

we have seen,[1] the court will determine aliment for children of the family, before considering claims by the parties to the marriage for financial provision on divorce. But in practice the parent who obtains custody may suffer economic disadvantages in looking after the children of the family: for example, he or she may not be able to take up full time employment or may have to hire the services of a nanny. In these circumstances, principle 9(1)(c) operates to ensure that the economic burden of child care is shared fairly between the parties. In practice this will usually mean that the custodial parent should receive additional financial provision in recognition of the economic burden of caring for the children of the family.

In determining this financial provision the court must consider a) any decree or arrangement for the aliment of the child of the marriage, b) any expenditure or loss of earning capacity caused by the need to care for the child, c) the need to provide suitable accommodation for the child, d) the age and health of the child, e) the education, financial or other circumstances of the child, f) the availability and cost of suitable child care facilities or services, g) the needs and resources of the parties, and h) all the other circumstances of the case.[2] The court may also take into account the fact that the spouse from whom financial provision is sought is supporting a person who is maintained as a dependant in his or her household, whether or not he or she owes an obligation of aliment to that dependant; for example, where a husband leaves his wife and is living with and supporting his mistress and her children.[3] If the court does so, this will reduce the resources available for financial provision under principle 9(1)(c). Moreover, a spouse's matrimonial misconduct is again irrelevant unless it has adversely affected the financial resources of the couple. This is because principle 9(1)(c) recognises that by contributing to the family by caring for the children, the custodial parent deserves financial provision.

Unlike orders under principles 9(1)(a) and (b), the court has the power when applying principle 9(1)(c) to make an order for a periodical allowance, provided it is satisfied that a capital sum or property transfer is inappropriate or insufficient to satisfy the requirements of s 8(2).[4] Thus where a couple have little or no capital assets so that it is not reasonable in the light of their resources to make a capital sum payment or a property transfer order, a periodical allowance may well be justified under principle 9(1)(c). If a periodical allowance is made,

---

1 *Supra* p 123.
2 Section 11(3).
3 Section 11(6).
4 Section 13(2).

it could – subject to recall or variation – last until the youngest child of the marriage reaches the age of sixteen.[1] If, however, the couple have extensive capital assets, financial provision under principle 9(1)(c) could take the form of the payment of a capital sum or property transfer order *in addition* to any financial provision under principles 9(1)(a) or (b). Alternatively, if the capital assets were not so extensive, principle 9(1)(c) could be used to justify, for example, the transfer of the matrimonial home to the spouse with custody of the children even although the custodial parent would thereby receive more than half the value of the matrimonial property to which he or she was prima facie entitled under principle 9(1)(a).[2]

Principle 9(1)(d):   A party who has been dependent to a substantial degree on the financial support of the other party should be awarded such financial provision as is reasonable to enable him to adjust over a period of not more than three years from the date of the decree of divorce to the loss of that support on divorce

The purpose of this principle is to provide financial support for a spouse, in practice, a wife, who has been financially dependent on her husband, to enable her to readjust to life as a single person after the divorce. The financial provision can take the form of a periodical allowance provided the court is satisfied that a capital sum or property transfer is inappropriate or insufficient to satisfy the requirements of s 8(2).[3] However, any payment of any periodical allowance is restricted to a maximum period of three years. It might be thought that a three year maximum period is too short to enable a spouse to readjust to life as a single person, but the view was taken that it was not the function of the law on financial provision on divorce to act as a panacea for the general problem of high unemployment. Moreover, it should also be noticed that any financial provision awarded under principle 9(1)(d) is *additional* to any capital sum or property transfer order awarded by virtue of principles 9(1)(a) or (b) and any financial provision awarded under principle 9(1)(c), which as we have seen,[4] can last until the youngest child reaches the age of sixteen.

1 A periodical allowance could be competent beyond the child's sixteenth birthday if the custodial parent had incurred a substantial economic burden until the child reached sixteen but the defender's means were not sufficient to pay the appropriate periodical allowance which would compensate the pursuer by the time the child reached sixteen: *Monkman v Monkman* 1988 SLT (Sh Ct) 37.
2 *Morrison v Morrison* 1989 SCLR 574.
3 Section 13(2).
4 *Supra.*

Before the s 9(1)(d) principle applies, the applicant must have been to a substantial degree financially dependent on the other spouse. Accordingly, where a wife has been able to find a job during the period between separation and divorce, the principle may not be triggered at all or any support awarded will not be for the maximum period of three years.[1] However, provided she has continued to receive aliment from her husband, a wife can expect some financial provision under this principle, even if she has obtained part-time employment.[2]

In making any order the court must have regard to a) the age, health and earning capacity of the applicant, b) the duration and extent of the dependence prior to divorce: thus for example, a wife, who has been a party to a short marriage and has given up her job only shortly before the divorce, is unlikely to receive a periodical allowance for the maximum three years as opposed to a wife who has been dependent for many years before the divorce, c) the applicant's intention to undertake a course of education or training, d) the needs and resources of the parties, and e) all the other circumstances of the case. The court may also take into account the fact that the spouse from whom financial provision is sought is supporting a person who is maintained as a dependent in his or her household whether or not he or she owes an obligation of aliment to that dependent.[3] Unlike s 9(1)(a), (b) and (c) principles, matrimonial misconduct will be taken into account not only when it has affected the couple's financial resources, but also if it would be manifestly inequitable to leave the conduct out of account.[4] This is because principle 9(1)(d) is based on equitable considerations and is not a recognition of what a spouse has earned or will earn as a result of his or her contributions to the marriage.

Given that financial provision under principle 9(1)(d) is *additional* to any financial provision awarded under principles 9(1)(a), (b) or (c), it is submitted that it will be useful in helping a spouse to readjust to being unmarried. It will be particularly valuable when the applicant intends to embark on a course of further education or retraining. But by restricting the payment of any periodical allowances under this principle to a maximum of three years, any order will not be perceived by the payer as an indefinite financial burden.

---

1 *Dever v Dever* 1988 SCLR 352 (6 month's support); *Muir v Muir* 1989 SCLR 445 (1 year's support).
2 *Tyrrell v Tyrrell* 1990 SLT 406.
3 Section 11(6).
4 Section 11(7)(b).

Principle 9(1)(e): A party who at the time of divorce seems likely to suffer serious financial hardship as a result of the divorce should be awarded such financial provision as is reasonable to relieve him of hardship over a reasonable period

Principle 9(1)(e) is intended to be a 'long stop' measure where adequate financial provision for a spouse cannot be achieved by applying the previous four principles. It deals with the situation where, *at the time of the divorce*, the applicant is old or is seriously ill[1] and, because he or she is unable to work, will suffer serious financial hardship. The principle does not apply if the spouse is overtaken by illness or other misfortune *after* the date of divorce: that is not the concern of a previous spouse.

Again financial provision can take the form of a periodical allowance provided the court is satisfied that a capital sum or property transfer is inappropriate or insufficient to satisfy the requirements of s 8(2).[2] In making any order, the court must have regard to a) the age, health and earning capacity of the applicant, b) the duration of the marriage, c) the standard of living of the parties during the marriage, d) the needs and resources of the parties, and e) all the other circumstances of the case.[3] The court may also take into account the fact that the spouse from whom financial provision is sought is supporting a person who is maintained as a dependent in his or her household, whether or not he or she owes an obligation of aliment to that dependent.[4] Moreover, matrimonial misconduct will be taken into account not only when it has affected the couple's financial resources but also when it would be manifestly inequitable to leave the conduct out of account.[5] This is because principle 9(1)(e) is clearly based on equitable considerations and accordingly, an applicant's responsibility for the breakup of the marriage should be a relevant consideration. Nevertheless, it should be stressed that conduct will only be relevant when it would be *manifestly* inequitable to ignore it.

Recourse to the s 9(1)(e) principle should be rare. For example, if there has been a long marriage during which a wife has given up employment to look after her family, then, even if at the date of the divorce she is too old to enter the labour market, the s 9(1)(e) principle should not be applicable. For, in the circumstances of this type of marriage, the wife should have obtained substantial financial provision

1 *Johnstone v Johnstone* 1990 SCLR 358.
2 Section 13(2).
3 Section 11(5).
4 Section 11(6).
5 Section 11(7).

under principles 9(1)(a) and (b), particularly when it is remembered that matrimonial property includes the husband's interests under any life policies or occupational pension scheme.[1] Nevertheless, the courts have made awards of periodical allowance to middle aged women who had already received generous capital settlements.[2] They had not, however, received an award under principle 9(1)(b) in recognition of their economic contributions in respect of caring for the children and running the household during a long marriage. The courts were concerned about their ability to survive comfortably without an income and accordingly, made an award of periodical allowance under s 9(1)(e). With respect, this is to distort the scope of s 9(1)(e) as the women were not in *serious* financial hardship since they had received substantial capital settlements. The proper course in these cases was to make an award under s 9(1)(b).

Moreover, since the serious financial hardship must arise *from the divorce* where a couple have very limited resources, principle 9(1)(e) should be inapplicable as any periodical allowance awarded thereunder simply reduces the amount of income support and other benefits to which the payee would otherwise be entitled as a divorced person. Once again, the courts have distorted the scope of s 9(1)(e) by awarding a periodical allowance in these circumstances. In *Stott v Stott*[3] the husband had a very low income and no capital assets. If there had been no divorce, the wife could have received an award of aliment which would have been no greater than the income support and other benefits she would have received if she divorced. Nevertheless the court awarded her a periodical allowance. In the present writer's view, s 9(1)(e) was inapplicable because her financial situation was the same whether or not she remained married and therefore no financial hardship arose from *the divorce*. The solution was to have recognised the wife's economic contribution in running the home and looking after the children by making an award of a capital sum under s 9(1)(b), payable by instalments over a long period.[4] The fact that matrimonial misconduct is generally irrelevant further restricts the scope of the principle.

1 Discussed *supra* p 129.
2 *Bell v Bell* 1988 SCLR 457; *Humphrey v Humphrey* 25 May 1988, (unreported).
3 1987 GWD 17–645.
4 On the use of s 9(1)(b) in these circumstances, see discussion *supra* p 137. In *Stott*, the sheriff awarded a periodical allowance under s 9(1)(d) to be followed after three years by a periodical allowance under s 9(1)(e). It is submitted that the order under s 9(1)(d) should not have been made; its purpose is to enable the payee to adjust to the loss of the payer's financial support: by awarding a periodical allowance under s 9(1)(e) to take effect three years later, the payer's financial support continues! In other words principles s 9(1)(d) and (e) are mutually exclusive. On principle s 9(1)(d), see *supra* pp 135 ff.

Thus it should only be in very exceptional circumstances that principle 9(1)(e) will be relevant. For example, if there has been a short marriage and the couple have few capital assets but H has a reasonable income, the s 9(1)(e) principle might apply if W was seriously physically handicapped at the time of the divorce, provided her conduct was not responsible for the break-up of the marriage. Even in these circumstances, if W was being divorced under s 1(2)(e) of the Divorce (Scotland) Act 1976,[1] she may have a s 1(5) defence to the action of divorce on the ground that the grant of decree would result in grave financial hardship to the defender.[2] If a periodical allowance was ordered under this principle, while subject to recall or variation, it is not limited to any maximum period and can continue until the payee remarries or dies.[3] The fact that it gives rise to a potentially life long financial burden for the payer is another reason why principle 9(1)(e) should only be applicable in the most exceptional circumstances.

Conclusion

The s 9 principles provide sophisticated guidelines which judges must use when exercising their discretion in making orders for financial provision on divorce. Principles 9(1)(a) and (b) give recognition, through the payment of capital sums and property transfer orders, of the economic and other contributions made by the spouses to the marriage and provide compensation for any economic disadvantages suffered by a spouse in the interests of the family. As such, Clive has suggested[4] that they constitute a major step towards a system of deferred community of property and, in effect, perceive marriage as basically an equal partnership between the spouses. It is therefore to be regretted that more use has not been made of s 9(1)(b). At the same time, principle 9(1)(c) recognises the need to provide financial provision for a spouse who suffers an economic burden as a result of continued involvement in caring for any child of the marriage after the divorce and principle 9(1)(d) is designed to help a spouse to readjust to life as a single person – though in this case a periodical allowance is restricted to a maximum period of three years. The final principle is a 'long stop' for very exceptional cases where at the time of the divorce serious economic hardship is likely to arise as a result of the divorce. Because of the underutilisation of s 9(1)(b), it is submitted that too

1 Non-cohabitation for five years: discussed *supra* p 115.
2 See *supra* Ch 7.
3 Section 13(7)(b); *Johnstone v Johnstone* 1990 SCLR 358.
4 *The financial consequences of divorce: reform from the Scottish perspective*, in *State, Law and The Family* (1984, ed Freeman) p 204.

great a reliance is currently being made of s 9(1)(e), thus undermining the economic 'clean break' between the parties which was one of the major aims of the 1985 Act. Finally, matrimonial misconduct, unless it has adversely affected the couple's financial resources, is irrelevant, except in relation to principles 9(1)(d) and (e), where it should only be taken into account in so far as it would be manifestly inequitable *not* to do so.[1] This is, of course, consistent with a non-fault system of divorce.

It is thought that the Act therefore provides a framework for a system of financial provision suited to the needs of Scottish society in the late twentieth century. But as the judges are inevitably left with considerable discretion, the effectiveness of the system ultimately depends on how willing the courts are to adhere to the policies inherent in the principles when making orders for financial provision on divorce. As we have seen, there is some ground for concern that the principles are being undermined as a result of the failure to apply s 9(1)(b) thus distorting the scope of s 9(1)(e).[2]

AGREEMENTS FOR FINANCIAL PROVISION

It was a cardinal principle of the previous law that a spouse could validly discharge his or her right to apply for financial provision on divorce.[3] Accordingly, spouses could agree for themselves the appropriate redistribution of their property and thus achieve an economic 'clean break' on divorce. The problem was, however, that because of the uncertainty on what financial provision a court was likely to order if the case was litigated, lawyers had difficulty in advising their clients on what in the circumstances of the marriage constituted a fair settlement. The introduction of the s 9 principles gives greater certainty as to the outcome of litigation and accordingly it is hoped that lawyers will now be in a better position to negotiate financial settlements on behalf of their clients.

Prior to the 1985 Act, an agreement on the financial provision to be made on divorce could not be set aside unless there was evidence of a vitiating factor such as error, fraud, undue influence or misrepresentation. Accordingly, it was and is important for the parties to be separately advised. Section 16 of the 1985 Act, however, gives the

1 It is also significant that periodical allowances are most likely to be awarded under these principles.
2 On the operation of the Act in practice, see *The Impact of the Family Law (Scotland) Act 1985 on Solicitors' Divorce Practice* Scottish Office Central Research Unit Papers (November 1990).
3 *Dunbar v Dunbar* 1977 SLT 169; *Thomson v Thomson* 1982 SLT 521; *Elder v Elder* 1985 SLT 471.

courts limited additional powers to set aside or vary agreements on financial provision to be made on divorce. First, any term in an agreement relating to the payment of a periodical allowance may be varied or set aside provided there is an express term in the agreement to this effect.[1] This can be done at any time after the divorce has been granted.[2] Second, any term relating to a periodical allowance can be varied or set aside if the payer has become bankrupt.[3] This can be done on, or at any time after, granting decree of divorce. Third, on granting decree on divorce,[4] the court may set aside or vary any agreement or any term of such an agreement that was not 'fair and reasonable' at the time when the agreement was made.[5] Thus, while the courts now have power 'to police' such agreements to ensure that they were fair and reasonable *at the time they were made*, because the power can only be exercised when granting decree of divorce,[6] the aim of achieving an economic 'clean break' between the parties after the divorce will not be frustrated. It is thought that while this power was desirable for the additional protection of parties to such agreements, its limited nature will ensure that it does not operate to discourage spouses from self-regulation of their financial arrangements on divorce.

VARIATION OF PERIODICAL ALLOWANCES AWARDED UNDER THE DIVORCE (SCOTLAND) ACT 1976

The court has power to vary awards of periodical allowance made under the Divorce (Scotland) Act 1976 where there has been a material change of circumstances.[7] This includes the power to vary the periodical allowance to run for a definite period, say 3 years, or until the happening of a specified event, for example, until the youngest child reaches the age of eighteen.[8] There has been a series of cases where a payer has sought to have an award of periodical allowance, originally made to run for an indefinite period, varied so that it will come to an end on the expiry of a definite period. In such cases, the s 9 principles are not strictly applicable, but may be indirectly relevant in so far as they constitute circumstances in a particular case.[9] There is no

1 Section 16(1)(a); *Mills v Mills* 1989 SCLR 213.
2 Section 16(2)(a); *Mills v Mills* 1989 SCLR 213.
3 Section 16(3).
4 Section 16(2)(b): the court may also exercise its power within such period as the court may specify on granting decree.
5 Section 16(1)(b).
6 Or within a period specified by the court when granting decree.
7 Section 5(4) of the Divorce (Scotland) Act 1976.
8 Section 28(3) of the Family Law (Scotland) Act 1985.
9 *Wilson v Wilson* 1987 SLT 721.

automatic right to have an order varied so that the payer's obligations cease after the expiry of a definite period[1] but such a variation will be ordered if the circumstances so demand. In practice, when the periodical allowance has been paid for a long time, the courts have been prepared to bring it, in effect, to an end:[2] but if the payee has forgone a capital sum payment in the expectation that periodical allowance would run indefinitely, it is most unlikely that such a variation would be made. A variation restricting the payment of a periodical allowance until the expiry of a definite period can itself be varied on a further change of circumstances.[3]

PROCEDURAL MATTERS

By s 18 a spouse who has made a claim for an order for financial provision[4] may, not later than a year from the date of disposal of the claim, apply to the court for an order setting aside or varying any transfer of, or transaction involving, property which was effected by the other party to the marriage not more than five years before the date of making the claim.[5] The court will make such an order if satisfied by the challenger that the transaction had, or was likely to have, the effect of defeating in whole or in part, the applicant's claim for financial provision. This is an objective criterion: there is no need to establish whether the transfer was intended by the transferor to defeat the applicant's claim. Transactions will cover not only dispositions or settlements of property but also gifts of money and other moveables.[6] An order under s 18 does not prejudice the rights of a third party in or to the property, where the third party has acquired the property or any rights therein in good faith and for value or has derived title to such property or rights from any person who has done so. Thus, for example, if three years before W's claim for financial provision H transferred £20,000 to his mistress, M, the court could set aside the

---

1 *Collins v Collins* 1989 SLT 194.
2 See, for example, *McCrae v McCrae* 1988 SLT 248; *Smith v Smith* 1988 SLT 840; *Macpherson v Macpherson* 1989 SLT 231.
3 *Macpherson v Macpherson* 1989 SLT 231.
4 The provisions also apply to an action for aliment, or variation or recall of a decree of aliment or order for financial provision.
5 The court has also the power to interdict the party from entering into such a transfer or transaction.
6 Cf the previous position in s 6 of the Divorce (Scotland) Act 1976: *Maclean v Maclean* 1976 SLT 86.

transfer unless M was in good faith and had given value in respect of the money, eg sold H a painting worth £20,000.[1]

Finally, in an action for financial provision,[2] the court can order either party to provide details of his or her resources.[3] It should also be remembered that before the determination of a divorce action or an action of declarator of nullity, the court has the power to make an award of interim aliment to a party to the action.[4] Only periodical payments can be awarded which are payable until the date of the disposal of the action[5] when, of course, the court will make orders for financial provision.

---

1 Warrants for inhibition or arrestment on the dependence are also possible, on cause shown, in respect of any property which could be relevant in a claim for financial provision or aliment: s 19.
2 Or actions for aliment or interim aliment.
3 Section 20.
4 Section 6. Interim aliment can also be awarded in actions for aliment.
5 Section 6(3).

8 Parents and children

INTRODUCTION

In the law of Scotland, children have passive capacity in the sense that they enjoy a plethora of legal rights. But, as we shall see,[1] they lack active capacity in that they are unable to enforce these rights during their childhood. This must be done on their behalf by an adult, who will usually be a parent. In family law, children's most important rights are those which are exigible against their natural parents. The primary purpose of this chapter is to discuss how parentage is established. Before doing so, however, it is proposed by way of introduction to consider when a child first obtains legal rights.

Once a child is conceived, Scottish criminal law provides protection for the foetus by prohibiting the inducement of an abortion.[2] However, as a result of s 1(1) of the Abortion Act 1967[3], a person will not be guilty of an offence if a pregnancy is terminated by a registered medical practitioner, provided two doctors in good faith are of the opinion—

(1) that the pregnancy has not exceeded its twenty fourth week and that its continuance would involve risk, greater than if it were terminated, of injury to the physical or mental health of the pregnant woman or any existing children of her family; or

(2) that the termination is necessary to prevent grave permanent injury to her physical or mental health; or

(3) that the continuance of the pregnancy would involve risk to her life, greater than if the pregnancy were terminated; or

(4) that there is a substantial risk that if the child were born it would suffer from such physical or mental abnormalities as to be seriously handicapped.

Where an abortion is sought in the first trimester, ie during the first three months of the pregnancy, then termination will involve a risk to the mother's health which is considerably less than the risks involved in childbirth: accordingly, it is not too difficult to establish ground (1) for a lawful termination in these circumstances.

---

1 *Supra* Ch 9.
2 See generally Gordon *Criminal Law* (2nd edn, 1978) Ch 28; Norrie 'Abortion in Great Britain' 1985 Crim LR 475.
3 As amended by s 34(1) of the Human Fertilisation and Embryology Act 1990.

As in all cases of medical treatment, the patient, ie the woman, must consent. However, where the grounds for a lawful termination under s 1(1) are established, the consent of the father is not required nor can he obtain an interdict to prevent the pregnancy being terminated.[1]

While ground (1) cannot be used after the twenty fourth week of the pregnancy, there is no time limit in relation to the other grounds. A later abortion may be necessary, for example, if there has been a delay in establishing that the foetus is abnormal for the purposes of ground (4). While not illegal *per se*, late termination *ie* beyond twenty four weeks, is not common in Scotland.[2]

While the Congenital Disabilities (Civil Liability) Act 1976 does not apply in Scotland, it is thought an action in delict will lie when a child is born physically or mentally handicapped as a result of injuries sustained in the womb.[3] While there is no authority directly in point it is submitted that, in theory at least, an action would lie even where the injuries were caused as a result of the mother's negligence.[4] To this extent, the Scottish common law position is wider than the provisions of the 1976 Act.[5] A child's right to the physical integrity of its person therefore extends to injuries suffered before he or she was born. This conclusion is consistent with the *nasciturus* principle, *viz* that, in matters of private law, a child who is *in utero* should be deemed to be already born when this would operate for the child's benefit.[6] The principle has, for example, been used when a posthumous child has not received provision in his father's will: after birth, the will may be challenged on the child's behalf as a result of the presumption that the testator would not wish his will to be given effect in the altered circumstances – the *conditio si testator sine liberis decesserit*. A successful challenge revokes the will completely.[7]

In spite of these developments, in general a child only obtains the passive capacity to enjoy rights when he or she is born alive and has acquired an existence separate from his or her mother.

---

1 *Paton v Trustees of BPAS* [1978] 2 All ER 987, [1979] 2 QB 276; noted by Kennedy (1979) 42 MLR 324; *Paton v UK* [1980] 3 EHRR 408; *C v S* [1988] QB 135.
2 Before the amendments made by the Human Fertilisation and Embryology Act 1990, there was no time limit for termination in Scotland.
3 See *Liability for Antenatal Injury*, Scot Law Com No 30; Norrie, 1983 SLT (News) 121.
4 It has long been accepted that actions in delict are competent between parent and child, for injuries sustained after the child's birth: *Young v Rankin* 1934 SC 499; *Wood v Wood* 1935 SLT 431.
5 Section 1(1) excludes the child's mother unless when the injury was the result of the mother's negligent driving: s 2.
6 See TB Smith *A Short Commentary on the Law of Scotland* (1962) p 246.
7 See, for example, *Elder's Trustees v Elder* (1894) 21 R 704; (1895) 22 R 505.

ESTABLISHING PARENTAGE

In the context of family law, the rights which a child enjoys are those which are prima facie exigible against his natural parents. It is therefore important to have rules which establish parentage.

At one time there was little difficulty in determining who was a child's mother: she was the woman who gave birth to the child. Recent advances in reproductive techniques do, however, raise difficulties. If, for example, an ovum is donated, then fertilised and the resulting embryo transferred to the donee's womb, is she to be regarded as the child's mother, although genetically unrelated to the child? It was the present writer's view that a woman's act in carrying a foetus from implantation to full term should be the criterion of motherhood, rather than genetic relationship. Like Mason and McCall Smith,[1] the present writer believed—

> 'that it should be an irrebutable presumption that a woman who has carried a child and given birth to it is its mother – no genetic niceties should obscure the fact that these are the essential features of motherhood'.

This principle has now been enacted in s 27(1) of the Human Fertilisation and Embryology Act 1990 which provides that 'The woman who is carrying or has carried a child as a result of the placing in her of an embryo or of sperm and eggs, and no other woman, is to be treated as the mother of the child'.

On the other hand, a child's father is determined solely by biological criteria: he is the man whose semen fertilised the ovum, leading to the birth of the child. In other words, he must be genetically related to the child. The difficulty, of course, is that more than one man may have had access to the mother at the probable date of conception. The law therefore proceeds on the basis of a series of presumptions which can, of course, be rebutted by evidence to the contrary.

By s 5(1)(a) of the Law Reform (Parent and Child) (Scotland) Act 1986[2] a man is presumed to be the father of a child if he was married to the mother of the child at any time during the period beginning with the conception and ending with the birth of the child. Thus the presumption applies when—

a) H and W were married both at the date of conception and birth;

b) H and W were married at the date of conception but not at the date of the birth: for example, if H had died before the child's birth – a

---

1 Mason and McCall Smith *Law and Medical Ethics* (2nd edn; 1987) at p 57.
2 In this chapter, references are to the Law Reform (Parent and Child) (Scotland) Act 1986 unless otherwise stated.

posthumous child, or the couple had divorced before the child's birth;

c) H and W were not married at the date of conception but were married at the date of the birth.[1]

The presumption does not apply where a child was conceived and born *before* H and W married.[2] The s 5(1)(a) presumption applies in the case of a void, voidable or irregular marriage in the same way as it applies in the case of a valid and regular marriage.[3]

However, even if s 5(1)(a) does not apply, a man will be presumed to be the father of a child, if *both* he and the mother of the child have acknowledged that he is the father and the child has been registered as such.[4] Thus, for example, a child of cohabitees will be presumed to be the child of the male cohabitee if he and the mother have acknowledged that he is the father and the child is registered as such.[5] The presumptions in s 5 may be rebutted by proof, on a balance of probabilities,[6] that the man was not the father of the child.

An interesting problem arises in relation to a child who is born as a result of artificial insemination from a donor (AID). If a married woman conceives as a result of AID, prima facie s 5(1)(a) will apply and her husband will be presumed to be the father of the child. However, as the husband is not the genetic father, the presumption could easily be rebutted. It is now provided however, that unless the husband has not consented to the AID, he is to be treated in law as the father of the child and the donor is not to be treated as the child's

---

1 Cf the position at common law in *Gardner v Gardner* (1876) 3 R 695; (1877) 4 R (HL) 56.

2 This was also the position at common law: *Imre v Mitchell* 1958 SC 439; *James v McLennan* 1971 SLT 162.

3 Section 5(2). A difficulty arises if W marries H1 and later goes through a ceremony of marriage with H2. If W has a child both H1 and H2 have the benefit of the s 5(1)(a) presumption as the presumption applies both to her valid marriage with H1 and her void 'marriage' with H2. In these circumstances it is submitted that the statutory presumptions cancel each other and H1 and H2 must attempt to establish paternity by evidence.

4 Section 5(1)(b) and para 8 of Sch 1 to the Act.

5 Cf the position at common law where no presumption applied from cohabitation: *A v G* 1984 SLT (Sh Ct) 65.

6 Section 5(4). At common law, the presumption *pater est quem nuptiae demonstrant*, ie the father is the man to whom the marriage points, applies when H was married to W at the date of conception. It is a presumption which can only be rebutted by evidence which establishes beyond reasonable doubt that H did not have access to W at the probable date of conception: see, for example, *S v S* 1977 SLT (Notes) 65.

father.[1] A marriage for this purpose includes a void marriage if either or both parties reasonably believed that the marriage was valid.[2]

Where the presumptions apply, the presumptive father – or the mother if she alleged her husband was not the father – can seek a declarator of non-parentage in the Court of Session or the sheriff court. Where the presumptions do not apply, a declarator of parentage may be sought in the Court of Session or the sheriff court.[3] Thus if a woman has a child, she can seek declarator that a particular man is the father of her child.[4] Conversely, a man can seek declarator that he is the father of a woman's child. If declarator of non-parentage is granted, the presumptions in s 5 are displaced: if declarator of parentage is granted, it will give rise to a presumption to the same effect as the decree.[5]

The court shall not grant decree of declarator unless it is satisfied that the grounds of action have been established by sufficient evidence.[6] Thus, in an action of declarator of parentage, the pursuer – who will usually be the mother of the child – must establish, by evidence, that on the balance of probabilities the alleged man is the father of the child. Corroborated evidence is no longer required[7]. Similarly, if a man seeks a declarator of parentage, he must establish, by evidence, that on the balance of probabilities, he is the father of the child.[8] Finally, in an action of declarator of non-parentage, it must be established, by evidence, that on the balance of probabilities the s 5

1 Sections 28(2), (4) and 29 of the Human Fertilisation and Embryology Act 1990. A similar rule applies when AID is provided in the course of joint treatment of a couple and s 28(2) is inapplicable: s 28(3) and (4).
2 Section 28(7). There is a rebuttable presumption that one of the parties reasonably believed the marriage was valid: *ibid*.
3 The Court of Session has jurisdiction if the child was born in Scotland or the alleged or presumed parent or the child a) is domiciled in Scotland on the date when the action is brought, or b) was habitually resident in Scotland for not less than one year on the date when the action is brought, or c) died before that date and either (i) was at the date of death domiciled in Scotland or (ii) had been habitually resident in Scotland for not less than one year immediately preceding the date of death: the sheriff court has jurisdiction if a) the child was born in the sheriffdom or b) an action could have been brought in the Court of Session and the alleged or presumed parent or the child was habitually resident in the sheriffdom on the date when the action was brought or on the date of his death: ss 7(2) and (3).
4 The action of affiliation is probaly no longer competent: *Canlon v O'Dowd* 1987 SCLR 771.
5 Section 5(3).
6 Section 8(1) of the Civil Evidence (Scotland) Act 1988.
7 Section 1(1) of the Civil Evidence (Scotland) Act 1988. The doctrine of corroboration by false denial has also been abolished: s 1(2).
8 See, for example, *Docherty v McGlynn* 1985 SLT 237; *Campbell v Grossart* 1988 GWD 24–1004.

presumptions of paternity have been rebutted, by, for example, evidence of non-access by the husband to his wife at the probable date of conception. In this context it should be noted that courts have recognised the possibility of abnormal gestation periods.[1]

BLOOD TESTS AND DNA 'FINGERPRINTING'

In actions of declarator of parentage or non-parentage, blood test evidence can be of immense importance. These have become extremely sophisticated and highly accurate. By taking blood tests from a child, his or her mother and the alleged or presumptive father, it is possible to establish that because of his blood group the man could not be the father of the child: ie blood tests can lead to an exclusionary result. However, if a non-exclusionary result was obtained, the blood tests merely establish that any man within that blood group *could* be the child's father: blood tests cannot yet establish that a man genetically *is* the child's father.

EXAMPLE

A and B could both be the father of C's child. If blood samples are taken from A, B, C and the child, it might be possible to obtain a result which showed that genetically A or B could not be the child's father. If an exclusionary result was obtained in respect of A and a non-exclusionary result in the case of B, while the non-exclusionary result per se would only establish that B could be the child's father, if evidence was brought that C only had sexual intercourse with A and B at the probable date of conception, this and the non-exclusionary result would establish that B was the father. If, however, non-exclusionary results were obtained for both A and B, it would remain difficult to establish which of the two men was the child's father if both had sexual intercourse with C at the probable date of conception.

However, the utility of blood test evidence has been overtaken by developments in relation to DNA 'fingerprinting'. By taking samples of bodily fluid or tissue from the child, the mother and the alleged or presumptive father, it is possible by DNA profiling to establish posi-

1 See, for example, *Currie v Currie* 1950 SC 10. (W gave birth 336 days after the couple last cohabited: held not to be an impossible period of pregnancy): cf *Preston-Jones v Preston-Jones* [1951] 1 All ER 124, [1951] AC 391, HL (alleged pregnancy of 360 days).

tively whether or not the man is the child's father *ie* an inclusionary result can be obtained.

The utility of blood test and DNA profiling evidence is obvious in determining issues of paternity. Nevertheless, at first the Scottish courts were sceptical of the value of blood test evidence because of the possibility of inaccuracies. More recently, however, they have begun to recognise the advances which have been made in serology and the increased evidential importance of blood tests.[1] But the law on the subject was uncertain[2] and has now been put on a statutory basis.

The first problem is to consider who has the power to consent to samples of blood, bodily fluid or tissue being taken from a child. In civil proceedings relating to the determination of parentage, where such a sample is sought from a pupil[3] by a party to the proceedings or a *curator ad litem*,[4] the child's tutor[5] or any person having custody or care of him may consent.[6] Where the child is a minor[7] the child will have capacity to consent provided he or she understands the nature and purpose of the blood test.[8] Where such a sample is sought from a person, for example, a pupil, who is incapable of giving consent, the court has power to consent to the taking of a sample where a) there is no person who is entitled to give such consent, for example, if the child has no tutor, and b) there is such a person but it is not reasonably practicable to obtain his or her consent, for example, if the child's

1 Contrast the attitude of the court in *Imre v Mitchell* 1958 SC 439 and *Sproat v McGibney* 1968 SLT 33 with *S v S* [1970] 3 All ER 107, [1972] AC 24, HL; *Allardyce v Johnstone* 1979 SLT (Sh Ct) 54 and *Docherty v McGlynn* 1983 SLT 645; 1985 SLT 237.
2 See *Torrie v Turner* 1990 SLT 718 where the Inner House held that a court has no power to make a direction that a person should give a sample for the purposes of DNA screening even though this could lead to a positive result of paternity. Leave has been given to appeal to the House of Lords. See generally, *Report on Evidence: Blood Group Tests DNA Tests and Related Matters* SLC No 120. The Law Commission's recommendations in Part III of the Report were enacted by s 70 of the Law Reform (Miscellaneous Provisions) (Scotland) Act 1990, discussed *infra* p 156.
3 Ie a boy below the age of 14 and a girl below the age of 12: discussed *infra* Ch 9.
4 A *curator ad litem* is a person appointed by the court to protect the interests of the child in the proceedings.
5 The child's tutor will usually be the child's mother and presumptive father: for full discussion, see *infra* Ch 9.
6 Sections 6(1) and (2) as amended by s 70(3) of the Law Reform (Miscellaneous Provisions) (Scotland) Act 1990.
7 Ie a boy between the ages of 14 and 18 and a girl between the ages of 12 and 18.
8 On the capacity of minors to consent to inter alia medical treatment; see *infra* Ch 10.

tutors are abroad, or he or she is unwilling to accept the responsibility of giving or withholding consent.[1]

A particular difficulty arises if the child's tutor is his or her presumptive father. Consider the following example. H and W are married at the date of the child's conception and birth: s 5(1) will operate so that H will be presumed to be the child's father and consequently the child's presumptive tutor. If H subsequently brings an action of declarator of non-parentage, can he consent to samples being taken from the child when the purpose of so doing is to rebut the s 5 presumption to establish on the balance or probabilities that he is not the father? While *Docherty v McGlynn*[2] is authority that a presumptive father may consent to samples being taken from a child, it is important to note that in this case he wished to do so to establish that he was in fact the child's genetic father. But could he rely on the presumption, if his purpose was to deny that he was in fact the child's genetic father? In spite of dicta in *Docherty v McGlynn*[3] that he cannot do so, it is submitted here that he can. Until the s 5 presumption is rebutted, H is the child's presumptive father and tutor and it is in that capacity that he has the power to consent to the blood or DNA test on the child. Even if his purpose is to establish that he is not the child's genetic father, this does not undermine the legality of his consent to samples being taken from the child, which was given in his capacity as the child's presumptive father and tutor. As we shall see,[4] the court may refuse to admit the evidence so obtained if it would be against the child's interests to do so.

The second problem is that it is a cardinal principle of Scots law that in civil proceedings the courts will not make an order to compel a person to submit to a blood or DNA test against his or her will.[5] Similarly, the court will not make an order to compel a tutor or person with care and custody of a child, to consent to samples of blood, bodily fluid or tissue being taken from the child.[6] Moreover it would appear

---

1 Section 6(3) as amended by s 70(3) of the Law Reform (Miscellaneous Provisions) (Scotland) Act 1990: it should be noted that s 6(3) applies to any person – not necessarily a child – who is incapable of consent, for example, a person suffering from mental illness.
2 1983 SLT 645.
3 Ibid at 746 per Lord President (Emslie) approving *Whitehall v Whitehall* 1958 SC 252 and *dicta* in *Imre v Mitchell* 1958 SC 439. But cf *Clive* p 502.
4 *Infra* p 156.
5 *Whitehall v Whitehall* 1958 SC 252; *Torrie v Turner* 1990 SLT 718.
6 *Docherty v McGlynn* 1983 SLT 645; *Torrie v Turner* 1990 SLT 718.

that at common law the court could not make a direction that a sample should be given and then draw adverse inferences if a sample was refused.[1] Section 70(1) of the Law Reform (Miscellaneous Provisions) (Scotland) Act 1990 now provides that in civil proceedings the court[2] may request a party to the proceedings to provide a sample of blood, bodily fluid or tissue or consent to such a sample being taken from a child in relation to whom the party has power to give consent. This provision still does not give the court the power to *compel* a person to give such a sample or consent to such a sample being taken from a child. However, if the person refuses or fails to provide such a sample or refuses to consent to such a sample being taken from a child, the court may draw such adverse inference as seems appropriate.[3]

Where a person has died, the Scottish courts are prepared to admit hospital records containing the blood group of the deceased, where the deceased's blood group is necessary to determine a child's paternity by the use of blood tests.[4]

Finally, in *Docherty v McGlynn*,[5] the Inner House of the Court of Session held that in the exercise of its inherent protective jurisdiction in relation to children the court could intervene and refuse to admit such evidence if it was not in the child's interests to do so. Moreover, while it is expressly enacted that a court cannot exercise its powers under s 6(3) to consent to a blood sample being taken from a child unless satisfied that it would not be detrimental to the child's health to do so,[6] it is submitted that a court would not consent if the results of the blood tests would be contrary to the child's interests. In reaching its decision in *Docherty v McGlynn*,[7] the Inner House relied upon the English case of *S v S*[8] where Lord Reid concluded that 'the court ought to permit a blood test of a young child to be taken unless satisfied that it would be against the child's interest'.[9]

---

1 *Torrie v Turner* 1990 SLT 718; cf the approach of Lord Cameron in *Docherty v McGlynn* 1983 SLT 645 at 650.
2 Ie the Court of Session or the sheriff court: s 70(4). The Court may make the request *ex proprio motu*: cf s 61.
3 Section 70(2) of the Law Reform (Miscellaneous Provisions) (Scotland) Act 1990.
4 *Docherty v McGlynn* 1985 SLT 237; s 7 of the Law Reform (Miscellaneous Provisions) (Scotland) Act 1966. Cf the position in English law in *The Ampthill Peerage* [1977] AC 547, HL per Lord Simon of Glaisdale at 583.
5 1983 SLT 645.
6 Section 6(4).
7 1983 SLT 645.
8 [1970] 3 All ER 107, [1972] AC 24, HL.
9 Ibid at 45.

In what circumstances will the courts either refuse to make a request under section 70(1) of the Law Reform (Miscellaneous Provisions) (Scotland) Act 1990 that a party to the proceedings should consent to a sample of blood, bodily fluid or tissue being taken from a child or refuse to admit the results of blood or DNA tests which had been carried out on a child with the appropriate consents? In *Docherty v McGlynn*[1] the Inner House considered that there was a 'delicate balance' between the desire for truth in litigation and the advantages for a child in continuing to be regarded as legitimate: Lord Cameron, in particular, thought that 'the stigma of illegitimacy is one which in many cases and ranks of society is a cause of pain and distress'.[2] Thus, there is authority that the court should not exercise its power to make such a request or admit such evidence, if it was likely thereby to establish that a child who was presumptively legitimate was in fact illegitimate. But as we shall see,[3] the marital status of a child's parents is no longer of any major legal significance in relation to the child's rights[4] and consequently the force of the court's observations in *Docherty v McGlynn*[5] now carry little, if any, weight. It is therefore submitted that merely because the s 5 presumption of paternity is likely to be rebutted, is not per se sufficient for a court to conclude that it would be contrary to a child's interests to make a request under s 70(1) of the Law Reform (Miscellaneous Provisions) (Scotland) Act 1990 or admit the results of blood or DNA tests as evidence. Only in very exceptional circumstances[6] will it now be contrary to a child's interests that the truth of his paternity should be known.

LEGITIMACY AND ILLEGITIMACY

Introduction

For centuries a child's rights in Scots law were dependent upon whether or not he was legitimate. A child is legitimate if his parents were validly married at the date of the child's conception or his birth or any

---

1 1985 SLT 237.
2 Ibid at 650.
3 *Infra*.
4 Section 1(1).
5 1983 SLT 645.
6 For example that the child is the product of an incestuous relationship.

time in between.[1] When the child is conceived during a valid marriage, the husband is presumed to be the child's father: *pater est quem nuptiae demonstrant*. Thus, for example, where a couple were validly married at the date of the child's conception he or she is presumed to be the legitimate child of the husband, even if the husband died before the child's birth. If a child is conceived and born out of wedlock, he or she is illegitimate.[2]

Where his or her parents' marriage is void, a child conceived or born during the void marriage can be regarded as legitimate as a result of the doctrine of putative marriage. Before this doctrine is applicable, at least one of the parties must have entered into the 'marriage' in the bona fide belief that the marriage was valid, ie in ignorance of any impediment to the marriage. However, the error has to be one of fact not of law: for example, if a man and woman married without realising they were uncle and niece, the doctrine is applicable (error of fact) but it does not apply if they had married in the belief that uncle and niece had capacity to marry each other under the law of Scotland (error of law).[3] A child who is conceived or born during a voidable marriage retains his legitimate status even if a declarator of nullity of marriage is subsequently obtained.[4]

When a child was born illegitimate, at common law, he or she would be legitimated by the subsequent valid marriage of his parents: legitimation *per subsequens matrimonium*. While the effect of the doctrine was retrospectively to treat the child as legitimate from the date of birth, it did not apply if the child's parents lacked the capacity to marry each other at the date of the child's conception.[5] The law was, however, changed by the Legitimation (Scotland) Act 1968. This provides that a child will become legitimated as a result of his or her parents' subsequent marriage, provided that the child was living at the date of the marriage and the father was domiciled in Scotland at that date.[6] It is irrelevant that the parents lacked capacity to marry at the date of the

---

1 Bell's *Principles* 1624. If the child is conceived before marriage, if the husband knew at the time of the ceremony that his wife was pregnant and he had intercourse with her at the probable date of conception, there is a strong presumption that the child was the legitimate child of the husband: *Gardner v Gardner* (1876) 3 R 695; (1877) 4 R (HL) 56.
2 *James v McLennan* 1971 SLT 162.
3 *Purves' Trustees v Purves* (1896) 22 R 513.
4 Section 4 of the Law Reform (Miscellanous Provisions) (Scotland) Act 1949: since the only ground of a voidable marriage is incurable impotency, the number of children involved was very small: see *supra* Ch 2.
5 Erskine *Institute* I 67.52; Bell *Principles* 1627; *Kerr v Martin* (1840) 2 D 752.
6 Section 1 of the Legitimation (Scotland) Act 1968.

child's conception,[1] but, unlike the common law position, the child is only treated as legitimate from the date of the marriage.[2] A marriage for the purposes of the Act includes a putative and void-able marriage.[3]

The law took pains to preserve a child's status of legitimacy. Thus, for example, the presumption *pater est* would only be rebuttable by proof beyond reasonable doubt that the husband was not the father of the child.[4] Moreover, because of the scope of the doctrine of putative marriage and the possibility of legitimation by the subsequent marriage of a child's parents, the range of persons who are treated as legitimate is wide. Nevertheless, the proportion of live illegitimate births to live legitimate births continues to rise in the United Kingdom.[5] It became increasingly obvious how reprehensible it was that the rights of children should continue to depend on the marital status of their parents. Indeed, the legal discrimination against illegitimate children appeared to be in breach of the United Kingdom's international obligations under the European Convention on Human Rights.[6] The matter was considered by the Scottish Law Commission[7] and its recommendations were enacted in the Law Reform (Parent and Child) (Scotland) Act 1986.

The current law

Section 1(1) of the Law Reform (Parent and Child) Scotland Act 1986 declares:

> 'The fact that a person's parents are not or have not been married to one another shall be left out of account in establishing the legal relationship between the person and any other person; and accordingly any such relationship shall have effect as if the parents were or had been married to one another'.

---

1 By s 4 of the Legitimation (Scotland) Act 1968, certain children who failed to be legitimated *per subsequens matrimonium* because their parents lacked capacity to marry at the date of their conception were to be treated as legitimate from the date of the commencement of the Act.
2 Section 1(1) of the Legitimation (Scotland) Act 1968.
3 Section 8(1) of the Legitimation (Scotland) Act 1968.
4 See, for example, *Ballantyne v Douglas* 1953 SLT (Notes) 10 per Lord Patrick at 11. Proof of non access by the husband to the wife at the probable date of conception would suffice: *Coles v Homer and Tulloh* (1895) 22 R 716. Now, of course, the s 5 presumption of paternity can be rebutted by proof on a balance of probabilities: s 5(4).
5 See Hoggett and Pearl *The Family, Law and Society* (2nd edn, 1987) 406 ff.
6 Arts 8 and 14: on these Articles, see *Marckx v Belgium* (1979) 2 EHHR 330.
7 See *Illegitimacy*, Scot Law Com No 82.

The effect of this provision is that children have legal equality regardless of their parents' marital status at the time of their birth. In other words, the status of legitimacy and illegitimacy is no longer to have any legal significance.

To ensure its purpose, the Act provides that in any future deeds or statutes a reference to any relative shall, unless the contrary intention appears in the statute or deed, be construed in accordance with s 1(1).[1] The Act amends previous legislation[2] to remove legal inequalties between legitimate and illegitimate children[3] and, so far as possible, references to illegitimate children.[4]

There are, however, areas where the distinction between legitimate and illegitimate children remains important. First, s 1(1) does not apply to any deed executed *before* the commencement of the Act.[5] However, if the deed was executed after the commencement of the Law Reform (Miscellaneous Provisions) (Scotland) Act 1968, any reference in the deed to a relative includes, unless the contrary intention appears, an illegitimate as well as legitimate relationship.[6] Second, s 1(1) does not apply to any deed executed *after* the commencement of the Act, where the deed (however expressed) refers to a legitimate or illegitimate relationship.[7] Thus, for example, if a testator makes a bequest in his will to his daughter's legitimate children, her illegitimate children cannot benefit, even if the testamentary deed was executed after the commencement of the Act. Third, the Act does not affect the right of legitim out of, or the right of succession to, the estate of any person who died before the commencement of the Act.[8] Finally, the Act does not apply to the succession or devolution of any title, coat of arms, honour or dignity transmissible on the death of the holder

---

1 Section 1(2).
2 Section 10(1) and Sch 1 to the Act.
3 For example, in relation to succession, para 7 of Sch 1 to the Act removes inequalities by the simple expedient of providing that any reference to relative in the Succession (Scotland) Act 1964 shall be construed in accordance with s 1(1) of the 1986 Act. On succession see *supra* p 56.
4 See, for example, Sch 1, para 15 in relation to the Damages (Scotland) Act 1976, para 17 in relation to the Marriage (Scotland) Act 1977 (discussed *supra* Ch 2), and para 18 in relation to the Adoption (Scotland) Act 1978. But cf para 10 where the expression 'illegitimate person' is used in an amendment to The Law Reform (Miscellaneous Provisions) (Scotland) Act 1968.
5 Section 1(4)(b).
6 Section 5 of the Law Reform (Miscellaneous Provisions) (Scotland) Act 1968. See, for example, *Russell v Woods* 1987 SCLR 207.
7 Section 1(4)(c).
8 Section 9(1)(d): on the rights of children on succession, see *supra* p 56.

thereof.[1] Thus, it will still be necessary to resort to the law on legitimacy and legitimation for these, admittedly limited, purposes.

There remains a major difficulty in equating the legal position of a legitimate and illegitimate child. As we shall see,[2] parents enjoy important rights over their children in respect of the child's care and upbringing. When a married woman has a child, the s 5 presumption will apply and both spouses will prima facie enjoy parental rights. But when an unmarried woman has a child, should the child's father as well as the mother have parental rights? While an illegitimate child should enjoy the same rights vis à vis his father and his family as a legitimate child, it does not follow that the father of an illegitimate child should automatically have parental rights in the same way as the father of a legitimate child. Any legislation purporting to achieve the legal equality of legitimate and illegitimate children must recognise that the relationship between the parents of an illegitimate child will often lack the stability and commitment of that of the parents of a legitimate child.

The Act faces this problem by providing that the mother of a child has parental rights whether or not she is or has been married to the child's father.[3] A child's father only has parental rights if he is or was married to the child's mother at the date of the child's conception[4] when, of course, he will also have the benefit of the s 5 presumption of paternity. However, if he was not married to the child's mother at the time of the child's conception, he will acquire parental rights if he marries her subsequently.[5]

EXAMPLES

a) If H marries W after the date of conception but before the date of birth, he will have the benefit of the s 5 presumption of paternity and will have parental rights as he married the child's mother after the date of conception.

b) If H marries W after the date of conception and birth, he will not have the benefit of the s 5 presumption:[6] but if his paternity is established, he will obtain parental rights when he subsequently marries.

1 Section 9(1)(c).
2 *Infra* Ch 10.
3 Section 2(1)(a).
4 Section 2(1)(b).
5 Ibid.
6 Unless both have acknowledged that he is father of the child and the child has been registered as such: s 5(1)(b).

However, if parents of a child never marry, the father – even if his paternity has been established – will not obtain parental rights over his child unless he has obtained an order granting him parental rights under s 3(1): in such proceedings, the welfare of the child is regarded as the paramount consideration.[1] Thus, where the parents of a child never marry, prima facie it is only the child's mother who has parental rights. Consequently, the Act does not alter the rule that a child born out of wedlock takes the domicile of his mother as a domicile of origin or dependence[2] nor the law of adoption, under which the father of a child born out of wedlock plays little part in the proceedings unless he has obtained parental rights[3]

Because a father will automatically have parental rights in respect of his child if he was married to the child's mother at the date of conception or married her subsequently,[4] it will be clear that marriage plays a crucial role in determining a father's entitlement to parental rights. The Act provides that marriage for this purpose includes (i) a voidable marriage,[5] and (ii) a void marriage, provided the father believed in good faith at the time of the marriage that it was valid, whether that belief was due to an error of fact or an error of law.[6] Where a couple are merely cohabiting, however, only the mother will automatically have parental rights: unless they subsequently marry, the father will enjoy no parental rights over his children unless and until he obtains parental rights by virtue of an order made under s 3.

In spite of the reforms in the 1986 Act, the status of illegitimacy still subsists in Scots Law. The Scottish Law Commission has recommended that since there are now virtually no legal differences between legitimate and illegitimate children, a separate status of legitimacy and illegitimacy is unnecessary, and in the case of the latter, offensive. Consequently the Commission suggests that section 1(1) of the Law Reform (Parent and Child) (Scotland) Act 1986 be amended so that it is expressly enacted that no person whose status is governed by Scots law shall be illegitimate.[7] However, where a person's parents have

1 Section 3(2). For full discussion of s 3, see *infra* Ch 11.
2 Section 9(1)(a): a child who is born in wedlock prima facie takes the domicile of his father as his domicile of origin or dependence.
3 On adoption, see *infra* Ch 12.
4 Section 2(1)(b).
5 Section 2(2)(a).
6 Section 2(2)(b): because an error of law will suffice, this is wider than the doctrine of putative marriage in Scots law.
7 *Family Law: Pre-consolidation Reforms* SLC Discussion Paper No 85, paras 11.1–11.10. As a consequence the Legitimation (Scotland) Act 1968 would be repealed as unnecessary and declarators of legitimacy, legitimation and illegitimacy would be incompetent.

never married, this would remain significant in relation to the exceptions to the general principle of legal equality[1] and in the context of parental rights.

1 *Supra* p 159.

9 Children's rights and duties

INTRODUCTION

The purpose of this chapter is to examine some of the most important legal rights enjoyed by children and how these rights are enforced. However, as a child matures, there may be a conflict between the child's 'right' to self-determination and his parents' rights in relation to his care and upbringing. Full discussion of this important and controversial issue will be left to the following chapter, where parental rights will be discussed in some detail. At present, we are therefore concerned with a child's capacity to enter into juristic acts and to seek redress when his or her rights have been infringed: we shall also consider when a child may incur liability in respect of his actions. At the outset it must be emphasised that the treatment of the substantive law on many of these issues is not intended to be exhaustive.

PUPILS AND MINORS: TUTORS AND CURATORS

Scots law makes an important distinction between pupils and minors. A pupil is a boy below the age of fourteen and a girl below the age of twelve. A minor is a boy between the ages of fourteen and eighteen and a girl between the ages of twelve and eighteen. At the age of eighteen, a minor becomes an adult in the eyes of the law.[1]

While a pupil has passive capacity ie he enjoys the full complement of legal rights, for example, the right of ownership of property, he or she has no active capacity.[2] This means that the pupil cannot enter into juristic acts, for example, make a will. Moreover, a pupil cannot pursue actions when his or her rights have been infringed. Instead, the pupil's tutor must enter into juristic acts for his or her benefit or pursue litigation on the pupil's behalf. A child's tutor is the pupil's mother and father, if the father was married to the mother at the date of the child's

---

1 Age of Majority (Scotland) Act 1969.
2 The fact that a pupil has passive capacity was overlooked by the Inner House in *Finnie v Finnie* 1984 SLT 439.

conception or subsequently.[1] Where the parents never marry, the father will not be the child's tutor unless he obtains that office by virtue of an order for parental rights under s 3 of the Law Reform (Parent and Child) (Scotland) Act 1986.[2]

On the other hand, a minor has active capacity. But unless he or she has been forisfamiliated ie has left home or set up in business on his or her own or has married, as a general rule the minor's active capacity is limited unless the consent of the minor's curator to the juristic act or the litigation has been obtained. A child's curator is the minor's mother and father, if the father was married to the mother at the date of the child's conception or subsequently.[3] Where the parents never marry the father will not be the child's curator unless he obtains that office by virtue of an order for parental rights under s 3 of the Law Reform (Parent and Child) (Scotland) Act 1986.[4]

Where a pupil or a minor is not represented in litigation by a tutor or curator, the court can appoint a *curator ad litem,* who is a person appointed by the court to ensure that the case is properly conducted and that the pupil's or minor's interests are fully protected.[5]

The parent of a child may appoint any person to be tutor or curator of the child after his or her death, provided the appointment is in writing and signed by the parent and the parent was tutor or curator of the child.[6] Any person so appointed to be a child's tutor, shall, unless the appointment otherwise specifies, become curator of the child when the child attains the age of minority.[7] Where both parents are dead and no tutor has been appointed, any person claiming interest may apply under s 3 of the Law Reform (Parent and Child) (Scotland) Act 1986 to be made the child's tutor and if he or she is appointed will become the

---

1 Section 2(1)(a) and (b) of the Law Reform (Parent and Child) (Scotland) Act 1986; discussed *supra* Ch 8.
2 Parental rights include tutory: s 8 of the Law Reform (Parent and Child) (Scotland) Act 1986.
3 Section 2(1)(a) and (b) of the Law Reform (Parent and Child) (Scotland) Act 1986.
4 Parental rights include curatory: s 8 of the Law Reform (Parent and Child) (Scotland) Act 1986.
5 McLaren *Court of Session Practice* (1916) p 185. A *curator ad litem* will be appointed, for example, if the child is suing his tutor or curator. Since the *curator ad litem* has no role regarding the person of the child he cannot consent to the taking of a sample of blood, bodily fluid or tissue from a pupil: *Imre v Mitchell* 1958 SC 439; on blood and DNA tests see *supra* Ch 8. A *curator ad litem* will also be appointed if there is a conflict of interest between the parent and the child: see, for example, *Briandon v Occidental Petroleum (Caledonia) Ltd* 1990 SLT 322.
6 Section 4(1) of the Law Reform (Parent and Child) (Scotland) Act 1986: such an appointment can also be made if the parent would have been the child's tutor if he or she had survived until after the child's birth.
7 Section 4(2) of the Law Reform (Parent and Child) (Scotland) Act 1986.

child's curator when the child reaches the age of minority, unless the court otherwise directs.[1] A minor who has no curator, may petition the Court of Session to appoint curators.[2]

CONTRACTUAL OBLIGATIONS

The general view is that a pupil has no legal capacity to perform juristic acts: accordingly any contract entered into by a pupil is null.[3] Consequently, a pupil who has purported to contract on his or her own behalf, cannot be sued on the contract. A tutor can, of course, enter into a contract on the pupil's behalf, but such a contract is liable to be set aside on the grounds of minority and lesion.[4]

A minor who has no curators or who has been forisfamiliated has full contractual capacity, but his or her contracts may be reduced on the grounds of minority and lesion.[5] If a minor has a curator, he or she can contract with the consent of the curator but again the contract is subject to reduction on the grounds of minority and lesion. Where, however, a minor who has a curator purports to contract without the curator's consent, the general rule is that the contract is null.[6] If necessaries are supplied to a minor, the minor must pay for them.[7] If a minor makes contracts in the course of trade or business, the minor is bound by these contractual obligations, whether or not he or she has a

---

1 Section 3(3) of the Law Reform (Parent and Child) (Scotland) Act 1986. If there is no application under s 3, the court can appoint a tutor-dative or factor *loco tutoris*: see TB Smith *A Short Commentary on the Law of Scotland* (1962) pp 383–388.
2 Section 12 of the Administration of Justice (Scotland) Act 1933.
3 Stair I 6.35: I 10.13; Bell *Principles* 2067. There is, however, an alternative view that while the contract is null against the pupil, it is enforceable by the pupil if the contract is in the pupil's interests. Where money is lent to a pupil and used for his or her benefit, the pupil is liable in so far as he or she is enriched: *Scott's Trustee v Scott* (1887) 14 R 1043. A pupil may also be liable to pay a reasonable price for 'necessaries' supplied to him or her.
4 See *infra* p 167.
5 A minor can, in effect, enter into all juristic acts, for example, make a gift of moveables. A minor cannot, however, make a gift of heritage: Erskine *Institute* 1.7.33. Nor can a minor insist that a debtor make a capital payment unless the minor gives security that the money will be properly invested: this is to protect the debtor if the receipt or discharge of the debt is later challenged on the ground of minority and lesion: on this see *infra* p 167.
6 Stair I 6.33; Bell *Principles* 2088; *Boyle v Woodypoint Caravans* 1970 SLT (Sh Ct) 34. Some authorities suggest that a minor may sue upon the contract if the contract is in the minor's interests.
7 This is the position at common law but there is now a statutory obligation to pay a reasonable price for 'necessary' goods.

curator and whether or not the curator has consented to the contract.[1] The contract must, however, be related to the minor's business.[2] Such contracts are not reducible on the ground of minority and lesion. Finally, a minor has capacity to enter into a contract of apprenticeship[3] or a contract of employment[4] without his or her curator's consent. These contracts are, however, reducible on the grounds of minority and lesion.[5] A minor will, however, be bound by a contract of any type if he or she fraudulently induced the other party to contract with him or her, for example, by misrepresenting that he or she is an adult: in these circumstances, a minor will also be barred from seeking reduction on the grounds of minority and lesion.[6]

As we have seen, where a tutor has contracted on behalf of a pupil or where a contract has been made by a minor who has no curators or has been made with the curator's consent, the contract may be reduced on the grounds of minority and lesion. An action of reduction must be brought in the Court of Session.[7] The onus is on the pursuer to show that he or she suffered 'enorm lesion' as a result of his immaturity when entering into the contract: in other words, it must be shown that the consideration which the minor got at the time the contract was made was immoderately disproportionate to that which the minor might have obtained.[8] Lesion will be presumed in certain transactions, for example, gratuitous obligations or loans to a minor.[9] Reduction must be sought before the expiry of the four year period after the pupil or minor has reached majority: this is known as the *quadriennium utile*. Thus the contract can be challenged at any time until the minor reaches the age of 22.[10] While the matter is not beyond doubt, it is thought that an action of reduction can be sought before the age of majority, and

---

1 Erskine *Institute* I 7.38.
2 Cf *O'Donnell v Brownieside Coal Co* 1934 SC 534 (Discharge of claim to damages for injuries sustained at work does not amount to a contract in the course of a business).
3 *Stevenson v Adair* (1872) 10 M 919.
4 *M'Feetridge v Stewarts & Lloyds Ltd* 1913 SC 773.
5 *Stevenson v Adair* (1872) 10 M 919 per Lord President (Inglis) at 920; per Lord Ardmillan at 922.
6 Stair I 6.44; Erskine *Institute* 1.7.36; *Kennedy v Weir* (1665) Mor 11658; *Wemyss v Creditors* (1637) Mor 9025.
7 A challenge on the ground of minority and lesion can also be made *ope exceptionis* ie as a defence to an action for breach of contract, in proceedings in either the Court of Session or the sheriff court.
8 *Robertson v Henderson & Sons Ltd* (1905) 7 F 776 per Lord President (Dunedin) at 785.
9 Stair I 6.44; Erskine *Institute* I.7.37.
10 Ie adding 4 years to the age of majority which is now 18: Age of Majority (Scotland) Act 1969.

therefore the pupil or minor need not wait until he or she reaches the age of eighteen before making the challenge.[1]

There is force in the contention that these rules are now anachronistic. Reform of the law on the legal capacity and responsibility of minors and pupils has been recommended by the Scottish Law Commission.[2] The Commission recommended that the current distinction between pupils and minors be abolished and replaced by a two tier system whereby young people under the age of 16 would generally have no active legal capacity while those aged 16 and 17 would have full legal capacity, subject to the right to apply before the age of 21 to have the court set aside prejudicial transactions which they had entered when 16 or 17 years old. While the general policy of this recommendation is to be welcomed, its simplicity is undermined by detailed exceptions to the general rule. For example, a person below the age of 16 could have capacity to enter transactions 'of a kind commonly entered into by persons of his age and circumstances' provided the terms were not unreasonable. Similarly, certain transactions could not be set aside on the grounds that they are prejudicial, for example, a transaction made in the course of the applicant's trade, business or profession. In these circumstances, reform of this area of the law should, perhaps, await a full scale reform of the law on children's rights.[3]

DELICT

Where a pupil is injured by the wrongous or negligent act of another, the child's tutor can sue for damages in delict on his or her behalf. Similarly, where a minor is injured he or she can bring an action for damages in delict with the curator's consent. Where a child is injured by his or her parent, an action for damages in delict is competent:[4] in these circumstances, a *curator ad litem* will be appointed.

Conversely, both pupils and minors can be liable in delict for their wrongful acts if the requisite intention or negligence can be established. Since children are rarely wealthy or insured, there are few, if any, cases where they have been sued for damages in delict. This will, of course, not apply if a minor motorist causes injury through negligent driving. More importantly, it has been held that a pupil or minor can be

---

1 Bell *Principles* 2098; *M'Feetridge v Stewarts & Lloyds Ltd* 1913 SC 733; *Patrick v William Baird & Co* 1926 SN 101; 1927 SN 32. The action will, of course, have to be brought by the child's tutor or curator.
2 *Report on the Legal Capacity and Responsibility of Minors and Pupils*, SLC No 110.
3 The Age of Legal Capacity (Scotland) Bill 1989, which would have implemented the Scottish Law Commission's recommendations, failed to be enacted.
4 *Young v Rankin* 1934 SC 499; *Wood v Wood* 1935 SLT 431.

guilty of contributory negligence, leading to a reduction of the pupil's or minor's damages when he or she has been injured. Thus in *McKinnell v White*,[1] for example, Lord Fraser reduced the damages of a five year old child by fifty per cent on the basis that the child had been contributorily negligent when he ran in front of a speeding motorist. Lord Fraser justified his decision on the basis that any child living in an urban area would be bound to be aware by the age of five of the danger of traffic.[2]

It should be noted that parents are not automatically vicariously liable for the delicts of their children[3] but a parent will incur personal liability if as a result of the parent's negligence, this caused or contributed to the child's delict, for example, failure to supervise a child properly.[4]

Where a child's parent has been killed as a result of the wrongous or negligent act of another, a child may claim damages in respect of the parent's death under the Damages (Scotland) Act 1976. The fact that the child's parents were never married to each other is irrelevant.[5] Damages are available for loss of support suffered or likely to be suffered as a result of the parent's death and also a 'loss of society award' is available for the loss of non-patrimonial benefits, for example, the parent's affection and guidance.

SUCCESSION

A pupil lacks capacity to make a will. At common law a minor could test on moveable property without a curator's consent: but a minor could not test on heritage. However, s 28 of the Succession (Scotland) Act 1964 gives a minor full legal capacity to dispose by will of heritable as well as moveable property without his or her curator's consent.[6]

A child's right to legitim out of a deceased parent's moveable estate has already been discussed.[7]

---

1 1971 SLT (Notes) 61.
2 Ibid at 62.
3 But, of course, the parents would be liable if they had authorised the child's action or the child was acting as an employee of his parents.
4 *Hastie v Magistrates of Edinburgh* 1907 SC 1102; *Hardie v Sneddon* 1917 SC 1.
5 Para 15 of Sch 1 to the Law Reform (Parent and Child) (Scotland) Act 1986.
6 There was a limited exception in respect of wills made during active service by virtue of the Wills (Soldiers and Sailors) Act 1918, s 3(2).
7 *Supra* p 56.

MARRIAGE

At common law, a minor had the capacity to marry without his or her curator's consent. It was only as a result of the Age of Marriage Act 1929, that the age of capacity to marry was raised to 16 for both sexes.[1]

CRIMINAL LIABILITY

In Scots law, the age of criminal responsibility is only eight.[2]

ALIMENT

Perhaps the most important right which a child enjoys vis à vis his parents is the right to aliment from them. The law of aliment of children has been radically reformed as a result of the Family Law (Scotland) Act 1985.[3]

By s 1(1)(c) an obligation of aliment is owed by a father or mother to his or her child. *Both* parents are under an obligation to aliment their children. Thus liability must be divided between the father and the mother: aliment is no longer the primary responsibility of the father of a child.[4] The fact that the parents have never married each other is irrelevant.[5] However, s 1(1)(d) also places an obligation on a person to aliment a child who has been accepted by him or her as a child of the family.[6] The absence of a blood tie is irrelevant. The obligation to aliment is therefore extended beyond parents and natural children to include, for example, step-parents and stepchildren. But s 1(1)(d) would equally apply where a grandparent brings up a grandchild or an uncle or aunt brings up a nephew or niece.[7] It is not clear whether the acceptor must have a family before the child is accepted but it is expressly provided by s 27 that family includes a one-parent family.

But before the obligation arises under s 1(1)(d) the child must have been 'accepted' as a child of the family. This could give rise to difficulties. Consider the following example.

---

1 See now the Marriage (Scotland) Act 1977, s 1, discussed *supra* Ch 2.
2 Children and Young Persons (Scotland) Act 1937, s 55; Criminal Procedure (Scotland) Act 1975, ss 170, 369.
3 In this section, references are to the 1985 Act unless otherwise stated.
4 *Scully v Scully* 1989 SCLR 757; *Howarth v Howarth* 1990 SCLR 162.
5 Para 21 of Sch 1 to the Law Reform (Parent and Child) (Scotland) Act 1986.
6 Foster parents are not obliged to aliment children who have been boarded out by a local or other public authority or a voluntary organisation: s 1(1)(d).
7 See, for example, *Inglis v Inglis and Mathew* 1987 SCLR 608.

EXAMPLE

H and W are married. W has a child. The presumption of paternity in s 5 of the Law Reform (Parent and Child) (Scotland) Act 1986 will apply. If, however, H later rebuts the presumption and establishes that he is not the child's father, does he owe the child an obligation of aliment? Section 1(1)(c) is inapplicable as H is not the child's father. Section 1(1)(d) may not apply if the court took the view that H did not accept the child as a child of his family because he did not know that the child was not his and had, therefore, not agreed with W to accept another man's child as a child of his family.[1]

It is hoped that the Scottish courts will construe s 1(1)(d) as objectively as possible but the difficulty could have been avoided if the criterion was whether a person had 'treated', as opposed to 'accepted', the child as a child of the family.[2]

A child for the purposes of aliment means a person under the age of eighteen or a person between the ages of eighteen and twenty-five who is reasonably and appropriately undergoing instruction at an educational establishment, or training for employment or for a trade, profession or vocation.[3] Thus, for example, while a parent's obligation to aliment a child continues while the child attends university,[4] the obligation to aliment a mentally handicapped child prima facie ceases when the child reaches the age of eighteen.

The obligation of aliment is to provide such support as is reasonable in the circumstances,[5] having regard to the factors which the courts use to determine the amount of aliment, *viz* the needs[6] and resources of the parties, their earning capacities and generally all the circumstances

---

1 There is English authority that a non-parent does not accept a child as a child of the family unless there was full knowledge on the part of the non-parent of the child's paternity and he agreed to accept the child as a child of his family: *P(R) v P(P)* [1969] 3 All ER 777, sub nom *P v P* [1969] 1 WLR 898; cf *Kirkwood v Kirkwood* [1970] 2 All ER 161, [1970] 1 WLR 1042, DC; *Snow v Snow* [1972] Fam 74, CA.
2 'Treated' is now the criterion for maintenance of a child in English law: see, for example, the Matrimonial Causes Act 1973, s 52(1).
3 Section 1(5)(a) and (b). See, for example, *Jowett v Jowett* 1990 SCLR 348.
4 Provided he or she is under the age of 25.
5 Section 1(2).
6 In *McGeachie v McGeachie* 1989 SCLR 99 the child was an infant and the mother was in receipt of child benefit: the court reduced an award of aliment on the ground that it was too generous in the light of the baby's existing needs! To be fair, this was an application for interim aliment.

of the case.[1] Where two or more parties owe an obligation of aliment to a child, while there is no order of liability, the court, in deciding how much, if any, aliment to award against any of those persons, must have regard to the obligation of aliment owed to the child by the other person(s).[2] The following examples illustrate how this provision operates in practice.

EXAMPLE 1

H and W are married. They had a child, C. Both H and W therefore have an obligation to aliment C: s 1(1)(c). In quantifying the amount of aliment H should pay, the court must have regard to the fact that W also owes an obligation of aliment to C. Thus, if H was unemployed and W was in well paid employment, the court could take the view that H should only be ordered to pay a fraction of the required aliment, or, indeed, no aliment at all, leaving C to pursue a claim against W.

EXAMPLE 2

A, mother, and B, father, have a child, C. Both A and B therefore have an obligation to aliment C: s 1(1)(c). A later marries H, who accepts C as a child of his family. H therefore has an obligation to aliment C: s 1(1)(d). In quantifying the amount of aliment H should pay, the court must have regard to the fact that both A and B owe an obligation of aliment to C. Thus, even if H was in employment, the court could take the view that H should only be ordered to pay a fraction of the required aliment, leaving C to pursue claims against A and his father, B.

1 Section 4(1). The court may take into account any support given by the defender to any person whom he maintains as a dependant in his household, whether or not the defender owes the dependant an obligation of aliment, for example, a mistress' children: s 4(3)(a). Conduct is irrelevant unless it would be manifestly inequitable to leave it out of account: s 4(3)(b). Section 4(3) is discussed in detail in the context of aliment between husband and wife, *supra* p 48.
2 Section 4(2). See, for example, *Inglis v Inglis and Mathew* 1987 SCLR 608 (action of aliment by uncle and aunt, who had accepted the child, against the child's parents: court took into account the fact that the aunt and uncle also owed an obligation to aliment the child).

An action for aliment can be brought by the child.[1] Thus, for example, an eighteen year old child who is attending university, can bring a claim for aliment against his or her parents if they have refused to make the appropriate parental contribution towards his or her grant.[2] Where a child is below the age of eighteen, an action can be brought on his or her behalf by the mother or father of the child, the child's tutor where the child is a pupil, or any person entitled to, seeking or having custody or care of the child.[3] Thus, for example, if a grandmother is caring for her daughter's child, she can bring an action of aliment on the child's behalf against the child's mother and father. A woman, whether married or not, may bring an action for aliment on behalf of her unborn child as if the child had been born, but no such action will be heard or disposed of prior to the birth of the child:[4] however, on granting decree after the birth, the court has power to backdate the aliment to the date of the child's birth.[5]

An action for aliment of a child can be brought even if the child is living with the defender: so, for example, a child can seek aliment from his or her parents while still living at home with them.[6] In these circumstances, however, the parents will have a defence if they can show that they are fulfilling their obligation of aliment and are continuing to do so.[7] Where a couple have separated and the mother, for example, has taken a child under the age of sixteen with her, then if the mother brings an action for aliment on behalf of the child against the father, it is no defence to the action that the father has offered to receive the child into his household and thereby fulfil the obligation of aliment.[8] This is because the question of where a child should live is prima facie an issue for custody proceedings where the child's welfare will be the paramount consideration.[9] However, where the child is over the age of 16, the father will have a defence to a claim for aliment, if he had offered a home to the child which it was reasonable to expect

---

1 Section 2(4)(a). Where the child is below the age of 18, a *curator ad litem* will be appointed if the action is not pursued by the tutor or brought with the consent of the child's curator: where a minor is incapax the action can be brought by the child's curator: s 2(4)(b). A minor without curators can, of course, sue alone. See, for example, *Wilson v Wilson* 1987 GWD 21–788.
2 See *Jowett v Jowett* 1990 SCLR 348.
3 Section 2(4)(c).
4 Section 2(5). This provision is important, if, for example, the father was about to remove himself from the jurisdiction.
5 Section 3(1)(c).
6 Section 2(6).
7 Section 2(7).
8 Section 2(8).
9 On custody proceedings, see *infra* Ch 11.

the child to accept.[1] In determining whether it was reasonable for the child to accept such an offer, <u>the defender's conduct will be taken into account.</u>[2] Thus, for example, it might not be reasonable for a daughter to accept her father's offer of accommodation if the father's unreasonable behaviour towards her mother had led to the breakdown of the marriage and had been a cause of distress to both the mother and the child.[3]

While an action for aliment *simpliciter* is competent in both the Court of Session and the sheriff court,[4] in practice, a claim is more likely to be made in the course of other proceedings, such as declarator of parentage, actions for parental rights, custody, separation, divorce and financial provision.[5] For example, when a woman has a child, if she seeks declarator of parentage,[6] she can bring a claim for aliment on behalf of her child against the alleged father in the same proceedings: if parentage is established, aliment can be ordered from the father of the child.

Similarly, in an action for divorce, the pursuer can bring claims for aliment on behalf of the children of the marriage: these will include not only the spouses' children but any children accepted by either of them as children of the family.[7] As we have seen,[8] any claims for aliment for the children must be satisfied before the court will order financial provision for the spouses. Where at any stage in the proceedings, an action for divorce or separation is dismissed, the court is not prevented from making inter alia an order for aliment for any children of the family.[9]

<u>Aliment takes the form of periodical payments</u>, whether for a definite or indefinite period or until the happening of a specified event.[10]

---

1 Section 2(8).
2 Section 2(9).
3 See, for example, *McKay v McKay* 1980 SLT (Sh Ct) 111. In *Bell v Bell* Sh Ct (unreported) the father's offer was held to be unreasonable as his daughter lived with her mother after the divorce and was currently engaged in higher education in a different town.
4 Section 2(1).
5 Section 2(2).
6 Section 7 of the Law Reform (Parent and Child) (Scotland) Act 1986.
7 Section 1(1)(c) and (d). Aliment can be awarded directly to the child but payable to the custodial parent: see *Huggins v Huggins* 1981 SLT 179. However, there are now no tax advantages in the 'Huggins' formula.
8 *Supra* Ch 7.
9 Section 9(1) of the Matrimonial Proceedings (Children) Act 1958; s 21 of the Family Law (Scotland) Act 1985.
10 Section 3(1)(a): for example, aliment could be ordered until the child reaches the age of 18.

The court cannot substitute a lump sum for a periodical payment.[1] But the court can order alimentary payments of an occasional or special nature to meet special needs which it would be unreasonable to expect the claimant to meet out of a periodical allowance:[2] this could, for example, be an order to pay school fees. It must be stressed, however, that this provision is not intended to enable a court to make an order for a substantial capital sum in lieu of a periodical allowance. Aliment is an obligation of a continuing nature reflecting, in this context, the continuing relationship between a parent and child. It is not to be used as a way of anticipating a child's rights of succession in respect of his or her parent's estate. On a material change of circumstances, an award of aliment can be varied or recalled.[3] The variation can be backdated to the date when the action is brought or, on special cause shown, to an even earlier date,[4] for example, to the date when the payer became unemployed.[5] These provisions are retrospective and therefore apply to awards of aliment made before the 1985 Act came into force.[6]

There is now no obligation on a child to aliment his or her parent, however wealthy the child or indigent the parent. Where a child is wealthy in his or her own right, a parent can use the child's income for his or her maintenance or education: resort will rarely be made to the child's capital for these purposes, unless the parent's circumstances are so reduced that he or she cannot aliment the child.[7]

Finally, the discretionary nature of awards of aliment must be emphasised. What a child will actually receive as an award of aliment depends not only on the child's needs but also the resources of his or her parents. For children of low income families, awards of aliment will be small. Increasingly, resort will have to be made to income support for basic maintenance of children whose parents are unemployed. Both parents are under a statutory obligation to maintain their natural children until the age of sixteen.[8] Where a parent has failed to aliment a child under the age of sixteen, the DSS can take proceedings against the parent for a contribution to any income support paid in respect of the child. It will be noted that this statutory obligation only

1 Section 3(2).
2 Section 3(1)(b).
3 Section 5(1).
4 Section 5(2) incorporating s 3(1)(c) by inference.
5 *Abrahams v Abrahams* 1989 SLT (Sh Ct) 11; *cf Hannah v Hannah* 1988 SLT 82.
6 Ie 1 September 1986. See s 5(1); *Nixon v Nixon* 1987 SLT 602; *Matheson v Matheson* 1988 SLT 238. This also applies in respect of actions for interim aliment: *Donaldson v Donaldson* 1988 SLT 243.
7 *Polland v Sturrock's Exors* 1952 SC 535.
8 Section 26(3) of the Social Security Act 1986.

continues until the child is sixteen, while the right to aliment under the Family Law (Scotland) Act 1985 prima facie continues until the child reaches the age of eighteen.[1]

1 Section 1(5): it will continue until the child reaches the age of 25, if the child is reasonably and appropriately undergoing instruction at an educational establishment, or training for employment or for a trade, profession or vocation.

10 Parental rights in respect of the care and upbringing of children

INTRODUCTION[1]

It is a hallmark of a democratic society that while parents have the primary responsibility for the care of their children, they are free to bring up their children in the manner which they deem best for their children's welfare. Accordingly, parents enjoy important rights in respect of the care and upbringing of their children. However, parental autonomy is not absolute. The criminal law protects children from serious physical, emotional or sexual abuse by their parents. Moreover, if a parent neglects or physically ill-treats a child, the child can be made subject to compulsory measures of care under the Social Work (Scotland) Act 1968 and can, if necessary, be removed from the care of the parent.[2] But within these parameters, Scots law gives parents the right to choose a child's religion, the right to decide how a child should be educated, the right to discipline the child, the right to consent to medical treatment on his or her behalf and the right to determine, generally, the place and manner in which the child's time is spent. These parental rights are given to parents to enable them to fulfil their responsibilities towards their children. As a child gains maturity, increasingly the child will wish to make important decisions in relation to such matters as medical treatment for him or herself. Accordingly, it is submitted that the nature of a parental right alters as the child matures: beginning with the right to take decisions on the child's behalf, it will become, in time, a right merely to give advice to the child, and, eventually, when the child gains sufficient maturity even that right will cease.

The purpose of this chapter is to examine the nature and extent of parental rights. We shall consider a) who is entitled to exercise

---

1 On proposals for reform, see generally *Parental Responsibilities and Rights, Guardianship and the Administration of Children's Property* SLC Discussion Paper No 88. The paper was published at too late a stage for detailed discussion in this edition.
2 On the Social Work (Scotland) Act 1968, see *infra* Ch 13.

parental rights, b) the duration of parental rights, and c) how parental rights must be exercised, illustrating the principle involved by considering several of the most important parental rights. It must, however, be emphasised at the outset, that this is one of the most controversial areas of contemporary family law and that many of the issues to be discussed have not been the subject of recent authoritative decisions in the Scottish courts.

WHO CAN EXERCISE PARENTAL RIGHTS?

When a child is born, the mother has parental rights.[1] The child's father will also have parental rights if he was married to the child's mother at the date of the child's conception or subsequently.[2] Where a child's father never marries the child's mother, he will not have parental rights in respect of the child unless these are granted to him under s 3 of the Law Reform (Parent and Child) (Scotland) Act 1986. In s 3 proceedings, the welfare of the child is the paramount consideration.[3] Moreover any person claiming interest, for example, a grandparent who has care of a grandchild, may apply for an order relating to parental rights under s 3. Where two or more persons have a parental right, each of them can exercise the right without the consent of the other(s).[4]

Parental rights are widely defined. They mean tutory, curatory, custody or access and 'any right or authority relating to the welfare or upbringing of a child conferred on a parent by any rule of law'.[5] But it is not at all clear in what capacity a parent exercises rights in respect of the care and upbringing of a child in Scots law. There is little difficulty where a child is born to parents who were married at the date of the child's conception and who together bring up the child. Both parents are the child's tutors and according to the traditional view, it is by virtue of being the child's tutor that each can exercise rights in respect

---

1 Section 2(1)(a) of the Law Reform (Parent and Child) (Scotland) Act 1986.
2 Section 2(1)(b) of the Law Reform (Parent and Child) (Scotland) Act 1986. A marriage for this purpose includes a voidable marriage and a void marriage provided the father believed in good faith that the marriage was valid, whether or not that belief was due to an error of fact or law: s 2(2). Cf doctrine of putative marriage, discussed *supra* p 158. See, generally, *supra* p 161ff.
3 Section 3(2) of the Law Reform (Parent and Child) (Scotland) Act 1986: s 3 proceedings are discussed *infra* Ch 11.
4 Section 2(4) of the Law Reform (Parent and Child) (Scotland) Act 1986.
5 Section 8 of the Law Reform (Parent and Child) (Scotland) Act 1986.

of the child's care and upbringing.[1] But what happens if the couple divorce and custody is granted to the mother?[2] Both parents will still remain the child's tutors but does it follow that the non-custodial parent retains the full complement of parental rights in respect of the care and upbringing of the child? In the present writer's view, parents enjoy these rights not because they are the child's tutors, but because they will usually have custody of their child. In other words, these parental rights cluster under the umbrella of custody, a concept relatively underdeveloped in Scots law. It follows, therefore, that if the father loses custody, he will no longer have these parental rights although he will remain the child's tutor and, in that capacity, he can continue to administer the pupil's property and represent the child in litigation.[3] The rights in respect of the child's care and upbringing will vest exclusively in the custodial parent, the mother. Similarly, if custody was granted to a third party, for example, a grandparent, he or she would have parental rights, not the child's parents even if they continued to be the child's tutors.

To summarise the argument: it is contended that parental rights in respect of the care and upbringing of a child are an integral part of the concept of custody. Parents exercise these rights not in their capacity as the child's tutors or curators, but because they prima facie have custody of the child. It follows, therefore, that if a parent loses custody, it will be the custodial parent – or any third party who has been granted custody – who will have parental rights in relation to the child's care and upbringing.

THE DURATION OF PARENTAL RIGHTS

According to the traditional theory that a parent exercises parental rights in his or her capacity as the child's tutor, these rights came to an abrupt end when the child reached minority ie twelve in the case of a girl, fourteen in the case of a boy. This conclusion followed from the proposition that while a tutor had power over a pupil's person, a curator had only rights in respect of the child's property: *tutor datur*

---

1 At common law, a father was the tutor of his legitimate children and exercised the *patria potestas* ie parental rights over him. It was only as a result of s 10(1) of the Guardianship Act 1973 that a mother became the tutor of her legitimate children: s 10 has now been repealed: Sch 2 to the Law Reform (Parent and Child) (Scotland) Act 1986. An illegitimate child had no tutors at common law – the mother of an illegitimate child only became the child's tutor as a result of a court order to that effect.

2 On custody disputes, see *infra* Ch 11.

3 And, it is thought, become the child's curator along with the mother when the child attains minority.

personae curator rei. According to this thesis, a minor is deemed to have capacity to determine his or her own life style and the parents, in their capacity as the child's *curators*, have no right to be involved in the minor's decisions. While there is considerable authority to support this view,[1] it is thought by the present writer to be too simplistic.

First, there is authority that some parental rights continue even although a child has reached the age of minority. In *Stewart v Thain*,[2] for example, it was accepted by the court that a parent had the right physically to chastise an unruly fifteen year old boy.[3] More importantly, in the leading case of *Harvey v Harvey*,[4] the Inner House of the Court of Session recognised that a parent's rights over a child who was not forisfamiliated did not cease when the child reached minority. The Lord Justice Clerk (Inglis) expressly stated that the court would be reluctant to give countenance to a doctrine which would allow a twelve year old girl, 'to desert the paternal mansion, and fix her own present residence, and thereby her future fate and course of life, in defiance of all parental control'.[5] Parents retained some rights over their child not from

> 'any notion of his [the minor's] incapacity to exercise a rational judgment or choice, but rather on the one hand, from a consideration of the reverence and obedience to parents which both the law of nature and the Divine law enjoin, and, on the other hand, from a regard to the *inexperience and immaturity of judgment* on the part of the child, which requires friendly and affectionate counsel and aid'.[6]

Thus a parent has the right to give advice to a minor who is not forisfamiliated, when as a result of his or her inexperience and immaturity, a minor is about to embark on a course of conduct which could be detrimental to the child's interests. Finally, the Law Reform (Parent and Child) (Scotland) Act 1986 recognises that some parental rights – though it does not specify which – continue until a minor reaches the age of eighteen.[7]

If, as has been contended,[8] parents exercise parental rights, not in their capacity as tutors, but because they have custody of their child,

---

1 See, for example, Norrie, 1985 SLT (News) 157; cf Thomson, 1985 SLT (News) 223.
2 1981 SLT (Notes) 2.
3 The case was concerned with a teacher's right of chastisement, but it is inherent in the judgments that a parent's right to discipline a child extends beyond pupillage.
4 (1860) 22 D 1198.
5 Ibid at 1208.
6 Ibid at 1209; italics added.
7 Section 8.
8 *Supra* p 179.

these rights will not automatically come to an end when the child reaches minority. Instead, as the authorities discussed in the previous paragraph suggest, they will continue throughout minority until the parents lose custody or the child is forisfamiliated or he or she reaches the age of eighteen. However, it must be emphasised, that parental rights over a minor are less extensive than those exercised over pupils. As we shall see in the next section,[1] parental rights must be exercised for the benefit of the child. Where a minor is mature in judgment, in determining a course of action which will further his interests, great weight must be given by parents to the child's own wishes. It is particularly important to emphasise this point as the most important right which a custodial parent has in respect of a minor is the right to give counsel and aid to the child to influence the minor from making a decision which would be prejudicial to his or her welfare.[2] In exercising their right to proffer advice, parents must therefore take the minor's own wishes into account. In the present writer's view, parents have no power to veto the minor's decision unless the child's proposed course of action is clearly against the minor's interests, but in determining whether or not the proposed conduct is in fact against the child's interests, the wishes of a mature minor will be crucial.[3] In this way, it is possible to reconcile the continuation of paternal rights in respect of minors and the child's 'right' to self-determination as he or she matures.

To summarise the argument, it is submitted that because parental rights are an integral part of the concept of custody, they do not automatically end when a child reaches minority. However, in exercising rights over minors, in particular the right to proffer counsel and advice, parents must give increasing weight to the child's own wishes as he or she matures. Where the minor understands the nature and effect of his or her proposed conduct, a parent has no right of veto unless the minor's proposed conduct would clearly be against his or her interests.

Whatever the extent of a minor's 'right' to self-determination at common law, a minor's freedom to determine his or her own life style is greatly restricted by a large number of statutes designed to protect a minor from consenting to acts which he or she might later regret. While at common law it was not an offence for a man to have sexual intercourse with a consenting minor, it is now a criminal offence to have sexual intercourse with a female under the age of sixteen, even if she

1 *Infra* p 182.
2 *Harvey v Harvey* (1860) 22 D 1198.
3 This point is more fully discussed in the context of the right to consent to medical treatment, *infra* p 188.

has consented.[1] A male cannot lawfully engage in private consensual homosexual acts until he and his partner are twenty-one.[2] There are general prohibitions on the sale of alcohol to persons under the age of eighteen[3] and the sale of tobacco to persons under the age of sixteen.[4] Stringent controls existed on the employment of young people, particularly those under the age of sixteen.[5] Moreover, it is, for example, an offence to tattoo a young person under the age of eighteen[6] or to hypnotise a young person at a public entertainment if he or she has not reached the age of eighteen,[7] or to admit a person under eighteen to a betting shop.[8] The minimum age for driving a motor car is, of course, seventeen.[9] As a result of such paternalistic legislation, the state attempts to prevent the exploitation of children and also endeavours to prevent children from engaging in conduct which is potentially damaging to themselves.

THE NATURE OF PARENTAL RIGHTS

In this section it is proposed to discuss some of the most important parental rights in relation to the care and upbringing of children. In the present writer's view the rights of parents over their children are only prima facie rights, in the sense that any purported exercise of such a right in relation to custody, access, discipline, education, religious training or the medical treatment of a child must further the child's welfare or, at least, must not be against the child's interests: this is known as the welfare principle. If a purported exercise of a parental right is against a child's interests, there will, in those circumstances, be no obligation on a third party, for example, a doctor or social worker, to act in accordance with the parent's wishes. The ultimate arbiter of whether or not a purported exercise of parental rights is in fact contrary to a child's welfare, should be a court of law. Although the Court of Session has inherent protective jurisdiction over children,[10]

---

1 Sexual Offences (Scotland) Act 1976, s 3 (sexual intercourse with a girl under the age of 13); s 4 (sexual intercourse with a girl between the ages of 13 and 16); s 5 (indecent behaviour towards a girl between the ages of 12 and 16).
2 Criminal Justice (Scotland) Act 1980, s 80.
3 Licensing (Scotland) Act 1976, s 68.
4 Children and Young Persons (Scotland) Act 1937, s 18.
5 See, for example, Children and Young Persons (Scotland) Act 1937, s 28, as amended by the Employment of Children Act 1973. These controls have been relaxed as a result of s 10 of the Employment Act 1989.
6 Tattooing of Minors Act 1969, s 1.
7 Hypnotism Act 1952, s 3.
8 Betting, Gaming and Licensing Act 1963, s 10(1) and Sch 4, para 2.
9 Road Traffic Act 1972, s 4(1).
10 See, for example, *Docherty v McGlynn* 1983 SLT 645.

petitioning the Court is inconvenient and will take time: this is particularly important in this context where time will often be of the essence. Not surprisingly, perhaps, recourse to the Court's inherent protective jurisdiction is rare. Scots law presently lacks the equivalent of the wardship jurisdiction of the High Court in England, where issues relating inter alia to the purported exercise of parental rights can speedily be determined. However, any person 'claiming interest' may apply to a court for an order '*relating* to parental rights':[1] this, it is submitted, is sufficiently wide for the court to entertain an application which is concerned with the wisdom of a purported exercise of parental rights, for example, a parent's consent to the sterilisation of a mentally handicapped daughter.

Physical possession of a child

A parent has the prima facie right to the physical possession of his or her child. But as this is only a prima facie right, it must be exercised according to the welfare principle. Thus a parent may lose the possession of a child if it would be against the child's interests to remain with or be returned to the parent.

This is illustrated by the leading case of *J v C*,[2] a decision of the House of Lords in an English appeal, but accepted as authoritative in Scotland.[3] When a couple had a child, they were advised that because of the child's health, he should remain with foster parents in England and not return with his parents to Spain where the family lived. The parents left their child in England, but retained contact with him through visits etc. When, several years later, the child's health had improved, the parents decided that the child should come to Spain and live there with the rest of the family. The child was made a ward of court. The court had then to determine whether or not the parents should be permitted to take their child to Spain. The proceedings were protracted and the case was eventually heard by the House of Lords. The House decided that in spite of the fact that the parents' conduct was unimpeachable, the child should nevertheless remain with his foster parents in England. After eight and a half years, the boy had become integrated into his foster parents' family and to remove him to Spain would be likely to cause him distress and possible long term psychological harm: and so the parents could not exercise their prima

---

1 Section 3(1) of the Law Reform (Parent and Child) (Scotland) Act 1986. For full discussion of s 3, see *infra* Ch 11.
2 [1969] 1 All ER 788, [1970] AC 668, HL.
3 See *Cheetham v Glasgow Corpn* 1972 SLT (Notes) 50.

facie right to the possession of their child because it would be contrary to the child's interests to allow them to do so.

J v C is therefore authority for the proposition that the parental right of custody of a child is governed by the welfare principle.[1] Accordingly, a parent cannot with validity exercise the right if it is not in the best interests of the child to do so.

Access

When a parent loses custody of a child, he or she will be denuded of most of the parental rights in respect of the child's care and upbringing. However, some rights will remain.[2] In the present writer's view the most important of these is the right of access to the child[3]. But again this is only a prima facie right in the sense that it must be exercised in accordance with the welfare principle[4]. This point was forcibly made by Lord Dunpark in *Porchetta v Porchetta*.[5] After the wife had divorced her husband, he sought access to their eighteen months old son. The child did not know his father who had had little, if any, contact with the child. The mother was hostile towards her husband because of his bad treatment of her. In these circumstances, Lord Dunpark held that access would be against the child's interests as, given the unhappy relationship between the parents, access would simply be the occasion of further ill-feeling and the child would suffer. In the course of his judgment Lord Dunpark said:—

'The father's application for access was made by him on his own admission, because he is the father. He gave no other reason for his application. A father does not have an absolute right to access to his child. He is only entitled to access if the court is satisfied that that is in the best interests of the child'.[6]

---

1 See, in particular, the speech of Lord McDermott, [1970] AC 668 at p 701. This is now enacted in s 3(2) of the Law Reform (Parent and Child) (Scotland) Act 1986.
2 For example, the right to refuse to agree to the child's adoption, see *infra* Ch 13: on rights in respect of education, see *infra* p 186.
3 The matter is not without difficulty: in *Girvan v Girvan* 1988 SCLR 493, Sheriff Mitchell suggested that a parent loses the right of access if custody is awarded to the other parent and no order for access was made: '. . . if there is no award of access to the non-custodial parent his or her legal rights as a parent are excluded. The court by making an award of access reinstates to the limited extent specified in the access order one of the rights which the parent formerly enjoyed'; ibid at 496. It is thought this analysis is unsound; see Thomson 1989 SLT (News) 109.
4 Access disputes are discussed in detail, *infra* Ch 11 at pp 205 ff.
5 1986 SLT 105.
6 Ibid at 105.

Moreover, section 3(2) of the Law Reform (Parent and Child) (Scotland) Act 1986[1] provides that in *inter alia* access proceedings the welfare of the child is the paramount consideration and the court cannot make an order unless satisfied that it would be in the child's interests to do so. Thus it would appear that in order to enforce the right of access, a parent must establish that contact with the child is positively in the child's best interests[2]. This undermines the value of treating access as a parental *right*[3] in the sense that it is to be assumed that access is for the benefit of the child unless the defender establishes that access would be against a child's interests in a particular case. In other words, access should be regarded as a *prima facia* right and the non-custodial parent should be allowed to exercise the right unless it would be contrary to the child's interests to do so.[4]

In spite of these theoretical problems, in practice the courts generally take the view that access by a non-custodial parent is in the child's best interests. When the child is a minor, the child's wishes on the matter must be taken into account: if the minor genuinely does not wish to retain contact with the parent, access will not be ordered as, in the circumstances, it will no longer be in the child's interests.

Discipline

A custodial parent has the right to discipline a child. This can include physical chastisement.[5] In theory, the exercise of this right must be in accordance with the welfare principle: in practice, physical chastisement must be reasonable. Excessive physical ill-treatment of a child will lead to criminal proceedings for cruelty[6] and will constitute grounds for compulsory measures of care under the Social Work (Scotland) Act 1968.[7] Thus, where the parent's intention is to punish the child, no crime is committed and no ground for compulsory measures of care exists, provided the force used is moderate: it is irrelevant

---

1 Discussed in detail *infra* Ch 11.
2 The position is the same in England: *Re KD (a minor)* [1988] AC 806. The 'right' exists but is without substance as the welfare principle ultimately prevails.
3 Access is defined as a parental 'right' in s 8 of the Law Reform (Parent and Child) (Scotland) Act 1986.
4 For full discussion, see Thomson 1989 SLT (News) 109.
5 The recognition of this right is inherent in the decision of the European Court of Human Rights in *Campbell v Cosans* (1982) 4 EHHR 293. In that case, the Court indicated that at least the threat of a strapping using the tawse did not amount to torture or inhuman or degrading treatment.
6 Section 12(1) of the Children and Young Persons (Scotland) Act 1937: s 12(7) provides that a parent's and teacher's right to discipline is not affected.
7 On the Social Work (Scotland) Act 1968, see *infra* Ch 13.

that the parent lost his or her temper at the time of the chastisement.[1]
On the other hand, a conviction was upheld when an angry parent
slapped her child on the face, knocking him over, since this was an act
'as remote from reasonable chastisement as one could possibly
imagine.'[2]

In Scots law, school teachers have an independent right from
parents physically to chastise school children.[3] This right is, however,
analogous to that of a parent.[4] In *Stewart v Thain*,[5] it was held that a
school teacher could lawfully physically chastise a fifteen year old boy.
Thus, it is submitted that a parent's right of discipline can also be
exercised over a minor. While the exercise of this right is limited by the
welfare principle,[6] it is thought that there are more practical limitations: a mother, for example, may find difficulty in disciplining her
son for refusing to dry the dishes if he is a fifteen year old, twelve stone
prop forward.

Education

Parents are under a duty to ensure that their children receive a suitable
education until they reach the age of sixteen.[7] In particular, they must
ensure that the child attends school.[8] In order to fulfil these obligations, a parent has the right to choose a child's education. This right
must be exercised in accordance with the welfare principle.[9] In practice, unless the parent has sufficient means to afford private education,
the exercise of this right will be limited. However, parents' rights to
choose a local authority school which is suitable for the needs of their
children have been strengthened as a result of legislation.[10]

1 *B v Harris* 1990 SLT 208. (Mother lost her temper and strapped daughter who had called her 'a fucking bastard'!)
2 *Peebles v MacPhail* 1990 SLT 245 at 246. In other words the inference of intention to assault or punish could be drawn from the seriousness of the parent's conduct. See also *Cowie v Tudhope* 1987 GWD 12–395 where a father who had hit his 15-year-old son with the leg of a table was convicted of assault.
3 Local authority schools have, however, banned the use of the tawse as a result of the decision in *Campbell v Cosans* (1982) 4 EHHR 293. See s 48A of the Education (Scotland) Act 1980.
4 *McShane v Paton* 1922 JC 26.
5 1981 SLT (Notes) 2.
6 For example, it would be contrary to a 17 year old girl's interests to be beaten by her father.
7 Sections 30–31 of the Education (Scotland) Act 1980.
8 Section 35 of the Education (Scotland) Act 1980: the parent is relieved of this obligation if the parent provides the child with effective education by other means.
9 *J v C* [1969] 1 All ER 788, [1970] AC 668, HL per Lord McDermott at 702
10 Sections 28 and 28 A–H of the Education (Scotland) Act 1980: see Seager 1982 SLT (News) 291. The right is not absolute: *Keeney v Strathclyde Regional Council* 1986 SLT 490. Note also the parental involvement in school boards: see School Boards (Scotland) Act 1988.

It should be noted that the rights and obligations in respect of a child's education vest not only in the custodial parent but also the child's guardian, any person obliged to aliment the child and any person having day to day care of the child.[1]

Religion

In an increasingly pluralistic society, religious toleration is of the first importance. Scots law recognises that a parent has a prima facie right to choose a child's religion. This right must be exercised in accordance with the child's welfare. Where, for example, a parent's – or, indeed, a child's – religious convictions will result in physical harm to the child, the parents' and the child's wishes will be overridden. Thus, for example, while parents are free to decide that a child should be brought up as a Jehovah's witness, if the child should require a blood transfusion, the law will not countenance the parent's refusal to consent to such an operation.[2]

The Scottish courts have accepted that where parents are of different religions,[3] it matters little to the child whether he or she is brought up in one faith rather than another: the matter will be decided in the light of all the circumstances of the case in accordance with the welfare principle. Thus, for example, in *McNaught v McNaught*,[4] a mother who was a Protestant had custody of the children of the marriage. In spite of the fact that she had agreed to bring up the children in her husband's Roman Catholic faith, the husband failed to obtain an order that at least his youngest child, a son, should continue to be brought up as a Roman Catholic. As it was otherwise in the child's best interests that the mother should have custody, she was free to bring up the child as a Protestant since either faith was for the benefit of the child.

Hitherto, the courts have been adamant that it is in a child's welfare to be brought up in a religious faith. In *M'Clements v M'Clements*,[5] the Lord Justice Clerk (Thomson) said that in his opinion a child 'ought

---

1 Section 135(1) of the Education (Scotland) Act 1980.
2 In practice the child will be removed to a place of safety and the local authority can then assume parental rights and consent on behalf of the child: see *infra* Ch 13. Alternatively, a person could apply for the parental right to consent to medical treatment by bringing proceedings under s 3(1) of the Law Reform (Parent and Child) (Scotland) Act 1986.
3 The cases are concerned with parents of different Christian denominations, but it is thought that the same principles would apply if, for example, one parent was Christian and the other Moslem.
4 1955 SLT (Sh Ct) 9.
5 1958 SC 286.

not to be denied the opportunity of being brought up in the generally accepted religious beliefs of the society in which he lives'.[1] While it is submitted that parents are entitled to bring up their children as atheists or agnostics, if the parents divorce it may be difficult for an aetheistical parent to obtain custody if the other parent will provide religious training. In *Mackay v Mackay*[2] the Lord President (Clyde) said:[3]

> 'Since the paramount consideration in custody cases is the welfare of the child, it would be almost impossible for a court in Scotland to award the custody to an atheist with the prospect of the child being brought up without the solace and guidance of any religious teaching at all.... For atheism and the child's welfare are almost necessarily mutually exclusive, according at least to our standards of civilised society'.

It is interesting to note in this context that religious instruction is a 'compulsory' element in the curricula of public, ie education authority, schools.[4]

A minor, who has sufficient understanding and maturity, can choose his or her own religion. While parents retain the right to advise their child on such matters, they have no power to veto the child's choice, unless the minor's purported course of action would clearly be against the child's interests. This could arise, for example, if the child proposed to join an extreme sect, for example, scientologists.

Medical procedures

Because a pupil has no active legal capacity, a parent has the prima facie right to consent to medical treatment on the child's behalf. However, this right is subject to the welfare principle. There is little Scottish authority on the point, but English decisions are instructive. In *Re D (a minor)*,[5] for example, a mother consented to the sterilisation of her mentally handicapped daughter who had reached the age of puberty. Before the operation took place the child was made a ward of court. The court overrode the mother's decision on the ground that the operation was not in accordance with the welfare of the child. Heilbron J based her decision on the grounds that while mentally handicapped, the child probably had sufficient capacity to enter into

---

1 Ibid at 289.
2 1957 SLT (Notes) 17.
3 Ibid at 17.
4 Education (Scotland) Act 1980, ss 8–10. Religious observance can only be discontinued after a poll of local government electors: s 8(2). Parents can, however, elect that their children should not take part in religious observance or education.
5 [1976] 1 All ER 326, [1976] Fam 185.

marriage, there was no evidence that she was promiscuous and any unwanted pregnancy could be terminated. In those circumstances, the proposed operation was not in the child's interests. On the other hand, in *Re B (a minor)*,[1] the House of Lords held that a sterilisation operation could be carried out on a mentally handicapped girl of 17 who had a mental age of 5. Pregnancy and childbirth would have been physically and mentally disastrous for the young woman and therefore it was in her best interests that the operation go ahead.[2]

The right to consent implies the right to refuse consent to medical treatment. This right must again be exercised in accordance with the welfare principle. Thus in *Re B (a minor)*,[3] the Court of Appeal overrode the parents' refusal to consent to an operation to remove an intestinal blockage from their new born infant who was suffering from Down's syndrome. The parents had taken the view that since the child was mentally handicapped, it was better for the child to die as a result of the blockage rather than live. The Court of Appeal held that this purported exercise by the parents of their prima facie right to withhold consent was not in accordance with the child's welfare. The child had the prospect of a reasonably happy life, albeit suffering from the syndrome. In these circumstances, the Court overrode the parents' decision and consented to the operation on behalf of the child. On the other hand, *Re B (a minor)* was distinguished in *Re C (a minor)*[4] where a new born baby, suffering from congenital hydrocephalus, was dying: it was in the infant's best interests to receive care which merely relieved her suffering and there was no need to give treatment which might achieve a short prolongation of life.

1 [1988] AC 199, [1987] 2 WLR 1213.
2 The court indicated that before such an operation was to be performed, the consent of the court should always be obtained: ibid at 1218, per Lord Templeman. In Scots law this could be done by an application under s 3 of the Parent and Child (Scotland) Act 1986: see Thomson 'Sterilisation of Mentally Handicapped Children' 1988 SLT (News) 1. Given that consent can only be given where it is in the child's best interests to do so, it could be argued that the consent of the court is otiose: however, it is thought that it would nevertheless be prudent to obtain the court's approval in such a sensitive area. In England, the court has approved such an operation on a mentally handicapped adult: in *Re F* [1989] 2 WLR 1025. In Scotland, this result could be obtained by the appointment of a tutor dative who could consent on behalf of the incapax adult.
3 [1981] 1 WLR 1421, CA.
4 [1990] Fam 26. See also *Finlayson (Applicant)* 1989 SCLR 601 where a ground for compulsory measures of care was established when parents refused medical treatment for their haemophiliac son even though they were genuinely concerned that the child might be infected with AIDS as a result of the treatment: the child's physical condition had deteriorated as a result of non-treatment.

Where the proposed treatment is generally accepted as therapeutic, it is thought that a parent's consent to such treatment on a child will be upheld as a valid exercise of the parent's prima facie right, since it would be in the child's best interests to consent. Conversely, where a parent refuses to consent to therapeutic medical treatment on a child, the purported exercise of the prima facie right will be overridden as it would be against the child's interests not to have the benefit of the treatment. More difficulties arise where the proposed medical procedures are not unarguably in the child's best interests. If an analogy be taken from the law on blood tests,[1] *S v S*[2] and *Docherty v McGlynn*[3] suggest that a medical procedure can be carried out on a child provided it is not positively *against* the child's interests to do so. Thus it is submitted that in Scots law parents can lawfully consent to medical procedures on their children which, while not in the child's best interests, are not positively against the child's interests. These would include, for example, non-therapeutic circumcision of male infants,[4] the taking of blood samples from healthy children for the purpose of medical research and the donation of regenerative tissue, for example, bone marrow.[5]

The necessity of parental consent to medical procedures being carried out on minors is a matter of controversy. Where the proposed medical treatment is therapeutic and unarguably for the benefit of the child, a minor who has capacity to understand the nature of the treatment[6] may consent on his or her own behalf and there is no need to obtain the consent of the parents. Thus, for example, a minor could consent to medical treatment for a broken arm or to have a tooth filled. The current medical practice to seek parental consent until the minor reaches the age of sixteen is without legal foundation in Scotland.[7]

But where the proposed medical procedure is not unarguably in the child's interests, for example, the prescription of contraceptives, the termination of a pregnancy, sterilisation, the donation of non-regenerative tissue or certain forms of treatment for mental illness, it is not at all clear that even if the minor understands the nature of the

---

1 Discussed *supra* p 153.

2 [1970] 3 All ER 107, [1972] AC 24 at 45, HL, per Lord Reid.

3 1983 SLT 645.

4 Non-therapeutic female circumcision cannot lawfully be carried out in the United Kingdom: Prohibition of Female Circumcision Act 1985.

5 The donation of non-regenerative tissue, for example, a kidney would be *against* the child's ie the donor's interests: consequently a parent cannot consent to this procedure on behalf of a child.

6 If the minor does not have this capacity, the consent of the parent will still be required.

7 See *Legal Capacity and Responsibility of Minors and Pupils*, SLC Consultative Memorandum No 65, paras 2.47–2.54.

proposed treatment, the minor's parents need not be involved.[1] It has been argued that parents have the right to give advice to a minor who is still in their custody, where the minor's proposed course of conduct could be prejudicial to the child's interests. This right must be exercised in accordance with the welfare principle, but in order that it can be exercised at all, the parents must be informed.

In the case of *Gillick v West Norfolk and Wisbech Area Health Authority*,[2] the House of Lords in an English appeal held that, in exceptional circumstances, a parent need not be informed when a girl under the age of sixteen seeks contraceptives or contraceptive advice from a doctor. There are two threads of reasoning in the speeches of the majority. Lord Scarman took the view that parental rights exist only in so far as a child lacks the capacity to take decisions for him or herself: thus when a girl has sufficient understanding, intelligence and maturity to make decisions in relation to inter alia sexual matters, the parent's rights cease.[3] But whether or not the child has gained this degree of maturity is a question of fact and it is difficult to see how this will be determined, particularly in relation to sexual matters. Parents will argue that a child has not reached that degree of maturity when the child's proposed course of conduct appears to be contrary to the parent's concept of what is in the best interests of the child. Lord Fraser, on the other hand, did not deny that the parents had a prima facie right to be informed. But he maintained that there could be exceptional circumstances where this was not necessary *viz* when the child (i) understood the nature and effect of contraceptives, (ii) had been persuaded to consult her parents but had refused, (iii) was likely to have or continue to have sexual intercourse without contraceptives, (iv) her physical or mental health would suffer without contraceptive advice, and (v) that it was in the child's best interests to be prescribed contraceptives without the parents' knowledge or consent. Whether an exceptional case had arisen could in his Lordship's opinion safely be left to the clinical judgment of the doctor concerned.[4] It should be noticed that before Lord Fraser's exception applies, the proposed course of treatment must be in the child's best interests. This could provide a solution to the problem where a minor refuses to have medical treatment which would be in the child's best interests, for example, a blood transfusion. Since the minor is acting *against* his or

---

1 On this difficult subject, see, for example, Skegg 'Consent to Medical Procedures on Minors', (1973) MLR 370.
2 [1985] 3 All ER 402, HL.
3 Ibid at 422.
4 Ibid at 413.

her interests, Lord Fraser's exception would *not* apply and the parental consent would be valid. In other words, if Lord Fraser is correct, a minor can in exceptional circumstances consent without the parent's knowledge to medical procedures which are in the minor's interests but cannot refuse to consent to such procedures if this would be clearly against the minor's interests.

Gillick was, of course, an English decision and is not binding on Scottish courts. However, to the extent that the House of Lords rejected the contention that parents have a right to veto such treatment on a minor, it is consistent with the present writer's view of the Scottish position outlined in this chapter. But, it is precisely because such medical procedures are not unarguably in the child's best interests that parents of minors who have not been forisfamiliated have the right to be informed and give advice to their minor children before they embark on a course of action which they might later regret. In the context of the prescription of contraceptives to girls under the age of sixteen, her parents have the right to proffer advice, to discuss, for example, whether or not it is in her long term interests to enter sexual relationships at such an early age. If they persuade her that this is not in her interests, then no further difficulties arise, but if they do not, they cannot prevent her obtaining contraceptives, unless it is clearly prejudicial to her interests to do so. In the case of a sexually active minor who is determined to continue to have sexual intercourse, it is the present writer's view that the Scottish courts would accept that it was not against her interests to be prescribed contraceptives without her parents' consent. But this would be a decision that the parents had purported to exercise their rights improperly, ie in a way which was contrary to the welfare principle – not that the right to be informed does not exist.[1]

It is thought that a similar approach would be taken in respect of other medical procedures. If, for example, a fourteen year old minor sought termination of a pregnancy, then even if she understood the nature of the proposed termination, her parents have the right to be informed in order to discuss with her the alternatives to termination and the possible long term effects on her of having an abortion. If the child was still determined to have the termination, it is submitted that any purported veto by her parents would be ineffective as it is surely against a child's interests to compel her to continue with an unwanted pregnancy.[2] On the other hand, if, for example, parents purported to veto a fourteen year old boy's decision to donate a kidney for a school

---

1 Cf the approach of Lord Scarman, ibid at 402.
2 See, for example, *Re P (a minor)* (1982) 80 LGR 301.

friend, the parent's decision would probably be upheld as the child will probably lack the maturity to understand the implications of such an operation and it is prima facie contrary to his interests to donate non-regenerative tissue.

Names

Parents have the right to name their children. It is customary for a child to take the surname of his father. Difficulties arise, however, when parents divorce and the mother obtains custody of the children of the marriage. If she remarries, can she lawfully change the children's surname to that of their step-father? While a custodial parent has the right to name a child, this is a prima facie right which must be exercised in accordance with the welfare principle. If, as a result of the retention of their surname, the children are experiencing difficulties at school or settling into their new family, it could be argued that it would be in their best interests to alter their surnames. On the other hand, the retention of their original surname is a valuable link in maintaining the children's relationship with their father: this would be particularly important, if the children knew their father before the divorce and access was operating satisfactorily. In those circumstances, unless there was evidence of genuine distress to the children in being known by their original surname, as opposed to inconvenience for the mother and step-father, it is submitted that it would be contrary to the children's interests to alter the surname and any purported exercise by the mother of her right to do so would be contrary to the welfare principle. On the other hand, if the children had had little contact with their father, there would be a strong case that a change of surname to that of their step-father would be in the children's interests as this would strengthen their relationship with their step-father who is, in the circumstances, the only father figure that they have known.[1]

---

1 *W v A* [1981] 1 All ER 100, [1981] Fam 14, CA; cf *Cosh v Cosh* 1979 SLT (Notes) 72.

11 Actions in relation to parental rights

INTRODUCTION

As we have seen, a mother has parental rights in relation to her child.[1] The child's father will also have the full complement of parental rights if he was married to the child's mother at the date of conception or subsequently.[2] But it is also possible for persons to acquire parental rights as a result of a court order. Indeed, the father of a child who has not married the child's mother has no parental rights unless and until such an order is successfully obtained. Moreover, where the parents are married, it is likely that in the event of a divorce, one of them will be deprived by court order of rights in relation to the care and upbringing of the child. The purpose of this chapter is to discuss the procedures which are applicable and the principles which are applied in litigation relating to parental rights.

Parental rights are widely defined to include 'tutory, curatory, custody or access . . . and any right or authority relating to the welfare or upbringing of a child conferred on a parent by any rule of law'.[3] It has been argued that the most important rights relating to the care and upbringing of a child, are clustered under the concept of custody.[4] Thus if a parent is awarded custody on divorce, the effect of the order is to deprive the other parent of these rights and to give the custodial parent the right to exercise them exclusively. Not surprisingly most litigation is concerned with the custody of the child.

PROCEDURE

Independent applications for parental rights

At common law, any person who had a proper interest in relation to a

---

1 *Supra* p 161.
2 Section 2(1)(a) and (b) of the Law Reform (Parent and Child) (Scotland) Act 1986.
3 Section 8 of the Law Reform (Parent and Child) (Scotland) Act 1986.
4 *Supra* pp 178 ff.

child domiciled in Scotland, could seek an order for custody or access. Originally an application had to be made to the Nobile Officium of the Inner House of the Court of Session[1] but later this jurisdiction was transferred to the Outer House.[2] As a result of s 5(2) of the Sheriff Courts (Scotland) Act 1907, the sheriff court had a similar extensive jurisdiction. Thus, for example, actions by grandparents for the custody of or access to grandchildren were competent.[3]

This traditional liberal approach to title to sue for custody is evident in s 3(1) of the Law Reform (Parent and Child) (Scotland) Act 1986 which provides:

> 'Any person claiming interest may make an application to the court for an order relating to parental rights and the court may make such order relating to parental rights as it thinks fit'.

Thus *any* person, for example, the father of a child who has not married the child's mother, other relatives of the child, a step-parent or foster parents, can apply under s 3 to obtain parental rights, including custody.[4] Moreover, s 3 applications can be brought by persons who already have parental rights. Thus, for example, if the parents of the child are married, either spouse could bring an application under s 3 for the exclusive custody of the child or for a ruling where there was disagreement over how a particular right should be exercised.[5] An application for a specific parental right, for example access, is competent: there is no need to apply for the full range of parental rights.[6]

For the purpose of s 3(1) applications relating to custody or access, a child is a person under the age of sixteen:[7] in relation to parental rights other than custody or access, a child is a person under the age of

---

1 *S v S* 1967 SC (HL) 46.
2 RC 189(a) as amended by Act of Sederunt of 30 January 1970.
3 *S v S* 1967 SC (HL) 46; *Syme v Cunningham* 1973 SLT (Notes) 40.
4 *M v Lothian Regional Council* 1989 SCLR 151 approved 1990 SLT 116. Cf the restrictive construction taken in *AB Petr* 1988 SLT 652 criticised by Thomson 1987 SLT (News) 165. See also *Whyte v Hardie* 1990 SCLR 23.
5 Where two or more persons have parental rights, each can exercise a parental right without the consent of the other(s): s 2(4) of the Law Reform (Parent and Child) (Scotland) Act 1986.
6 *Nolan v Lindsay* 1990 SCLR 56.
7 Section 8 of the Law Reform (Parent and Child) (Scotland) Act 1986.

eighteen.[1] An application can be brought in the Court of Session or the sheriff court.[2]

Notwithstanding the generality of s 3(1), s 47(2) of the Children Act 1975 imposes restrictions on the award of custody to a person other than the child's parent, tutor, curator or guardian. Where the parents of a child have never married, 'guardian' includes the father if he has obtained an order granting him parental rights.[3] Section 47(2)[4] provides that custody of a child shall not be granted in any proceedings to a person other than a parent, tutor, curator or guardian of a child unless

a) the applicant being a relative or a step-parent of the child, has the consent of a parent, tutor, curator or guardian of the child and has had care and possession of the child for the three months preceding the making of the application for custody: a relative means a grand-parent, brother, sister, uncle or aunt, whether of the full-blood or half-blood or by affinity;[5] or

b) the applicant, not being a relative or a step-parent of the child, has the consent of a parent, tutor, curator or guardian of the child and before making the application, has had care and possession of the

1 Section 8 of the Law Reform (Parent and Child) (Scotland) Act 1986: where the parental rights in issue relate to tutory or curatory, the child must be a pupil or minor respectively.
2 Section 8 of the Law Reform (Parent and Child) (Scotland) Act 1986; s 5(2C) of the Sheriff Courts (Scotland) Act 1907. Jurisdiction is based on the child's habitual residence in Scotland (or sheriffdom): s 9 of the Family Law Act 1986. The presence of the child in Scotland (or sheriffdom) will suffice if the child is not habitually resident in any part of the United Kingdom and, in the case of an application in the sheriff court, the pursuer or defender is habitually resident in the sheriffdom: s 10 of the Family Law Act 1986. In an emergency, jurisdiction can be taken on the presence of any child in Scotland (or sheriffdom) if it is necessary to make such an order immediately: s 12 of the Family Law Act 1986. Habitual residence of the child in Scotland (or sheriffdom) is a basis for jurisdiction in an application for tutory or curatory: s 16 of the Family Law Act 1986.
3 Section 47(5)(a) of the Children Act 1975 which provides that guardian has the same meaning as in the Adoption (Scotland) Act 1978, s 65: s 65 has been amended by para 18(4) of Sch 1 and Sch 2 to the Law Reform (Parent and Child) (Scotland) Act 1986. Thus, for example, a father of an illegitimate child who has obtained access under s 3, would be a guardian for the purposes of the Adoption (Scotland) Act 1978 and his agreement is prima facie necessary for the adoption. On adoption, generally, see *infra* Ch 12. Guardian also includes a person appointed to that office by deed or by an order of a competent court.
4 As amended by para 14 of Sch 1 and Sch 2 to the Law Reform (Parent and Child) (Scotland) Act 1986.
5 Section 55 (1) of the Children Act 1975 as amended by para 14 of Sch 1 to the Law Reform (Parent and Child) (Scotland) Act 1986: in determining whether a person is a relative, the fact that the child is illegitimate is irrelevant: s 55(2) as amended by para 14 *supra*, which provides that s 1(1) of the 1986 Act applies when construing these provisions in the Children Act 1975.

child for a period or periods which amounted to at least twelve months and included the three months preceding the application; or

c) where the consent of a parent, tutor, curator or guardian of the child has not been obtained, the applicant before making the application, has had care and possession of the child for a period or periods which amounted to at least three years and included the three months preceding the application; or

d) while not falling within paragraph a), b) or c), the applicant can show cause why an order should be made awarding him or her custody of the child.

The existence of s 47(2)(d) renders the other provisions unnecessary.[1] As we shall see,[2] custody will only be granted to an applicant if it is established that it is in the child's best interests to do so; if it can be shown that it would be in the child's best interests for the court to be awarded custody to the applicant, then s 47(2)(d) will be satisfied.

More importantly, where an application for custody is made by a person who is not a parent of the child, notice must be given of the application to the child's parents, if known.[3] Notice must also be given to the local authority where the child resides within seven days of making the application:[4] the local authority can then carry out an investigation into all the circumstances and make a report to the court on the proposed arrangements for the care of the child. While the application is pending, if the applicant has had care and possession of the child for at least three years, the child cannot be removed from the applicant's custody against the applicant's will.[5] This protection extends to local authority foster parents who apply for custody of a child who has been fostered with them.[6]

If in an application for custody under s 3(1) of the Law Reform (Parent and Child) (Scotland) Act 1986, the court takes the view that there are exceptional circumstances making it impracticable or undesirable for the child to be entrusted to either of the parents or to any

---

1 See Wilkinson, 1976 SLT (News) 221 and 237 at p 241; *Clive* pp 553ff.
2 *Infra* p 200.
3 Section 48(1) of the Children Act 1975: as s 1(1) of the Law Reform (Parent and Child) (Scotland) Act 1986 applies to the construction of this section, parent includes the father of a child who has never married the child's mother.
4 Section 49 of the Children Act 1975.
5 Section 51 of the Children Act 1975. It is a criminal offence to do so: s 51(3). The child can, however, be removed on the authority of a court or by virtue of authority under another enactment, for example, a place of safety order: see *infra* Ch 13.
6 Section 51(2) of the Children Act 1975.

other individual, it has the power to commit the child to the care of a specified local authority.[1]

Ancillary actions for parental rights

Section 9(1) of the Conjugal Rights (Scotland) (Amendment) Act 1861[2] provides that

> 'In any action for divorce, judicial separation or declarator of nullity of marriage the court may make, with respect to any child of the marriage to which the action relates, such order (including an interim order) as it thinks fit relating to parental rights, and may vary or recall such order'.

This provision gives the courts jurisdiction to make ancillary orders in relation to parental rights, including custody and access,[3] in actions for divorce, judicial separation or declarator of nullity of marriage.[4] A 'child of the marriage' includes not only a child of both parties to the marriage but also a child of one party to the marriage who has been accepted by the other party as a child of the family.[5] However, there must be a blood tie between the child and at least one of the parties to the marriage: the mere fact that the child has been accepted as a child of the family does not suffice.[6] When the action is concerned with custody or access, the court has jurisdiction to make or vary orders until the child reaches the age of sixteen.[7]

In practice, most actions for custody will be brought in actions for divorce. As we have seen,[8] the effect of an award of custody in this situation is to deprive the non-custodial parent of rights in relation to

---

1 Section 11(1)(a) of the Guardianship Act 1973, as amended by s 48(3) of the Children Act 1975: alternatively, the child can be placed under the supervision of the local authority: s 11(1)(b) of the 1973 Act. The court has the power to order a local authority to make a report into the child's circumstances before making its decision: s 12(2) of the 1973 Act.
2 As substituted by para 2 of Sch 1 to the Law Reform (Parent and Child) (Scotland) Act 1986. Such an order can be varied, recalled or set aside by the court: s 9(2) of the 1861 Act, as substituted by para 1 of Sch 1 to the Family Law Act 1986.
3 Parental rights has the same meaning as in the Law Reform (Parent and Child) (Scotland) Act 1986: s 9(2)(a) of the 1861 Act.
4 An order can be made even if the action is dismissed provided an application for a custody order was made before the action was dismissed: s 9 of the Matrimonial Proceedings (Children) Act 1958; s 13 of the Family Law Act 1986.
5 The difficulties inherent in the concept of acceptance as a child of the family are discussed in the context of aliment, *supra* pp 170 ff.
6 *Bradley v Bradley* 1987 SCLR 62.
7 Child has the same meaning as in the Law Reform (Parent and Child) (Scotland) Act 1986: s 9(2)(b) of the 1861 Act: discussed *supra* p 195.
8 *Supra* p 194.

the care and upbringing of the child – with the result that the custodial parent will exercise these rights exclusively. Custody is therefore a crucial issue when a marriage breaks down. Its importance is reflected in s 8(1) of the Matrimonial Proceedings (Children) Act 1958, which provides that a court shall not grant a decree of divorce, judicial separation or declarator of nullity of marriage, unless and until the court is satisfied as respects every child for whose custody the court has jurisdiction to make provision in that action:

'a) that arrangements have been made for the care and upbringing of the child and that those arrangements are satisfactory or are the best which can be devised in the circumstances; or

b) that it is impracticable for the party or parties appearing before the court to make any such arrangements.'

However, this provision can be ignored if there are circumstances making it desirable that decree should be granted without delay and the court has obtained a satisfactory undertaking from either or both of the parties to bring the question of the arrangements for the children before the court within a specified time.[1] The court has the power to appoint an appropriate local authority 'to investigate and report to the court on all the circumstances of the child and the proposed arrangements for the care and upbringing of the child'.[2] The report will often contain recommendations with regard to the residence and custody of the child and, while the decision is that of the court alone,[3] in practice the recommendations will usually be followed.[4] However, the use made of this power is not extensive,[5] though it is more likely to be used in the small number of cases where custody is disputed by the parties. Because of this, it is unlikely that in practice s 8 does ensure that the best custodial arrangements are made for children who are potentially at risk. Even if social background reports were made mandatory in all cases, it is considered that in the vast majority of cases they would simply confirm the custody arrangements agreed by the parties. In

1 Section 8(2) of the Matrimonial Proceedings (Children) Act 1958.
2 Section 11 of the Matrimonial Proceedings (Children) Act 1958, as amended by para 43 of Sch 8 to the Social Work (Scotland) Act 1968. The judge may also interview the children: *Blance v Blance* 1978 SLT 74; *Cosh v Cosh* 1979 SLT (Notes) 72; *Fowler v Fowler* 1981 SLT (Notes) 9; *Mason v Mason* 1987 GWD 27–1021; *Carlyon v Carlyon* 1987 GWD 38–1349. In *Mooney v Mooney* 1987 GWD 3–80 the child's views were ignored as too young.
3 *MacIntyre v MacIntyre* 1962 SLT (Notes) 70.
4 Eekelaar and Clive *Custody After Divorce* (1977, Oxford) p 53. Hereafter referred to as *Eekelaar and Clive*.
5 *Eekelaar and Clive* found that the use varied between 3% and 20% of cases depending on the court.

these circumstances, the resources involved would be better spent on supporting child welfare agencies.[1]

Provision for custody and access is made in the decree of divorce but the court has the power to make provision relating to parental rights even if the action for divorce etc is dismissed.[2] Interim orders are competent. As the court has the power to make such order relating to parental rights as it thinks fit,[3] it can award custody to a person other than one of the parties to the marriage. In exceptional circumstances, the child can be committed to the care of a local authority[4] or placed under the supervision of the local authority.[5] Orders for custody or access can be varied or recalled until the child reaches the age of sixteen.[6]

THE WELFARE PRINCIPLE[7]

Section 3(2) of the Law Reform (Parent and Child) (Scotland) Act 1986 provides that:

> 'In any proceedings relating to parental rights the court shall regard the welfare of the child involved as the paramount consideration and shall not make any order relating to parental rights unless it is satisfied that to do so will be in the interests of the child'.

Like its predecessor, s 1 of the Guardianship of Infants Act 1925, s 3(2) applies to *all* proceedings which are concerned with parental rights.[8] Accordingly, the child's welfare is the paramount consideration both in proceedings under s 3(1) of the Law Reform (Parent and Child) (Scotland) Act 1986 and ancillary proceedings in an action of divorce,

---

1 For discussion of the issues, see *Clive* pp 560–562. The court now has power to recommend conciliation in relation to custody issues: Rules 170B(15) and 260D(10) (Court of Session): Rule 132F (Sheriff Court).

2 Section 9 of the Matrimonial Proceedings (Children) Act 1958; s 21 of the Family Law (Scotland) Act 1985.

3 Section 9(1) of the Conjugal Rights (Scotland) (Amendment) Act 1861.

4 Section 10 of the Matrimonial Proceedings (Children) Act 1958 as amended by Sch 8 to the Social Work (Scotland) Act 1968.

5 Section 12 of the Matrimonial Proceedings (Children) Act 1958 as amended by Sch 9 to the Social Work (Scotland) Act 1968.

6 Section 9(1) of the Conjugal Rights (Scotland) (Amendment) Act 1861. See for example, *Beaney v Beaney* 1987 GWD 36–1268.

7 For a full discussion of the development of this principle in the context of divorce proceedings, see *Clive* pp 564–574.

8 *J v C* [1969] 1 All ER 788, [1970] AC 668, HL: followed in *Cheetham v Glasgow Corpn* 1972 SLT (Notes) 50; *G v H* 1976 SLT (Sh Ct) 51.

judicial separation or declarator of nullity of marriage. In particular, the welfare of the child is the paramount consideration in relation to actions for custody or access. While the welfare of the child is the paramount consideration, all the factors of the case are considered to the extent that they point to the course of action which is best for the child. As Lord MacDermott explained in *J v C*,[1] the welfare principle connotes

> 'a process whereby, when all the relevant facts, relationships, claims and wishes of parents, risks, choices and other circumstances are taken into account and weighed, the course to be followed will be that which is most in the interests of the child's welfare . . .'[2]

Thus specific factors remain relevant in so far as they pertain to the child's welfare. However, in determining what is best for the child's welfare, a judge will be influenced not only by medical and psychological knowledge of the development of children but, inevitably, by his or her own conception of how a child should be brought up. This is recognised in the rule that in a custody case, an appellate court will not interfere with the decision of the judge at first instance unless the court is satisfied either that the judge exercised his or her discretion upon a wrong principle, or that the decision is so plainly wrong that the judge must have exercised his or her discretion wrongly.[3]

It was the earlier practice of the Court of Session in divorce actions to apply a presumption that the 'innocent' spouse whose conduct was not responsible for the breakup of the marriage, should be granted custody: this presumption was rebuttable on evidence that it would be against the child's welfare to award custody to the innocent spouse.[4] However, such a presumption is incompatible with the s 3(2) principle that the welfare of the child is to be the paramount consideration in parental rights proceedings and is anachronistic given that the Scots law of divorce is now, theoretically at least, based on the non-fault concept of irretrievable breakdown of marriage.[5] Instead, a person's 'conduct' should only be relevant in so far as it suggests that it would not be in the child's best interests to award that person custody of the

---

1 [1969] 1 All ER 788, [1970] AC 668, HL at 710–711.
2 In *Campins v Campins* 1979 SLT (Notes) 41 at 42, Lord Cameron emphasised that nothing can override or be superior to the child's welfare.
3 *Britton v Central Regional Council* 1986 SLT 207; *Early v Early* 1990 SLT 221.
4 *Hume v Hume* 1926 SC 1008.
5 See *supra* Ch 6. In *Clark v Clark* 1987 GWD 35–1240 the court suggested that a child's parents had a pre-eminent right to custody unless they were unwilling, unable or unfit to retain control of the child. It is submitted that this approach is also inconsistent with the s 3(2) principle.

child. So, for example, if all other factors suggest that it would be in a child's interest that the mother should have custody, the fact that the mother was an adulterous wife is irrelevant. Similarly, it should also be irrelevant that a woman is a prostitute provided she is a competent mother and has satisfactory accommodation for the child: but if the accommodation was such that the child was in danger of physical or sexual assault by the woman's clients then the prostitution would be relevant because of its probable effects on the welfare of the child. It is submitted that a similar approach should be taken when the person seeking custody or access is homosexual. However, it is clear that a parent's sexual orientation has been considered to be an important factor. In *Early v Early*,[1] a mother lost custody of her child who had lived happily with her for several years: the court held, *inter alia*, that the boy who was approaching adolescence required a suitable male role model and could better adjust to his mother's sexuality if he lived with his father and siblings.[2]

In weighing up the factors which determine what is best for the child, the Scottish courts have given considerable importance to ensuring that a child obtains a religious upbringing. The 'solace and guidance' of a religious faith is regarded as so important for the welfare of a child, that on divorce it may be difficult for an atheist spouse to obtain custody if the other spouse is prepared to provide a religious upbringing. Thus, for example, in *M'Clements v M'Clements*,[3] an adulterous mother was awarded custody rather than an atheist father because she would give the children a religious upbringing.[4] When both parties are prepared to offer the child a religious upbringing, there is no bias in favour of any particular Christian denomination, and custody will be determined by weighing up other factors in accordance with the welfare principle.[5]

The Scottish courts have rejected any presumption that the custody of a young child should prima facie be awarded to the child's mother. In the leading case of *Hannah v Hannah*,[6] the Lord Ordinary in a divorce action had proceeded on the basis that it was 'more in accord-

1 1989 SLT 114, approved 1990 SLT 221.
2 However, in *Hill v Hill* 1990 SCLR 238, a child was returned to his homosexual father in Canada on the ground that the father was not a danger to the child, with whom he had had a good relationship.
3 1958 SC 286.
4 Cf *Mackay v Mackay* 1957 SLT (Notes) 17 when the atheist father was awarded custody on condition that the child's grandmother gave the child religious instruction.
5 *McNaught v McNaught* 1955 SLT (Sh Ct) 9: discussed *supra* Ch 10 in the context of parental rights.
6 1971 SLT (Notes) 42.

ance with nature' that a child should be removed from the custody of her father and his mistress where she had been for several years after the marriage had broken down, and be returned to the mother. In reversing the judge's decision, in the Inner House of the Court of Session, Lord Walker observed[1]

> 'What exactly the Lord Ordinary meant by nature, or what precisely nature has to do with it, I must confess I find difficulty in appreciating as a proper test in matters of this kind. It is not nature but the welfare of the child which is the material matter'.

The evidence established that the child, who had lived with her father for six years, was happy and well adjusted: in these circumstances, the Court held that it was in her best interests that custody be awarded to her father.[2]

It is submitted that *Hannah v Hannah* illustrates the most important factor which the court will take into account in determining custody disputes between a child's parents whose marriage has broken down *viz* the preservation of the status quo. Provided a child is secure in the environment where he or she has lived since the breakdown of the marriage, prima facie it is in the child's best interests to remain in the custody of that parent. Thus, for example, in *Whitecross v Whitecross*[3] a mother failed to obtain the custody of a young child who had lived with his father since the breakup of the marriage: the court took the view that it was in the child's best interests not to disturb the continuity of the child's relationship with his father with whom he had been living:

> 'To disturb the situation which admittedly is satisfactory in all respects and would involve removing the child from the custody of a parent with whom he has lived in family since his birth inevitably involves a certain degree of disturbance of his life, the effects of which it is impossible to assess or estimate with any accuracy.'[4]

Consequently, other things being equal, it is considered to be in a child's best interests to preserve the status quo and award custody to

1 Ibid at 43.
2 Nevertheless 'motherly love' can still be an important factor: see, for example, *Clark v Clark* 1987 GWD 35–1240; *Beaney v Beaney* 1987 GWD 36–1268; *McCluskey v Gardiner* 1988 GWD 16–680.
3 1977 SLT 225.
4 Ibid at 228 per Lord Cameron.

the parent who had looked after the child since the breakup of the marriage.[1]

However, it must be stressed that this is only a prima facie presumption. If it is established that it is in the best interests of the child to be moved, the courts will not hesitate to do so. Thus in _Hastie v Hastie_,[2] a child aged nine had been in the care of his father's mother ie the child's grandmother for four years. The grandmother who was 63, attempted to indoctrinate the child against his mother. In these circumstances, Lord Davidson ordered that the custody of the child should be awarded to his mother because this would restore a 'normal' parent-child relationship which was in the child's best interests.[3] Similar concern for a 'normal' family relationship has resulted in a child being removed from the care of his homosexual mother to that of his father.[4] Other factors, for example, if a child would be removed from a school where he was settled, may result in custody being awarded to a parent who has not hitherto had care and control of the child.[5]

Because it is generally accepted that the preservation of the status quo operates for the benefit of the child, an important consequence follows. When a marriage breaks down, the children will, in the vast majority of cases, remain in the care of their mother. Therefore, custody should be awarded to the mother in order to preserve the status quo. In practice, there are few disputed custody cases.[6] Instead, the couple agree that the child should remain in the custody of the parent who has cared for the child since the breakup of the marriage: in the vast majority of the cases, this will be the mother. The award of

1 See, for example, _Jordan v Jordan_ 1983 SLT 539; _Mooney v Mooney_ 1987 GWD 3–80; _Geddes v Geddes_ 1987 GWD 11–349; _Sinclair v Sinclair_ 1987 GWD 16–587; _Carlyon v Carlyon_ 1987 GWD 38–1349; _McDevitt v McDevitt_ 1988 GWD 3–95; _Abernethy v Abernethy_ 1988 GWD 19–811; _Higgins v Higgins_ 1989 GWD 11–454; _Robertson v Robertson_ 1990 GWD 19–1041; _Davidson v Connor_ 1990 GWD 23–1264. The preservation of the status quo is consonant with the 'least detrimental' criteria for custody disputes advocated by Goldstein, Freud and Solnit in their influential book, _Beyond the Best Interests of the Child_ (1973, New York).
2 1985 SLT 146.
3 See also _Clark v Clark_ 1987 GWD 35–1240 (Child removed from grandparents to mother).
4 _Early v Early_ 1989 SLT 114, approved 1990 SLT 221.
5 _Clark v Clark_ 1987 GWD 13–441. See also _Smith v Smith_ 1988 GWD 20–854 (bad influence of mother's lover).
6 _Eekelaar and Clive_ p 52. In the Scottish sample, custody was disputed at the time of the divorce proof in only 1% of the cases.

custody simply reflects this arrangement.[1] Even in the few contested cases, the courts are reluctant to disturb the status quo.[2]

Where parental rights are sought in an independent application, the status quo principle will also be significant. Thus, for example, if a child is living with its mother, it is unlikely that in an application for parental rights, brought under s 3(1) of the Law Reform (Parent and Child) (Scotland) Act 1986, the child's father will obtain custody:[3] he may, of course, be made the child's tutor or be awarded access, as this will not disturb the status quo. Conversely, an award of custody is likely to be made if the child was living with the applicant, for example, a grandmother, for some time before the application. Where a child's parents are cohabiting but are not married, the father should have little difficulty in obtaining full parental rights: but the status quo principle will again be predominant in determining custody if the couple's relationship subsequently breaks down.

In relation to access, the child's welfare will again be the paramount consideration.[4] The courts have accepted that on the breakdown of a marriage, it is prima facie in a child's best interest to retain contact with the non-custodial parent and his or her family, as this reinforces the child's sense of identity.[5] Access will, however, be denied if it would not be conducive to the welfare of the child.[6] In *Porchetta v Porchetta*,[7] for example, a father who had had little, if any, contact with his eighteen month old son before the divorce, was refused access on the ground that given the unhappy relationship between the parents, access would simply be the occasion of further ill-feeling and the child would suffer. Because the father had had no contact with his child before the breakdown of the marriage, *Porchetta* is an exceptional case. Normally *both* parents will have formed relationships with the

---

1 Thus *Eekelaar and Clive* found that the wife was awarded custody in 76% and the husband awarded custody in 9% of the cases: ibid p 56 and Table 34.
2 It is irrelevant whether or not the preservation of the *status quo* favours the child's father or mother. For full discussion, see Maidment, *Child Custody and Divorce* (1984, Croom Helm) pp 61–66.
3 See, for example, the approach taken in *A v N* 1973 SLT (Sh Ct) 34.
4 Section 3(2) of the Law Reform (Parent and Child) (Scotland) Act 1986.
5 *Cooper v Cooper* 1987 GWD 39–1411; *McCabe v Goodall* 1989 GWD 3–114.
6 *Naismith v Naismith* 1987 GWD 17–628; *Puddinu v Puddinu* 1987 GWD 4–105 (access refused for fear child might be wrongfully removed to Italy); *McCash v Toal* 1990 GWD 5–239 (access distressing to the child). The court may, however, suggest that steps be taken so that an award of access can be made at a later date: *Middleton v Middleton* 1987 GWD 27–1020; *Winton v Winton* 1987 GWD 15–551.
7 1986 SLT 105: see also *Johnson v Francis* 1982 SLT 285 when the custodial parent was permitted to take the children to Australia even though this frustrated the non-custodial parent's access: the court took the view that the emigration of the family was in the children's interests. This decision was followed in *Borland v Borland* 1990 GWD 33–1883.

children of the marriage and any natural hostility between the parents resulting from the breakup of their marriage should not per se be sufficient to deny one of the parties from having access to the child and, in this situation, the court should proceed in the usual way and take the view that prima facie access is always in the best interests of the child.[1] Nevertheless, if s 3(2) of the Law Reform (Parent and Child) (Scotland) Act 1986 is read literally, it would appear that access should not be awarded unless there is evidence that access would positively further the child's best interests. While this may be criticised where the applicant already enjoys a prima facie right to access,[2] there is force in the view that an applicant who does not enjoy parental rights, for example, the father of an illegitimate child, should adduce evidence that contact would be in the child's best interests.[3]

In determining whether access is conducive to a child's welfare, the child's own wishes must be taken into account. If a child refuses to see the non-custodial parent, the court will take pains to ensure that the refusal is genuine, before ordering that access should cease.[4] While accepting that it is pointless physically to compel a child to see the non-custodial parent, the Scottish courts have taken the view that it is the duty of the custodial parent,

> 'to tell the child, if necessarily firmly, to go with the person to whom access has been is granted. In other words, the person having custody should do his or her best to ensure that the access granted is in fact enjoyed'.[5]

In practice, the Scottish courts will not grant access unless it is sought by a parent or relative: accordingly, access awards are made in very

---

1 *Porchetta v Porchetta* 1986 SLT 105 is discussed in the context of parental rights *supra* p 184.
2 See discussion *supra* p 185.
3 *Montgomery v Lockwood* 1987 SCLR 525; *McEachan v Young* 1988 SCLR 98. In *McEachan* it was suggested that the standard of proof in s 3(2) is higher than on the balance of probabilities: followed in *Mann v Glending* 1990 SCLR 137. It is submitted that this is incorrect as applications for access are civil proceedings. The approach taken in *Sloss v Taylor* 1989 SCLR 407 and *Crowley v Armstrong* 1990 SCLR 361 that the standard is the balance of probabilities is therefore to be preferred.
4 *Cosh v Cosh* 1979 SLT (Notes) 72; *Clement v Clement* 1987 GWD 18–660; *Brooks v Brooks* 1990 GWD 2–62.
5 *Blance v Blance* 1978 SLT 74 per Lord Stewart at 75; *Brannigan v Brannigan* 1979 SLT (Notes) 73.

few divorce cases.[1] It is thought that this is because the parties will have made their own informal arrangements: research has shown that the existence of an access order bears little relation to the actual factual situation.[2]

CONCLUSION

We have seen how, in theory, any proceedings in relation to parental rights are determined by the welfare principle. But in relation to the custody of children whose parents' marriage ends in divorce, Maidment[3] has concluded that British socio-legal studies have produced three findings:

> 'Firstly, about 94 per cent of divorcing parents agree between themselves the arrangements for the care of their children after the divorce. Secondly, about 90 per cent of these arrangements provide for the mother being the main caretaker in that the children live with her. Thirdly, the court, which need not but usually is asked to confirm the private consensual arrangements, rarely disturbs parents' agreements and almost invariably preserves the residential status quo of the child . . .'

Whatever the theoretical powers of the court, in practice, they will 'rubber stamp' the arrangements which have been negotiated by the parties. In so far as these arrangements will normally confirm that the mother should have custody where she has had the care of the child since the breakup of the marriage, this preserves the status quo. This is thought to be conducive to the child's welfare as it does not disturb the continuity of the child's relationship with the de facto custodial parent. However, an award of custody deprives the non-custodial parent, usually the child's father, of exercising any rights in relation to the care and upbringing of the child. It will often have been agreed that the non-custodial parent should have access but, in practice, this will often become irregular, particularly if the parents subsequently enter into new family relationships. Moreover, the normal custody arrangement

1 *Eekelaar and Clive* found that access awards were made in only 7.9% of divorce cases: ibid p 59 and Table 36. See, for example, *Speirs v Peat* 1988 SCLR 369 at 370. If, however, a non-custodial parent does indeed lose his right of access when custody is awarded, he should be advised to apply for access on divorce: see discussion at p 185, *supra*.
2 Maidment (op cit *supra* p 205 n 2) at p 68.
3 Ibid.

whereby custody is awarded to the mother, operates to reinforce the traditional view that women should bear the major burden of the child-rearing function.

There is growing evidence that children will make a better recovery from the traumatic effects of the breakdown of their parents' marriage when they can sustain an emotional tie with both parents. It has been argued[1] that this can be achieved if parents were given joint custody of their children after divorce, enabling the child to feel secure with both of them – and their new families. While joint custody orders are competent,[2] little use has hitherto been made of them by Scottish courts. The recognition that children continue to need both parents after divorce hopefully will lead to an increase in such orders.[3]

INTERNATIONAL ASPECTS

In recent years there has been growing concern over the problem of child abduction. When, for example, a court has awarded custody to a parent in State A and the non-custodial parent 'kidnaps' the child to State B, it would appear desirable that there should be a quick and easy procedure by which the child should be returned to the custodial parent in State A, always provided that it is not against the child's interests to do so. This matter has been the subject of international conventions which have been enacted in Scotland.[4] These and related issues will be discussed in this section.

Common law

At common law, the Scottish courts will recognise custody decrees granted by the court of the country where the child was habitually resident.[5] However, that decree will only be enforced if it is in the child's best interests to do so as the welfare principle in section 3(2) of the

---

1　Ibid Chs 8–12. This book provides an excellent comprehensive account of the current literature.

2　*Mackenzie v Hendry* 1984 SLT 322; *McKechnie v McKechnie* 1990 SCLR 153. Of course, if no custody order is made in respect of spouses, the result will be joint custody.

3　A similar result to a joint custody order has, however, been achieved by awarding custody to one parent but extensive residential access to the other on a regular basis, for example, a week every fortnight: see *Sinclair v Sinclair* 1987 GWD 18–587.

4　The Child Abduction and Custody Act 1985 implementing (i) the European Convention on Recognition and Enforcement of Decisions concerning Custody of Children (the European Convention) and (ii) the Convention on the Civil Aspects of International Child Abduction (the Hague Convention).

5　Section 26 of the Family Law Act 1986. Previously the courts recognised decrees of the court where the child was domiciled.

Law Reform (Parent and Child) (Scotland) Act 1986 applies in this situation. Accordingly, if it is in the child's best interests to do so, a Scottish court can refuse to enforce the foreign decree and instead make its own order in relation to the custody of the child.[1] In *Sinclair v Sinclair*,[2] for example, Lord Prosser refused to order the return to Germany of children who had been abducted by their father to Scotland in breach of an interim custody order in favour of their mother, on the ground that he was not satisfied that the German court had made sufficient inquiries: the welfare of the children was the paramount consideration and it was in their best interests that the children should remain in Scotland.

United Kingdom Decrees

The common law position has now been overtaken where the 'foreign' decree emanates from a court in another part of the United Kingdom. In these circumstances the custody order[3] is to be automatically recognised by the Scottish courts as having the same effect as an order of the Court of Session.[4] When the custody order has been registered in the Court of Session,[5] proceedings can be brought for its enforcement.[6] The Court of Session has the same powers to enforce the order as if it was its own order.[7]

The European Convention

The European Convention provides for the mutual recognition and enforcement of custody decisions[8] between contracting states. Where a person has obtained a custody decision in a contracting state, he can seek to have it recognised and enforced in Scotland. He can approach 'the central authority' for help in tracing the child and securing the recognition and enforcement of the decision. In Scotland the central authority is the Secretary of State.[9] The custody decision is to be recognised as if it was made by a Scottish court unless there are

---

1 *Campins v Campins* 1979 SLT (Notes) 41.
2 1988 SLT 87.
3 Technically the term 'Part I order' should be used: this defines the relevant orders for parental rights including custody. See s 1 of the Family Law Act 1986 as amended by para 62 of Sch 13 to the Children Act 1989.
4 Section 25(1) of the Family Law Act 1986: the Court of Session is the 'appropriate court' in Scotland: s 32(1).
5 An application for registration is made to the court which made the order and then passed on to the Court of Session: s 27.
6 Section 29 of the Family Law Act 1986.
7 Ibid.
8 Access decisions are also included: article 11.
9 Section 14(1) of the Child Abduction and Custody Act 1985.

grounds upon which the Court of Session can refuse recognition.[1] Once registered in the Court of Session, the decision can be enforced as if it was an order of that Court.[2]

There are several grounds upon which the Court of Session can refuse to recognise or enforce a decision. For the present purpose, the most important are to be found in Article 10.[3] First, a decision will not be recognised if its effects are manifestly incompatible with fundamental principles of the law of Scotland.[4] For example, a decision reached on the basis that the custody of a child should automatically be awarded to the father, would not be recognised as it was made without reference to the welfare of the child and therefore manifestly incompatible with s 3(2) of the 1986 Act. Secondly, a decision will not be recognised if by reason of a change of circumstances, including the passage of time but *not* a mere change in residence, the effects of the decision are manifestly no longer in accordance with the child's welfare.[5] In other words, it must be established that the enforcement of the decision by, for example, returning the child to the custodial parent, would be *manifestly* against the child's interests: the fact that the Court of Session, applying the welfare test, would have reached a different decision from the foreign court is not enough to refuse to recognise or enforce the decision on this ground.

The Hague Convention

The Hague Convention is concerned with the wrongful removal of a child from one contracting state to another. Where a child has been wrongfully removed to or wrongfully retained in Scotland, the parent can seek the help of the Secretary of State, as the central authority in Scotland,[6] to obtain the return of the child. Proceedings for recovery of the child take place in the Court of Session.[7] The removal or retention of the child is wrongful if it is in breach of a parent's rights of custody. These rights can arise *ex lege* or as a result of a custody order.[8] Thus the Convention applies where a person automatically enjoys parental

---

1 Child Abduction and Custody Act 1985, s 15.
2 Ibid, s 18. The Court of Session is 'the appropriate court': ibid, s 27(2).
3 For full discussion see *The Laws of Scotland: Stair Memorial Encyclopaedia* vol 10, paras 1328 ff.
4 Article 10(1)(a).
5 Article 10(1)(b). See generally *Campins Coll* 1989 SLT 33.
6 Section 3(1) of the Child Abduction and Custody Act 1985.
7 The Court of Session is 'the appropriate court': ibid, s 4.
8 Article 3 of the Convention.

rights under the law of a contracting state:[1] there is no need to have obtained parental rights as the result of a custody order.[2] Before the court can proceed to order the return of the child, it must be satisfied that the removal or retention was wrongful ie in breach of the applicant's custody rights.[3]

When satisfied that the removal or retention was unlawful, the court *must* order the return of the child if a period of less than one year has elapsed since the date of the wrongful removal or retention.[4] If more than a year has elapsed, the court should still order the child to be returned unless it is demonstrated that the child is now settled in Scotland.[5] The court can refuse to return the child if satisfied (1) that the applicant did not have custody rights at the time of the removal or retention or had consented to the child's removal or retention *or* (2) that there is a *grave* risk that the child's return would expose the child to physical or psychological harm or otherwise place the child in an intolerable situation.[6] In establishing that there is such a risk, the onus rests on the person objecting to the child's return. The risk has to be greater than that normally to be expected when a child passes from the care of one parent to another: moreover there must be a risk of substantial harm which amounts to the child being placed in an *intolerable* situation. The court can consider what is likely to happen to the child if the child was returned.[7] However, it will only be in exceptional circumstances that such a risk would occur.[8] The fact that the Court of Session, applying the welfare principle, does not think that it is in the child's best interests to be returned is insufficient.[9] The exception must be kept within these strict limits: otherwise the purpose of the Convention *viz* the speedy return of wrongfully abducted children, would be frustrated.[10]

---

1 As, for example, the mother and married father enjoy under Scots law: see *supra* Ch 10. Of course, the applicant must have parental rights: *C v S* [1990] 2 All ER 449.
2 This point appears to have been overlooked in *Hill v Hill* 1990 SCLR 238.
3 Retention is a 'one-off' act of omission or commission: accordingly, the Convention does not apply where a child was retained before the 1985 Act came into force: see *Kilgour v Kilgour* 1987 SCLR 344.
4 Article 12.
5 Ibid.
6 Ibid, Article 13.
7 *Macmillan v Macmillan* 1989 SLT 350.
8 See, for example, *Re E (a minor)* [1989] 1 FLR 135; *C v C* [1989] 1 FLR 11.
9 *Viola v Viola* 1988 SLT 7, in particular at 10, per Lord McCluskey.
10 For the criminal aspects of the law on child abduction, see the *Laws of Scotland: Stair Memorial Encylopaedia* vol 10, paras 1342–1343.

12 Adoption

INTRODUCTION

Adoption is the legal process by which the relationship of parent and child is created by the order of a court. The law has been consolidated in the Adoption (Scotland) Act 1978.[1] The effect of an adoption order is to vest parental rights and duties in relation to the child in the adoptive parents.[2] An adopted child is treated in law as the legitimate child of the adopters, as if he or she had never been the child of any person other than the adoptive parents.[3] Thus the rights and duties of the natural parents towards their child are extinguished when the child is adopted and the child's rights are enforceable against the adopters and not the natural parents.

There are exceptions to the general principle that on adoption the child is no longer regarded as the child of his or her natural parents. In determining prohibited degrees of relationship for the purpose of the law of marriage and incest, the child remains the child of his or her natural parents:[4] in addition, an adopted child cannot marry an adoptive parent.[5] A child who is a citizen of the United Kingdom and Colonies retains that status even if adopted by aliens.[6] A child who is not, will, however, acquire that status if adopted by a citizen of the United Kingdom and Colonies.[7]

---

1 As amended by Part II of Sch 10 to the Children Act 1989 and para 4 of Sch 4 to the Human Fertilisation and Embryology Act 1990. References in this chapter are to the 1978 Act unless otherwise stated. On the law generally, see PGB McNeill *Adoption of Children in Scotland* 2nd edn, 1986

2 Section 12(1).

3 Section 39(1). Where, however, an illegitimate child is adopted by one of his or her natural parents as sole adopter, the child will be treated as the legitimate child of both parents if they subsequently marry: s 39(2). The adoption order can then be revoked: s 46.

4 Section 41(1).

5 Adoptive siblings can marry. For full discussion see *supra* p 22.

6 Section 41(2).

7 Section 40: in the case of a joint adoption, the adoptive father must be a citizen of the United Kingdom and Colonies.

An adopted child remains entitled to certain social security benefits in respect of his or her natural family, for example, death grant:[1] similarly, adoption does not affect a child's entitlement to a pension which was in payment at the time of the adoption.[2] Finally, while, as a general rule, an adopted child is treated for the purposes of the law of succession as the child of the adopters and no other person,[3] the child retains rights in relation to a natural parent's estate if the adoptive parent died before the commencement of the Succession (Scotland) Act 1964 and the natural parent died after the commencement of the Law Reform (Miscellaneous Provisions) (Scotland) Act 1966.[4]

In spite of these exceptions, it must be emphasised that the effect of an adoption order on the child's relationship with his or her natural parents is drastic. Put simply, the natural parents lose all parental rights when their child is adopted. Because of this, the law of adoption must have regard to the rights of parents as well as the interests of the child. While traditionally considered as a way of providing a home for a newborn infant – usually with a childless couple, adoption is increasingly perceived as a long term solution for children in need of care.[5] In these circumstances, adoption orders should not be made without the agreement of the natural parents unless they have clearly forfeited their prima facie rights to bring up their child.

ADOPTION AGENCIES

It is the duty of every local authority to establish and maintain a comprehensive adoption service to meet the needs of all those who are involved in adoption – the children, their parents and the adoptive parents.[6] The facilities to be provided include temporary board and lodging for pregnant women, arrangements for assessing children and prospective adopters, placing children for adoption and providing counsel and advice.[7] The adoption service is to be provided in conjunction with the local authority's other social services, so that help can be given in a co-ordinated manner.[8] Where a local authority does not have an adoption service, it may use the services of an adoption society

1 Sections 41(3), (4) and (5).
2 Section 42.
3 Section 23(1) of the Succession (Scotland) Act 1964.
4 Section 5 of the Law Reform (Miscellaneous Provisions) (Scotland) Act 1966.
5 See *infra* Ch 13.
6 Section 1(1).
7 Section 1(2).
8 Sections 1(3) and (2).

which has been approved by the Secretary of State.[1] For the purpose of the 1978 Act, the local authority adoption service and an approved adoption society is known as an adoption agency.[2]

It is a fundamental tenet of the 1978 Act that all the preliminary arrangements for an adoption should be made by an adoption agency. Accordingly, it is a criminal offence for a person other than an adoption agency to make arrangements for the adoption of a child or place a child for adoption.[3] Both the person who makes the placement and the person who receives the child can be prosecuted.[4]

There are two exceptions where arrangements made by persons other than an adoption agency are lawful. First, a private person can place a child for adoption where the proposed *adopter* is a relative of the child.[5] Thus, for example, a mother can place her child for adoption by her sister ie the child's aunt. Secondly, a children's hearing is entitled to make a requirement that a child who is in need of compulsory measures of care should live with persons who are suitable prospective adoptive parents.[6] This recognises the increasing importance of adoption as a way of providing a long term solution for at least some children in need of care.

WELFARE OF CHILDREN

Section 6 of the Act provides:

> 'In reaching any decision relating to the adoption of a child, a court or adoption agency shall have regard to all the circumstances, first consideration being given to the need to safeguard and promote the welfare of the child throughout his childhood; and shall so far as practicable ascertain the wishes and feelings of the child regarding the decision and give due consideration to them, having regard to his age and understanding'.

Thus at *every* stage of the adoption proceedings, the *first* consideration is the welfare of the child. This means that the child's welfare must

---

1 Section 1(1): on approval, see ss 3–5.
2 Section 1(4). The services maintained by local authorities are to be known collectively as 'the Scottish Adoption Services'.
3 Section 11(1) and (3).
4 Section 11(3).
5 Section 11(1).
6 Section 27 of the Law Reform (Miscellaneous Provisions) (Scotland) Act 1985; cf *R v Children's Hearing for the Borders Region* 1984 SLT 65. In spite of s 27, *R v Children's Hearing for the Borders Region* has continued to be followed. See *A v Children's Hearing for Tayside Region* 1987 GWD 20–755: *sed quaere*. On children in need of compulsory measures of care, see *infra* Ch 13.

always be taken into account and be given greater weight than any other consideration. But it is only the first, not the paramount consideration.[1] Thus, in exceptional circumstances, a court or adoption agency may take a decision on the basis that the child's welfare has been outweighed by a combination of other factors, for example, parental wishes and public policy. It is submitted, however, that in the vast majority of cases, the decision will be determined by what is best for the child.

In placing a child for adoption, an adoption agency must have regard (so far as is practicable) to any wishes of the child's parents and guardians in relation to the religious upbringing of the child.[2] Nevertheless, the child's welfare is the first consideration[3] and the adoption agency should give effect to parental wishes in relation to religion only when it is consistent with the child's welfare to do so. Only children who are under the age of eighteen[4] and have not been married,[5] can be adopted in Scots law. An adopted child can be adopted again.[6] Where the child is a minor, an adoption order cannot be made without the minor's consent.[7] However, in reaching any decision, a child's wishes and feelings must be given due consideration by a court or adoption agency.[8]

PROSPECTIVE ADOPTERS

An unmarried person aged 21 or over may apply to adopt a child alone.[9] Applications can be made to adopt a child *jointly* only if (1) the applicants are a married couple *both* of whom are 21 or over or (2) one of the spouses is the child's parent and is 18 or over and the other spouse is 21 or over.[10] A married person can adopt the child alone if the court is satisfied that (i) the other spouse cannot be found or (ii) the spouses have separated and are living apart and the separation is likely

---

1 This point was emphasised by the Inner House in *P v Lothian Regional Council* 1989 SLT 739.
2 Section 7.
3 Section 6.
4 Section 65(1).
5 Section 12(5).
6 Section 12(7).
7 Section 12(8). The court may dispense with the minor's consent if satisfied that he or she is incapable of giving consent.
8 Section 6.
9 Section 15(1)(a).
10 Section 14(1), (1A), (1B) as substituted by para 33 of Sch 10 to the Children Act 1989.

to be permanent or (iii) the other spouse is incapable of making a joint application because of physical or mental ill health.[1]

While a parent can adopt his or her own child,[2] an adoption order shall not be made

> 'on the application of the mother or father of the child alone unless the court is satisfied that
> a) the other natural parent is dead or cannot be found or by virtue of section 28 of the Human Fertilisation and Embryology Act 1990, there is no other parent, or
> b) there is some other reason justifying the exclusion of the other natural parent.'[3]

Two major problems arise where the prospective adopters are related to the child. First, if, for example, a woman adopts her daughter's child, the effect of the adoption is to distort the natural family relationship with the result that the child may suffer distress on discovering that his or her 'mother' is in fact the child's grandmother and the child's 'sister' is in fact his or her mother. Second, in approximately forty per cent of adoptions in Scotland, the applicants are the child's natural parent – usually his or her mother – and his or her spouse, the child's step-parent. The effect of an adoption order in this situation will be that the non-applicant parent will lose parental rights in relation to the child, for example, the right of access. If the child has had a good relationship with the non-applicant parent, it will be contrary to the child's welfare to lose all contact with the natural parent.

To alleviate these problems, applications for adoptions by relatives and step-parents were to be discouraged. Section 53(1) of the Children Act 1975 provides:[4]

> '. . . where on an application for an adoption order in respect of a child the court is of opinion–
> a) in the case of an applicant who is a relative of the child or a husband or wife of the mother or father of the child (whether applying alone or jointly with his or her spouse)

---

1 Section 15(1)(b).
2 This might be done if, for example, it was important for succession purposes that the child be treated as legitimate and there was no other way in which the child could be legitimated.
3 Section 15(3) as amended by para 4 of Sch 4 to the Human Fertilisation and Embryology Act 1990. Where such an order is made the reason justifying the exclusion of the other natural parent must be recorded by the court. As to s 28 of the 1990 Act, see *supra* pp 151, 152.
4 As amended by Sch 2 to the Law Reform (Parent and Child) (Scotland) Act 1986 and Sch 2 to the Family Law Act 1986.

(i) that the child's welfare would not be better safeguarded and promoted by the making of an adoption order in favour of the applicant than it would be by the making of a custody order in his favour; and
(ii) that it would be appropriate to make a custody order in favour of the applicant; or
b) in any other case, that the making of a custody order in favour of the applicant would be more appropriate than the making of an adoption order in his favour,
the court shall direct that the application is to be treated as if it had been made for custody of the child'.

The effect of s 53(1)(a) is that where the applicants are relatives or step-parents of the child, there is a presumption that the court should treat the adoption application as one for custody. Only if the applicants can show that, in the circumstances of the case, the child's welfare would be better safeguarded and promoted by adoption, should the court, in the light of the welfare principle in s 6 of the Adoption (Scotland) Act 1978, allow the adoption application to proceed. In contrast, where the applicants are not relatives or step-parents of the child, there is no presumption that the court should treat the adoption application as one for custody: s 53(1)(b) merely empowers the court to treat the application as one for custody, when, in the light of the welfare principle in s 6 of the Adoption (Scotland) Act 1978, custody would be more appropriate than adoption in the circumstances of the particular case.

As a result of s 53(1)(a), adoption applications by relatives or step-parents should not be allowed to proceed unless the court is satisfied that adoption would better promote and safeguard the child's welfare. Because of the danger in distorting family relationships and cutting ties with the child's natural parents, it is only in very exceptional circumstances that adoption by relatives and step-parents will be better for the child than making a custody order in the applicants' favour. The custody order gives the applicants parental rights and provides security for the child without the dangers or disadvantages inherent in adoptions by relatives or step-parents. However, s 53(1)(a) has been largely ignored in practice and relative and step-parent applications continue to be common and proceed with little difficulty in Scotland.[1] In the present writer's view this is a matter of regret.

---

1 See, for example, *A v B* 1987 SLT (Sh Ct) 121. The parallel provisions in England *viz* s 37(1) and (2) of the Children Act 1975 were emasculated by judicial interpretation and have been repealed: *In Re S (a minor)* [1987] 2 WLR 977; *In Re M (a minor)* [1987] 1 WLR 162; s 108(7) and Sch 15 to the Children Act 1989.

PROCEDURE

Where the child was placed with the applicants by an adoption agency or where the applicant is a parent, step-parent or relative of the child, the child must be at least nineteen weeks old before an adoption order can be made and have lived with the applicant at all times during the preceding thirteen weeks.[1] If, however, a child was not placed with the applicants by an adoption agency and they are not related to the child, the child must be at least twelve months old before an adoption order can be made and have lived with the applicants at all times during the preceding twelve months:[2] this would apply, where, for example, foster parents want to adopt a child who has been left in their care.

Where a child has not been placed with the applicants by an adoption agency, the applicant must give notice to the local authority within whose area the child has his or her home of their intention to adopt the child. The notice must be given at least three months before the date of the order. During that period the local authority investigates the suitability of the adoptive parents etc and makes a report to the court.[3] The child is 'a protected child'[4] and the officers of the local authority are obliged to satisfy themselves as to the child's well being and have the power to inspect the premises where the child is living.[5] If the child's surroundings are unsuitable, on a complaint by the local authority, the sheriff can make an order removing the child to a place of safety.[6] Where a child has been placed by an adoption agency, the adoption agency submits a report to the court on the suitability of the adoptive parents etc.[7] An adoption order will not be made unless the court is satisfied that the applicants have afforded the adoption agency or the local authority sufficient opportunities to see the child in the home environment.[8]

Where an application for an adoption order is made by a person with whom the child has had his or her home for the preceding five years, no person can remove the child from the applicant's custody while the application is pending, except with the leave of court or under auth-

---

1 Section 13(1).
2 Section 13(2).
3 Section 22. Any change of address during that period must be notified to the local authority: s 35.
4 Section 32.
5 Section 33. It is an offence to refuse to allow an officer to visit the protected child: s 36(1)(b).
6 Section 34. It is an offence to refuse to comply with such an order: s 36(1)(c).
7 Section 23.
8 Section 13(3).

ority conferred by any enactment.[1] This protection extends to foster parents who decide to adopt a child who is in the care of a local authority but who has lived with the applicants for the preceding five years.[2]

An application can be made to the Court of Session or the sheriff court of the sheriffdom where the child lives.[3] The proceedings are heard in private.[4] A *curator ad litem* must be appointed with the duty of safeguarding the child's interests: in particular it is the curator's duty to provide the court with a comprehensive report dealing with all the circumstances of the adoption application.[5] Thus the court will have an independent assessment of whether the adoption will be in the interests of the child.

PARENTAL AGREEMENT

It is a fundamental principle of the law of adoption that an adoption order cannot be made unless the court is satisfied that each parent or guardian of the child 'freely, and with full understanding of what is involved, agrees unconditionally to the making of an adoption order'.[6] Parent includes the mother of the child and the child's father who has parental rights by virtue of marriage, ie who is or was married to the child's mother at the date of conception or subsequently.[7] Where the father does not have parental rights as the result of marriage to the child's mother, his agreement is not required.[8] However, he will be

---

1 Section 28(1). Similar protection exists for the period during which a prospective adopter has given notice of intimation to adopt to a local authority but before the application is made: the child must have lived with the prospective adopters for the preceding 5 years: s 28(2).
2 Section 28(3).
3 Section 56.
4 Section 57.
5 Section 58(1)(a). For full discussion, see PGB McNeill op cit *supra* p 212 n 1, Chs 7 and 8. A reporting officer must also be appointed for witnessing agreements etc: s 58(1)(b). The same person can be both *curator ad litem* and reporting officer.
6 Section 16(1)(b): agreement is necessary whether or not the parent or guardian knows the identity of the applicants.
7 Section 2(1)(b) of the Law Reform (Parent and Child) (Scotland) Act 1986, discussed *supra* p 178. Where a father has the full complement of parental rights by virtue of marriage, it is submitted that he retains the right to refuse to agree to adoption even if he is no longer married to the child's mother at the time of the application. He does not therefore have to rely on the definition of guardian in s 65(1).
8 *A v B and C* 1971 SC (HL) 129. In *A and B v C* 1987 SCLR 514, the Inner House stressed that the father of an illegitimate child has no *locus standi*: in adoption proceedings and should not therefore be asked whether or not he would consent to the adoption of his child.

treated as the child's guardian and his agreement will be necessary if he has obtained parental rights by virtue of a court order,[1] for example, under s 3 of the Law Reform (Parent and Child) (Scotland) Act 1986. There is no need for him to have obtained the full complement of parental rights under s 3: a right of access, for example, would suffice. A mother's agreement is ineffective if given less than six weeks after the child's birth.[2]

Freeing a child for adoption

When a parent or guardian agrees to an adoption, while the application is pending the child cannot be removed from the custody of the adoptive parents against their will except with leave of court.[3] But if the parent or guardian withdraws agreement before the order is made, the adoption cannot go ahead unless the court is prepared to dispense with the parent's or guardian's agreement.[4] To alleviate the difficulties which can arise if agreement is withdrawn, the Act provides a procedure whereby an order can be obtained which 'frees' the child for adoption.

An application for an order freeing a child for adoption is made by an adoption agency with the consent of the child's parent[5] or guardian.[6] If, however, the child is already in the care of the adoption agency, an application can be made without such consent provided the agency is applying to the court to dispense with the agreement of the parent or guardian.[7] Thus this procedure facilitates the adoption of children received into care by a local authority or who have been subject to a supervision requirement because they are in need of compulsory measures of care.[8] While an application is pending in these circumstances, the parents cannot without leave of court remove the child from the

---

1 Section 65(1) as amended by para 18(4) of Sch 1 to the Law Reform (Parent and Child) (Scotland) Act 1986. 'Guardian' also includes persons appointed to that office by deed or will or court order.
2 Section 16(4).
3 Section 27(1).
4 On dispensation, see *infra* p 221.
5 A mother's consent is ineffective if given less than 6 weeks after the child's birth: s 18(4).
6 Section 18(2)(a): the consent of one parent or guardian will suffice.
7 Section 18(2)(b). No dispensation will be made unless the child is already placed for adoption or the court is satisfied that it is likely the child will be placed for adoption: s 18(3). Dispensation of agreement is discussed *infra* p 221.
8 Section 28 of the Law Reform (Miscellaneous Provisions) (Scotland) Act 1985. On care proceedings generally, see *infra* Ch 13.

custody of the person with whom the child is living while in the care of the adoptive agency.[1]

If the requisite agreements have been obtained or dispensed with, the court will make an order if this is in accordance with the welfare principle in s 6.[2] Where the child is a minor, the child's consent is also required.[3] If the child's father has no parental rights by virtue of marriage, before making the order the court must satisfy itself that any person claiming to be the child's father has no intention of applying for parental rights under s 3(1) of the Law Reform (Parent and Child) (Scotland) Act 1986 or that if he did apply, his application would be refused.[4]

The effect of a freeing order is to vest in the adoption agency all the parental rights and duties in relation to the child.[5] Accordingly, once the child has been freed for adoption, the agreement of the parents or guardian to the adoption order is no longer required. But unless the parents or guardian have made a declaration before the order is made that they prefer not to be involved in future questions concerning the adoption of the child,[6] they are entitled after a year to progress reports from the adoption agency informing them whether the child has been adopted or placed for adoption.[7] If the child has not been adopted or placed for adoption, the parent or guardian may apply to a court to revoke the freeing order and so recover their parental rights.[8] A freeing order will only be revoked if this would be in accordance with the welfare principle in s 6. As a general rule, an application for revocation of an order freeing a child for adoption can only be made once.[9]

Dispensation with agreement

If a child has been freed for adoption, there is no need to obtain the parent's or guardian's agreement to the adoption order.[10] But where the child has not been freed for adoption, the agreement of the child's parent or guardian is necessary before an adoption order can be made.

1 Section 27(2).
2 Section 18(1).
3 Section 18(8).
4 Section 18(7) as amended by para 18(1) of Sch 1 to the Law Reform (Parent and Child) (Scotland) Act 1986.
5 Section 18(5).
6 Section 18(6).
7 Section 19.
8 Section 20.
9 Sections 20(4) and (5). If unsuccessful, the adoption agency is no longer obliged to make progress reports.
10 Section 16(1)(a).

However, the court has power to dispense with their agreement in certain circumstances;[1] these will be discussed in this section. It should be noted that this power also exists to dispense with the agreement of a child's parent or guardian in relation to an order freeing the child for adoption.[2]

Section 16(1) provides that:

> 'An adoption order shall not be made unless
> a) the child is free for adoption . . .; or
> b) in the case of each parent or guardian of the child the court is satisfied that–
>> (i) he freely, and with full understanding of what is involved, agrees unconditionally to the making of an adoption order . . .; or
>> (ii) his agreement to the making of the adoption order *should* be dispensed with on a ground specified in subsection (2)'.[3]

The grounds specified in s 16(2) are that the parent or guardian—
a) cannot be found or is incapable of giving agreement;
b) is withholding his agreement unreasonably;
c) has persistently failed without reasonable cause to discharge the parental duties in relation to the child;
d) has abandoned or neglected the child;
e) has persistently ill-treated the child;
f) has seriously ill-treated the child.[4]

It has recently been emphasised that dispensation with agreement involves the court in a two-stage process.[5] First, the court must be satisfied that a s 16(2) ground exists. This is primarily a question of fact.[6] If a ground is established, the court must then consider whether the agreement of the parent or guardian *should* be dispensed with on that ground. In reaching this decision, the court must apply the welfare principle in s 6. But it must be emphasised that s 6 is only relevant at this second stage ie *after* a s 16(2) ground has been established. In considering the s 16(2) grounds, it is proposed to leave discussion of s 16(2)(b) until the end, as this is the ground which has caused considerable controversy.

1 Sections 16(1)(b) and (2).
2 Section 18(1)(b). See, for example, *P v Lothian Regional Council* 1989 SLT 739; *L v Central Regional Council* 1990 SLT 818.
3 Italics added.
4 This ground cannot be used unless the rehabilitation of the child within the household of the parent or guardian is unlikely: s 16(5).
5 *L v Central Regional Council* 1990 SLT 818 (Inner House).
6 *Re P (infant)* [1977] 1 All ER 182, [1977] Fam 25, CA.

a) *Cannot be found or is incapable of giving agreement*

Whether a parent or guardian cannot be found is usually decided on the information contained in the report of the *curator ad litem* and the productions. The court must be told what steps were taken to find the parent or guardian, and in particular, it is important to 'follow up' evidence that relatives or friends may still be in contact with the missing person.[1] Evidence of incapacity to give agreement will usually be a medical report on the parent's or guardian's physical or mental condition.

Once the ground is established, the court must apply s 6 to determine whether agreement *should* be dispensed with. Consider the following examples.

EXAMPLE 1

A mother is unconscious in hospital after a road accident. Clearly the s 16(2)(a) ground is established as she is incapable of giving agreement. The medical prognosis is that she is likely to regain consciousness within a month. This evidence is relevant to the second stage ie whether the court *should* dispense with her agreement on the ground that she is incapable of giving agreement. This issue is determined by s 6. Since it is prima facie in a child's best interests to be brought up by his or her mother, giving first consideration to the welfare of the child, it is thought that the court should *not* dispense with the mother's agreement and the adoption order should therefore not be made.

EXAMPLE 2

A mother is unconscious in hospital after a road accident. Clearly, the s 16(2)(a) ground is established as she is incapable of giving agreement. The medical prognosis is that she is severely brain damaged and unlikely to regain consciousness. This evidence is relevant to the second stage, ie whether the court *should* dispense with her agreement on the ground that she is incapable of agreement. The issue is determined by s 6. Giving first consideration to the welfare of the child, it is thought that the court should dispense with the mother's agreement on this ground and make the adoption order.

1 *Re F (R) (infant)* [1969] 3 All ER 1101, [1970] 1 QB 385, CA.

b) *Persistently failing without reasonable cause to discharge the parental duties in relation to the child*

What is required for this ground is a pattern of behaviour which amounts to rejection of the child. The court must consider the past history of the case, not the child's future prospects.[1] An important factor in such behaviour will be failure to pay aliment, but all the circumstances of the case should be considered. A temporary withdrawal from the household when a marriage was breaking down has been held to lack the element of permanancy inherent in the concept of *persistent* failure.[2] Provided the parent aliments the children and attempts to keep the relationship alive, the ground is unlikely to be established.[3] It might be thought that the phrase 'without reasonable cause' suggests that an element of culpability is required: however it has been held[4] that the standard is objective, ie whether by the standard of a reasonable parent there was a reasonable cause for the failure. By that standard, ill health would probably amount to a reasonable cause while imprisonment would not. It has been held that a father who had failed to aliment his child because he was unemployed had reasonable cause for his failure to do so.[5]

Even if the ground is established, the court must apply s 6 to determine whether the agreement should be dispensed with. Thus, for example, if the ground was established but the reason for the failure was the parent's imprisonment, if the parent had been released from prison and was anxious to retain contact with the child, the court could hold that even giving first consideration to the welfare of the child, it should not dispense with the parent's agreement.

c) *Abandoning or neglecting the child*

Abandonment requires that the parent or guardian leaves the child, intending never to return.[6] Neglect is established by failure adequately to care for the child, for example, failure to provide food, clothing, care and attention. It is thought that the standard is objective. However, even if the ground is established, the court must consider whether the agreement of the parent should be dispensed with in accordance with the welfare principle in s 6.

1 *L v Central Regional Council* 1990 SLT 818. The child's future prospects are, of course, relevant under s 6 in determining whether agreement should be dispensed with if the ground is established.
2 *Re D (minors)* [1973] 3 All ER 1001, [1973] Fam 209, DC, cf *H and H v Petitioners* 1976 SLT 80 where the father had 'washed his hands' of the child.
3 *A and B v C* 1977 SLT (Sh Ct) 55.
4 *Central Regional Council v B* 1985 SLT 413, construing the phrase in the context of s 16(2)(e) of the Social Work (Scotland) Act 1968; discussed *infra* p 235.
5 *A v B* 1987 SLT (Sh Ct) 121.
6 *Watson v Nikolaisen* [1955] 2 All ER 427, DC.

d) Persistently ill-treating the child

This ground requires a consistent or repeated course of behaviour, which amounts to ill-treatment of the child: it need not be wilful.[1] The court must then consider whether the agreement of the parent should be dispensed with in accordance with the welfare principle in s 6. The court might refuse to dispense with the agreement if the parent's conduct had been the result of mental illness or alcoholism and evidence was brought that the parent had successfully undergone treatment and the child's rehabilitation within the family was likely and would be in the child's interests.

e) Seriously ill-treating the child

Unlike d), this ground is established by evidence of *one* incident which caused the child serious harm. However, this ground cannot be used 'unless (because of the ill-treatment or for other reasons) the rehabilitation of the child within the household of the parent or guardian is unlikely'.[2]

Thus, if, for example, a child was assaulted by his father when he was under the influence of LSD, the ground cannot be used unless it can be shown that the father is an addict and consequently rehabilitation within the father's household is unlikely.

Where rehabilitation is likely, it would, of course, be in accordance with the welfare principle in s 6 to refuse to dispense with parental agreement. The proviso to s 16(2)(f) goes further and prevents serious ill-treatment from being a ground at all if rehabilitation of the child in the household of the parent or guardian is likely.

Withholding agreement unreasonably

It has been argued that the question of dispensation of agreement falls into two stages *viz* i) does a s 16(2) ground exist and ii) *should* agreement be dispensed with on that ground.[3] The s 6 welfare principle is only relevant *after* the ground is established. Thus a parent or guardian is not withholding agreement unreasonably merely because, giving first consideration to the welfare of the child ie applying s 6, adoption would be better than living with the natural parent or guardian. If that were the law, whenever a court considered that an adoption order was in the interests of a child, it could dispense with agreement under s 16(2)(b) and the right of a parent or guardian to refuse to agree to the adoption of a child would be rendered nugatory. As Lord Hodson emphasised in the leading case of *Re W (infant)*,[4] 'it has been repeat-

---

1 *Central Regional Council v B* 1985 SLT 413.
2 Section 16(5).
3 *L v Central Regional Council* 1990 SLT 818 supports this approach, at least, in the context of dispensation based on s 16(2)(c).
4 [1971] 2 All ER 49, [1971] AC 682, HL at 718.

edly held that the withholding of consent could not be held unreasonably merely because the [adoption] order, if made, would conduce to the welfare of the child'. For these reasons, it remains the present writer's view that s 6 is irrelevant in determining whether the s 16(2)(b) ground exists. However, in *P v Lothian Regional Council*[1], the Inner House unanimously held that s 6 was relevant. The Lord Justice-Clerk (Ross) explained:[2]

> 'In my opinion "any decision relating to the adoption of a child" clearly includes the decision as to whether or not to make an adoption order. It also, in my opinion, includes the decision whether or not to dispense with parental consent on the ground that it is being withheld unreasonably. . . . The result of all this is that in determining whether a parent has unreasonably withheld consent a number of factors must be laid in the balance. The test is an objective one. The question is–would a reasonable parent have withheld consent? Regard must be had to the interests of the child, of the natural parents, and of the prospective adopter. The welfare of the child is the first consideration, and in the particular case may be the paramount consideration.'[3]

Although there is Scottish and English authority that s 6 does not operate until after the s 16(2)(b) ground has been established,[4] it seems clear that courts should follow the approach taken in *P v Lothian Regional Council*[5] until the issue is resolved by the House of Lords. It should be stressed, however, that the child's welfare is only the first, not the paramount consideration, unless the latter is justified by the particular circumstances of the case.[6]

A parent or guardian is withholding agreement unreasonably when in the particular circumstances of the case a reasonable parent would not have withheld agreement. In *A v B and C*,[7] Lord Guest took the view that 'other things being equal, it is in the best interests of a child to be with its natural parents . . .'. Accordingly it is reasonable for a parent or guardian to refuse to agree to the adoption. But a reasonable parent will regard the child's welfare to be the first factor to be taken

1 1989 SLT 739.
2 Ibid at 741.
3 See also ibid at 744, per Lord Wylie and at 745 per Lord Cowie.
4 *L v Central Regional Council* 1990 SLT 818 (Extra Division); *Re P (an infant)* [1977] 1 All ER 182; [1977] Fam 25, CA.
5 1989 SLT 739.
6 Ibid. The sheriff had misdirected himself in this case by regarding the child's welfare as the paramount and not merely the first consideration in determining whether or not the s 16(2)(b) ground existed.
7 1971 SC (HL) 129 at 143.

into account in determining whether or not to agree to the adoption of the child. While it is the first consideration the weight to be given to the child's welfare is is *not* the paramount consideration, but will depend on the circumstances. If, for example, the child had been with the adoptive parents for only a short period, a reasonable parent could take the view that natural ties of love and affection outweighed any possible disadvantage to the child in being removed from the adoptive parents' home:[1] on the other hand, if the child had been with the adoptive parents for a long period, a reasonable parent would give great weight to the disruptive effects on the child of removing him or her from that environment and would regard the child's welfare as outweighing natural ties of love and affection.[2]

All the circumstances of the case must be considered including the personal characteristics of the parents. Thus in *A v B and C* itself, while at the date of the appeal the child's parents were married and had a home available for the child, because there was evidence that they were emotionally unstable and since the child had been with the adoptive parents for several years, the House of Lords held that a reasonable parent would not, in those circumstances, have withheld agreement. There is, of course, a degree of artificiality involved. In *R v Lothian Regional Council*[3] the court was faced with the question whether a mother who was an alcoholic was withholding her agreement unreasonably. In the course of his judgment, the Sheriff Principal (O'Brien) said:[4]

'I readily accept that the question is what a reasonable woman in the place of the appellant [the mother] would do in all the circumstances, but do not find myself much nearer the answer in a case where a reasonable woman has to put herself in the shoes of an alcoholic mother claiming to have given up drinking'.

In *Re D (infant)*,[5] the House of Lords upheld a decision that a father who was homosexual was withholding his agreement unreasonably when his former wife and her husband applied to adopt his son. The trial judge had taken the view that the father who had had a series of homosexual relationships with males under the age of 21, had nothing to offer his child. In these circumstances, a reasonable parent –

1 *A v B* 1987 SLT (Sh Ct) 121.
2 *O v Central Regional Council* 1987 GWD 22–813; *Lothian Regional Council v R* 1988 GWD 28–1172.
3 1987 SCLR 362.
4 Ibid at 363.
5 [1977] 1 All ER 145, [1977] AC at 617, HL.

whether homosexual or heterosexual – who had nothing to offer his child, would not have withheld agreement, much as he loved his child. It will be clear that it is not necessary for there to be any degree of culpability on the part of the parent or guardian: on the other hand, because the child's welfare is not the paramount consideration, the ground is not established merely because adoption is in the child's best interests. As Lord Hailsham said in *Re W (infant)*:[1]

'Two reasonable parents can perfectly reasonably come to opposite conclusions on the same set of facts without forfeiting their rights to be regarded as reasonable. The question in any given case is whether a parental veto comes within the band of possible reasonable decisions and not whether it is right or mistaken. Not every reasonable judgment is right, and not every mistaken exercise of judgment is unreasonable. There is a band of decisions within which no court should seek to replace the individual's judgment with his own'.

Accordingly, it is only when the refusal is outwith the band of reasonable responses that the s 16(2)(b) ground is established.[2]

When a parent or guardian is withholding agreement unreasonably, it will automatically follow that the court should dispense with their agreement in the light of the welfare principle in s 6.

THE ADOPTION ORDER

If the child is freed for adoption or the relevant agreements have been obtained or dispensed with, the court can then proceed to make the adoption order.[3] It will do so having regard to s 6, ie giving first consideration to the welfare of the child. A court has refused to make an order, for example, when the purpose of the adoption was to avoid immigration requirements and not to integrate the child into the proposed adopters' family.[4] But the most common situation where an

1 [1971] 2 All ER 49, [1971] AC 682, HL at 700.
2 Cf *A B v C B* 1985 SLT 514: father refused to agree to the adoption of his children by his former wife and her husband. Although the court was doubtful, it dispensed with his agreement inter alia on the basis that informal access should be agreed by the mother to the younger child and that adoption was in the child's long term welfare. It is submitted that the father's refusal was not outwith the band of reasonable responses and therefore the s 16(2)(b) ground was not established. It should also be remembered that in the light of s 53(1) of the Children Act 1975, there is a presumption against adoption applications in these circumstances: see *supra* p 216.
3 Interim orders are possible: s 25(1).
4 *In re W (a minor)* [1985] 3 WLR 945, CA; cf *Re H (minor)* [1982] 3 All ER 84, [1982] Fam 121.

adoption order would not be made would be if the court was not satisfied with the verification of the statements in the petition. If an order is refused, the child is returned to the adoption agency[1] or in exceptional circumstances the child, if under the age of 16, can be placed under supervision or committed to the care of a local authority.[2]

Adoption orders are registered in the Adopted Children Register. On reaching the age of 17, an adopted person is entitled to obtain information in respect of his birth and counselling services are available for adopted persons who have received such information.[3]

---

1 Section 30.
2 Section 26.
3 See generally s 45 and Sch 1 to the Act.

13   Children in need of care

INTRODUCTION

While family autonomy may be regarded as a hall mark of a democratic society, it is accepted that there is a duty on a modern state to make provision through its social work agencies for the care and protection of children who are vulnerable when the family of which they are part becomes dysfunctional. At one extreme, this provision may simply take the form of advice, guidance and assistance to the family: at the other, it might involve the compulsory removal of a child from the family into the permanent care of a local authority. In the latter situation, two points must be stressed. First, not only are parental rights being overridden but the child is being deprived of his liberty. It is therefore important that the law should provide procedural safe-guards to ensure that these interests are adequately represented before a decision is made which would deprive parents of their child and the child of his or her family – even if, ultimately, this step must be taken to secure the welfare of the child. Second, while a large degree of dis-cretion must be given to social work agencies, their decisions in relation to a child in their care may have serious consequences for the child and the child's family: it is therefore crucial that the parameters in which this discretion can lawfully be exercised are clearly laid down. In the following account of the powers – and duties – of the state in relation to the care and protection of vulnerable children, the extent to which contemporary Scots law achieves these two important policies will also be considered. The law in this area is currently the subject of a wide ranging review and proposals for reform have been published.[1]

---

1 See *Review of Child Care Law in Scotland* (1990) (Scottish Office). Discussion of the Review proposals is outwith the scope of the present Chapters.

CHILDREN IN CARE

Reception into care

By s 12 of the Social Work (Scotland) Act 1968,[1] it is the duty of a local authority to give assistance to a child and his family, if this is likely to diminish the need to receive the child into the local authority's care or the child's referral to a children's hearing.[2] This assistance can take the form of assistance in kind or, in exceptional circumstances, cash.[3] However, even with this help the family may have become so dysfunctional that further steps must have to be taken to protect the children.

By s 15(1) of the Social Work (Scotland) Act 1968, a local authority has a *duty* to receive a child under the age of seventeen into their care where it appears that
a) the child has neither parent nor guardian or has been abandoned or is lost: or
b) that the child's parent or guardian is temporarily or permanently unable as a result of physical or mental illness or any other circumstances, to provide the child with proper accommodation, maintenance and upbringing; and
c) in either case, the intervention of the local authority is necessary in the interests of the welfare of the child.

Although the need for care will – hopefully – only be temporary, the local authority has a duty to keep the child in their care if the child's welfare so requires until the child reaches the age of 18.[4] In reaching any decision relating to the child, the local authority must give first consideration to the need to safeguard and promote the child's welfare, taking into account the child's own wishes and feelings when appropriate to do so.[5] The case of every child received into care must be reviewed by the local authority at least every six months.[6]

It is important to stress that when a child is received into care under s 15, the parent or guardian retains the full complement of parental rights and duties. Indeed, the local authority is under a duty to attempt to make contact with parents whose whereabouts are unknown.[7] Moreover, it is expressly provided in s 15(3) that:

---

1 References in this chapter are to the Social Work (Scotland) Act 1968 (as amended) unless otherwise stated.
2 On referral to a children's hearing, see *infra* pp 240 ff.
3 Section 12(2)(a) and (b).
4 Section 15(2).
5 Section 20.
6 Section 20A.
7 Section 15(8).

'. . . nothing in this section shall authorise a local authority to keep a child in their care under this section if any parent or guardian desires to take over the care of the child, and the local authority shall, in all cases where it appears to them consistent with the welfare of the child so to do, endeavour to secure that the care of the child is taken over either –
a) by a parent or guardian of his, or
b) by a relative or friend of his, being, where possible, a person of the same religious persuasion as the child . . .'

It is clear therefore that not only does a parent or guardian retain parental rights in relation to the child but that the local authority must endeavour to return the child to the care of his or her parents when this is in accordance with the welfare of the child. Consequently, the parent or guardian of a child received into care under s 15 retains the prima facie right to the possession of the child[1] and can call upon the local authority to return the child. However, when a child has been in the local authority's care for six months or more, a parent or guardian cannot lawfully obtain the possession of the child without the authority's consent until the parent or guardian has given the local authority 28 days notice in writing of his or her intention to seek the return of the child.[2] During that 28 days period, the local authority can consider whether to take over the permanent care of the child.

Assumption of parental rights

When a child has been received into care under s 15, the family environment may be so unsatisfactory that it is in the child's welfare that the local authority's care of the child should be put on a stable, long term basis. This is done by the local authority, acting through its social services committee, passing a resolution under s 16 of the Social Work (Scotland) Act 1968, assuming parental rights in respect of the child.

First, a s 16 resolution can only be passed in respect of a child who is in the local authority's care by virtue of s 15.[3] In the leading case of *Lewisham LBC v Lewisham Juvenile Court Justices*,[4] the House of Lords considered the meaning of 'care' in the parallel English legislation. The decision has, however, been accepted as authoritative in Scotland on the meaning of 'care' in s 15 of the Social Work (Scotland)

---

1 On prima facie parental rights, see *supra* Ch 10.
2 Section 15(3A). For penalties for unlawful removal of the child, see s 17(8).
3 Section 16(1)(a).
4 [1979] 2 All ER 297, [1980] AC 273, HL.

Act 1968.[1] In *Lewisham*, the House of Lords held that for the purpose of a s 16 resolution, care under s 15 continues in the following circumstances:

(i) where a child has been in care for six months or more, care continues under s 15 during the period of the 28 days notice which the parent or guardian must give the local authority: the local authority can therefore pass a s 16 resolution at any time during that period;

(ii) where a child has been in care for less than six months, care continues under s 15 until the child is physically given up to the parent or guardian. Provided the latter give the local authority *some* notice of their intention to seek the return of the child, the local authority can pass a s 16 resolution at any time before the parent or guardian arrives to collect the child: if they wish to do so, the social services committee will, obviously, have to move quickly;

(iii) where the child has been in care for less than six months, a difficulty remains if the parent or guardian simply turns up at a children's home, or the foster parents' house or the child's school and demands the immediate return of the child. As the child has been in care under s 15 for less than six months, there is no need to give 28 days notice and the parent or guardian has the prima facie right to the possession of the child.[2] If, however, the local authority considered it would be contrary to the child's welfare to be returned to the parent or guardian, can the authority lawfully hold on to the child and pass a s 16 resolution? This question was raised but not settled by the House of Lords in *Lewisham*.[3] But Lord Salmon thought[4] that in these circumstances, while legally obliged to return the child, the local authority would be under a *moral* obligation not to do so. In practice, the solution is that the child should be returned but that the local authority would immediately seek a place of safety order[5] under which the child could be removed to a place of safety. However, it is submitted that in theory the local authority is not legally obliged to return the child to the parent or guardian if it would *in fact* be against the child's interest to do so. The parental right to possession of a child is only a prima facie right. Where its purported exercise would not

1 *Central Regional Council v B* 1985 SLT 413.
2 *Supra.*
3 [1979] 2 All ER 297, [1980] AC 273, HL.
4 Ibid at 291.
5 On place of safety orders, see *infra.*

be in the child's welfare, no corresponding *legal* obligation on the local authority to return the child is created: s 15 care would therefore continue and a s 16 resolution could be passed.[1]

Secondly, not only must the child be in care under s 15, but one or more grounds must exist upon which the s 16 resolution can be based. The grounds are the following:

a) that the parents of the child are dead and the child has no guardian;[2] or

b) that there exists in respect of a parent or guardian any of the following circumstances:[3]

 (i) the parent or guardian has abandoned the child.[4] 'Abandonment' involves the intention permanently to leave the child and never to return.[5] But a parent or guardian will be deemed to have abandoned a child, if their whereabouts have remained unknown for twelve months and throughout that period the child has been in the care of the local authority under s 15.[6]

 (ii) the parent or guardian suffers some permanent disability rendering him or her incapable of caring for the child.[7] The disability can be either physical or mental but must be permanent.

 (iii) the parent or guardian suffers from a mental disorder rendering him or her unfit to have the care of the child.[8] A temporary mental disorder suffices.[9]

 (iv) the parent or guardian is of such habits or mode of life as to be unfit to have the care of the child.[10] This will usually cover a parent or guardian who is an alcoholic or drug addict or a prostitute. But in *Lothian Regional Council v T*,[11] the Sheriff Principal (Caplan) held that while 'habits' probably did, 'mode of life' did not have any moral connotations or involve voluntary behaviour on the part of the parent or guardian: 'mode of life' could be situational. A religious hermit has a mode of life which is as

---

1 If it could be shown that the purported exercise of the right was in the child's interests and that the local authority ought to have returned the child to the parent or guardians, the s 16 resolution could be challenged on the ground that the child was not lawfully in care under s 15 at the time it was made.
2 Section 16(1)(i).
3 Section 16(1)(ii).
4 Section 16(2)(a).
5 *Watson v Nikolaisen* [1955] 2 All ER 427, DC.
6 Section 16(12).
7 Section 16(2)(b).
8 Section 16(2)(c).
9 If the mental disorder was permanent, the resolution would be based on s 16(2)(b).
10 Section 16(2).
11 1984 SLT (Sh Ct) 74.

unsuited to bringing up a child as that of an alcoholic. Consequently, the local authority had been correct to assume a father's rights on the ground of his mode of life when, as a result of his temperament and through no fault of his own, he was unable to keep a job and provide adequate housing for his family.

(v) the parent or guardian has so persistently failed without reasonable cause to discharge the obligations of a parent or guardian as to be unfit to have care of the child.[1] In the leading case of *Central Regional Council v B*,[2] Lord Brand considered[3] that 'persistently' had the connotation of 'consistent or repeated behaviour which need not necessarily be wilful'. Moreover, the court took the view that 'without reasonable cause' was to be construed by applying the objective standard of a reasonable parent and deciding whether by that standard, the particular parent or guardian had reasonable cause for failure to discharge their obligations.[4] Thus, for example, if a mother's inability to look after her children is a result of low intelligence, this will not constitute reasonable cause for her failure as she has objectively not met the standards of a reasonable parent and her lack of fault is irrelevant;

c) that a s 16 resolution, based on one of the grounds in b), is already in force in relation to a parent who is or, is likely to become, a member of the household comprising the child and his other parent.[5] Consider the following example.

EXAMPLE

H and W have a child, C. When W enters a mental hospital, C is received into the care of a local authority under s 15. A s 16 resolution is passed assuming W's parental rights on the basis of s 16(2)(c) (temporary mental disorder). The local authority later agree that while the child remains in care, C should live with H.[6] If W then discharges herself from hospital still mentally ill, the local authority can assume H's parental rights if W becomes or is likely to become a member of the household comprising H and C.

1 Section 16(2)(e).
2 1985 SLT 413.
3 Ibid at 421.
4 Ibid per Lord Robertson at 418; per Lord Stewart at 422.
5 Section 16(1)(iii).
6 This is possible if it appears to the authority to be for the benefit of the child: s 17(3).

d) that the child has been in the care of the local authority under s 15 throughout the three years preceding the passing of the resolution.[1]

It is one of the most controversial features of the current s 16 procedure that it is only *after* the resolution has been passed, ie *after* the local authority has assumed parental rights, that the local authority is obliged to give the parents or guardian notice in writing that their rights in respect of the child have been assumed.[2] It has been held/that although s 16(5) provides that the local authority 'shall *forthwith* after the passing of the resolution' serve the notice, this obligation is directory not mandatory: accordingly, a notice given a month after the resolution was passed was valid.[3] The notice must also inform the parents of their right to object to the resolution.[4] If parents or guardians wish to object, they must, not later than one month after receipt of the notice, serve a counter-notice in writing on the local authority objecting to the resolution.[5] The resolution will lapse after fourteen days from the service of the counter-notice[6] unless the local authority makes a summary application to the sheriff.[7] On hearing the application, the sheriff has power to order that the resolution should *not* lapse by reason of the service of the counter-notice provided he is satisfied that:

a) the ground upon which the local authority purported to pass the s 16 resolution existed at the date upon which the resolution was made;[8] and

b) at the time of the hearing in the sheriff court there exists a ground upon which a s 16 resolution could be made: this ground does not need to be the same as the ground upon which the resolution was originally based;[9] and

c) it is in the interests of the child that the resolution should not lapse.

---

1 Section 16(1)(iv).
2 Section 16(5).
3 *Dumfries and Galloway Regional Concil v M* 1990 SCLR 49.
4 Section 16(6).
5 Section 16(7).
6 Ibid.
7 The resolution will then not lapse until the determination of the application: s 16(8).
8 There is no need for corroborated evidence that the ground existed: *Central Regional Council v B* 1985 SLT 413; section 1(1) of the Civil Evidence (Scotland) Act 1988.
9 *Central Regional Council v B* 1985 SLT 413. *Quaere* whether a local authority could use s 16(1)(iv) (3 years in care) if it had deliberately procrastinated: cf *Strathclyde Regional Council v M* 1982 SLT (Sh Ct) 106 where the sheriff thought that s 16(1)(iv) could not be used because s 15 care ceased when the parents began their objections: this point is now doubtful in the light of *Central Regional Council v B*.

The sheriff can appoint a *curator ad litem* to safeguard the child's interests in the proceedings.[1] An appeal to the Inner House of the Court of Session from the sheriff's decision is competent.[2]

While it is accepted that a s 16 resolution can be challenged by the counter-notice procedure and that the onus is on the local authority to convince the sheriff that the resolution should not lapse, nevertheless, a s 16 resolution will stand unless the parent or guardian triggers the counter-notice procedure. When it is remembered that in many of these cases the parents will be among the most vulnerable in our society, doubts must arise whether their interests are sufficiently safeguarded by the current law. There is force in the contention that a local authority should only obtain parental rights *after* judicial proceedings where the parents and child have been separately represented.

The effect of a s 16 resolution is drastic. The local authority acquires *all* the rights and powers in relation to the child which the parent or guardian on whose account the resolution was passed had enjoyed. As Lord Fraser observed in the leading case of *Beagley v Beagley*,[3]

'. . . it is clear beyond argument that [the parent] is automatically divested of any rights and powers which are now vested in the [local authority] by virtue of the resolution'.

In other words, while the resolution subsists the parent or guardian is denuded of all parental rights in relation to the child. Three points should, however, be noted. First, the parent retains the right to refuse to agree to an adoption order or an order freeing the child for adoption.[4] But in practice, this is of limited value as the grounds upon which the s 16 resolution was passed will often[5] constitute grounds for dispensing with parental agreement under s 16 of the Adoption (Scotland) Act 1978.[6] Second, the local authority cannot cause the child to be brought up in a religious persuasion different from that in which he or she would have been raised if the s 16 resolution had not been

---

1 Section 18A.
2 *Central Regional Council v B* 1985 SLT 413.
3 1984 SLT 202 at 205.
4 Section 16(3): *Lothian Regional Council v H* 1982 SLT (Sh Ct) 65.
5 Particularly if the resolution was based on s 16(1)(ii) – see *supra* p 206.
6 Discussed *supra* Ch 12. A s 16 resolution has been used as a preliminary step towards the adoption of the child: *Cheetham v Glasgow Corpn* 1972 SLT (Notes) 50.

passed: ie the child's religion cannot be changed.[1] Third, the parent or guardian retains any obligation to aliment or maintain the child.[2]

Apart from these exceptions, the local authority has the full complement of parental rights in relation to a child who has been the subject of a s 16 resolution and the parent or guardian is denuded of their rights in relation to the child. Thus, in *Beagley v Beagley,*[3] the House of Lords held that a parent whose rights had been assumed by a s 16 resolution, could not seek a court order for the custody of the child because having been divested of parental rights by the resolution, the natural parent had no longer any title to sue.

However, in exercising its rights, the local authority must give first consideration to the welfare of the child.[4] The child's case must be reviewed by the local authority at least every six months.[5] Where it is in the child's interests to do so, the local authority can allow a child to live with his or her parents,[6] but more often a child will live with foster parents or in a residential establishment. All decisions in relation to the child's care and upbringing are matters for the local authority. If a local authority's decision is *ultra vires*, for example, if it purported to alter the child's religion,[7] or is made in bad faith, for example, to punish the parents rather than further the child's welfare, then the decision will be subject to judicial review; but otherwise there is no procedure by which a parent or guardian can appeal from the merits of a decision taken in good faith by the local authority in relation to the child. Thus, for example, if the local authority took the view that it was in the child's interests that he or she should be inoculated against whooping cough, the merits of this decision cannot be challenged in the courts as the local authority has been given by statute the power to make such a decision in relation to the child.[8]

The injustice inherent in this principle became obvious when the courts refused to review a local authority's decision that a parent should not be allowed access to a child who had been subject to a s 16 resolution. This was held to be a matter entirely within the discretion of the local authority and could not be challenged if the local authority

---

1 Section 17(7): but what if the child was being brought up as an atheist?
2 Section 17(6). The parents can be obliged to make a contribution towards the child's maintenance while in care: Part VI of the Social Work (Scotland) Act 1968. These provisions do not extend to recovery of arrears of maintenance: *Tayside Regional Council v Thaw* 1987 SLT 69.
3 1984 SLT 202.
4 Section 20(1).
5 Section 20A.
6 Section 17(8).
7 Section 17(7).
8 *Beagley v Beagley* 1984 SLT 202 per Lord Templeman at 208.

genuinely believed that access was not in the child's interests.[1] This unsatisfactory situation has been overtaken by a series of amendments to the Social Work (Scotland) Act 1968.[2] Before terminating arrangements for access to a child who is subject to a s 16 resolution or refusing to make such arrangements, the local authority must give the child's parent or guardian notice of their intention to do so.[3] The notice must inform the parents or guardian of their rights to apply for an access order in the sheriff court.[4] If the parent or guardian makes a summary application, the sheriff has power to order the local authority to allow the parent or guardian access to the child and can make detailed conditions as to commencement, frequency, duration and place of the access.[5] The welfare of the child is the court's first and paramount consideration in determining access issues.[6] Where an access order has been made, a local authority can apply to the sheriff for an emergency order suspending access for up to seven days, where it can be established that continued access will put the child's welfare seriously at risk. During the period of suspension, the local authority can apply to the sheriff to have the access order varied or discharged: variation or discharge is again determined by the welfare principle.[7] A code of practice is published in respect of access to children in care.[8]

As a result of these provisions, parents and guardians now have the right to have the question of access to a child who is subject to a s 16 resolution determined by a court in accordance with the welfare principle. This is a marked improvement on the previous position. However, these provisions only relate to access: in all other matters, the bona fide exercise by the local authority of the parental rights it has assumed in respect of a child cannot be challenged in a court.[9]

A s 16 resolution continues until the child reaches the age of 18.[10] However, the local authority may rescind the resolution at any time if this would be for the benefit of the child.[11] Moreover, a parent or

---

1 Ibid.
2 The amendments were introduced by s 7 of the Health and Social Services and Social Security Adjudications Act 1984.
3 Section 17A(1). Variation of existing access arrangements does not constitute termination of access for this purpose: s 17A(4).
4 Section 17A(2).
5 Section 17B.
6 Section 17D. A *curator ad litem* can be appointed to safeguard the child's interests: s 18A.
7 Section 17C.
8 Section 17E.
9 *Beagley v Beagley* 1984 SLT 202.
10 Section 18(1).
11 Section 18(2).

guardian can apply to the sheriff court for an order that the resolution should cease to have effect because *either* there had been no grounds for passing the original resolution *or* it was in the child's interests at the date of the hearing that the resolution should be determined.[1] The onus is on the parent or guardian to establish either of these conditions: the latter in particular will be difficult to establish when local authority social workers maintain that the resolution should continue. If the sheriff refuses to determine the resolution, he can order the local authority to allow the parent or guardian to have the care of the child for set periods.[2]

COMPULSORY MEASURES OF CARE

We have hitherto been discussing the situation where a local authority assumes parental rights in relation to a child already in its care under s 15. Usually a child will have been received into care with the agreement of the child's parent or guardian, for example, where the parent feels that he or she can no longer cope with the child because of illness etc. In this section, we shall consider the provisions of the Social Work (Scotland) Act 1968, whereby a child can compulsorily be removed from his or her family and enter the care of a local authority.

Place of safety orders

By s 37(2) a police constable or any person authorised by a court or a justice of the peace[3] may take a child[4] to a place of safety if
a) the child has been or is believed to have been the victim of any offence in Sch 1 to the Criminal Procedure (Scotland) Act 1975 (a Sch 1 offence): these offences involve physical and sexual abuse of the child; or
b) the child has not been a victim of a Sch 1 offence but is a member of the same household as a child who has been or is believed to have been a victim of such an offence; or
c) the child is, or is likely to become, a member of the same household as a person who has committed or is believed to have committed a Sch 1 offence; or
d) the child has been or is believed to have been the victim of an

---

1 Section 18(3). A *curator ad litem* can be appointed to safeguard the child's interests: s 18A.
2 Ibid: see *Beagley v Beagley* 1984 SLT 202 at 206, per Lord Fraser.
3 For example, a social worker.
4 A person under the age of 16: s 30(1)(a).

offence under s 21(1) of the Children and Young Persons (Scotland) Act 1937: for example, a truant child of vagrants; or

e) the child is likely to be caused unnecessary suffering or serious impairment of health because there is, or is believed to be, a lack of parental care in respect of the child.

A place of safety is any residential or other establishment provided by a local authority, a police station, hospital or surgery, or any other suitable place.[1] The child can be detained at the place of safety for up to seven days,[2] during which arrangements can be made for a children's hearing to determine whether or not the child is in need of compulsory measures of care.[3]

Information to a local authority

By s 37(1A), if a local authority receives information, for example, from its social workers or the police, that a child may be in need of compulsory measures of care, the local authority must make enquiries and if it appears that the child may in fact be in need of compulsory measures of care, the local authority must give the reporter such information about the child as they have been able to discover, to enable the reporter to decide whether the case should be referred to a children's hearing.[4]

The role of the reporter

When a place of safety order has been made or a local authority has obtained information that a child may be in need of compulsory

---

1 Section 94(1).
2 Section 37(3)(c).
3 The reporter is informed as soon as possible and arranges for a children's hearing to sit not later than during the first lawful day after the commencement of the child's detention: if the children's hearing is unable to dispose of the case, they can issue a warrant requiring the child to be detained in a place of safety for up to 21 days: s 37(4). This warrant can be renewed only once: s 37(5). However, the reporter can then apply to the sheriff for a warrant detaining the child for a further maximum of 21 days: s 37(5A). The sheriff's warrant can be renewed only once: s 37(5B). The discretion to extend the duration of a place of safety order is not restricted to the situation where it is necessary for the child's protection in respect of the child's mental, physical and moral wellbeing. The fact that a child if allowed free would worsen his own position by committing further offences has been held to be sufficient: *Humphries v S* 1986 SLT 683. Resort has been made to the *nobile officium* to obtain a further extension beyond the statutory limits in very exceptional circumstances: *Ferguson v P* 1989 SLT 681 (father charged with culpable homicide of another child who was a member of the household).
4 Where any person has reasonable cause to believe that a child may be in need of compulsory measures of care, he may give the reporter such information about the child as he may have been able to discover: s 37(1).

measures of care, the decision whether or not to take the case to a children's hearing is that of the reporter. The reporter, while an officer of the local authority, acts independently of it and normally cannot work for the authority in any other capacity.[1] The reporter may have a legal background but this is not essential. After making an initial investigation, the reporter may take the view that no further action is necessary.[2] Alternatively, the reporter may consider that the family may be able to cope with social work support: in these circumstances, the reporter refers the case to the local authority concerned.[3] However, if the reporter feels that the child is in need of compulsory measures of care, it is the reporter's duty to arrange a children's hearing to consider the case[4] and to call upon the local authority for a report on the child and his social background. As we shall see, the reporter has important powers and duties in relation to the conduct of the children's hearing and subsequent proceedings. The reporter is, in effect, the lynch pin of the whole system and the importance of the reporter's role cannot be over-emphasised.

The children's hearing

Whether or not a child is in need of compulsory measures of care and if so, what steps should be taken to further the child's care and protection, are prima facie issues for a children's hearing. In every local authority, there is a children's panel consisting of persons with a knowledge or interest in social work and child care who are appointed by the Secretary of State to serve on the panel for the purposes of the 1968 Act.[5] A children's hearing consists of three members of the panel, one of whom acts as a chairman;[6] both a man and a woman must be among the members.[7]

It must be emphasised that a children's hearing is not a court. Its proceedings are informal and conducted in private with the reporter, the child and the parents present. The parties are not normally legally represented. The usual rules of evidence do not apply. Indeed it has been held that the rules of natural justice are suspended in the interests

1 Sections 36(1) and (5).
2 Section 39(1).
3 Section 39(2).
4 Section 39(3).
5 Section 33(1): the training, performance etc of the members of the panel are monitored by the relevant Children's Panel Advisory Committee (CPAC) which can also recommend persons to act on a panel.
6 The chairman may have a legal background.
7 Sections 34(1) and (2).

of the child:[1] thus, for example, the parents are not entitled to see the documents which have been made available to the reporter.[2] The rationale of the system is to enable the hearing to reach a decision which is the best in the circumstances for the child and the family. While the expertise and experience of the reporter and the members of the hearing are obviously crucial, the informality of the proceedings does lead to a danger that the parents' rights and, more importantly, the child's liberty, may too easily be overridden to achieve a solution which the hearing considers to be in best interests of the child.

Compulsory measures of care

Before a child[3] will be considered to be in need of compulsory measures of care, one or more of the following conditions must be applicable at the time of the hearing.[4] These 'grounds of referral' are listed in s 32(2) *viz*:
a) the child is beyond the control of his or her parents; or
b) the child is falling into bad associations or is exposed to moral danger. A child will probably be regarded as falling into bad associations or exposed to moral danger if his or her parents or friends are prostitutes, drug addicts, alcoholics or homosexuals;[5] or
c) lack of parental care is likely to cause the child unnecessary suffering or seriously to impair the child's health or development. Earlier incidents of parental neglect can be used to show the likelihood of the child's suffering or impairment of health or development.[6] In *McGregor v L*,[7] the Inner House of the Court of Session held that this ground was established in relation to a new born infant who had never left hospital but whose parents had a history of neglecting their children. It was not necessary for the child to have actually suffered parental neglect before the ground was made out:

> 'If it is proved that the habits and mode of life of these parents are such as to yield the reasonable inference that they are unlikely to care for this child in a manner likely to prevent unnecessary suffering or serious impairment of her health or development, the ground of referral would be established'.[8]

1 *Kennedy v A* 1986 SLT 358.
2 The chairman may, however, tell them of the substance of the report it if is not against the interests of the child to do so.
3 A child is usually a person under the age of 16: s 30(1)(a).
4 *Kennedy v B* 1973 SLT 38.
5 See, for example, *B v Kennedy* 1987 SLT 765.
6 *Kennedy v S* 1986 SLT 679. The fact that the child was put out of the house at night by the fathers' cohabitee did not prevent the court establishing the ground against the father.
7 1981 SLT 194.
8 Ibid at 196.

The test whether lack of parental care is likely to cause a child unnecessary suffering or seriously impair a child's health or development is objective, ie whether a reasonable person could draw that inference from the nature and extent of the parental lack of care;[1] or d) the child is a victim of a Sch 1 offence,[2] or the child is a member of the same household as a child who has been a victim of a Sch 1 offence. The extent of the latter ground is illustrated by *McGregor v H*.[3] Child A's brother, B, had been a victim of a Sch 1 offence. At the date of the hearing, B was in the care of foster parents ie was no longer physically in the same house as A. However, the Inner House of the Court of Session was prepared to give 'household' an extended meaning. In the Court's view, 'household' connotated a family unit, ie a group of persons held together by a particular tie, usually a blood relationship: while a family unit normally lived together, it did not cease if individual members were temporarily separated. Although at the time of the hearing, B was physically separated from A, they were still a part of the same family unit and therefore the same household. Accordingly, the ground of referral was applicable as A was a member of the same household as B, who had been the victim of a Sch 1 offence. As the ground is established on the balance of probabilities, the alleged perpetrator of the offence should not be identified in the case: indeed, the ground is established even if the perpetrator of the offence cannot be identified;[4] or

1 *M v McGregor* 1982 SLT 41. Thus the ground was established in *Finlayson (Applicant)* 1989 SCLR 601, although the parents refusal to allow conventional medical treatment on their haemophiliac child was the result of concern that the child might thereby be infected by AIDS.
2 Ie an offence listed in Sch 1 to the Criminal Procedure (Scotland) Act 1975: they include physical and sexual abuse of a child. The ground can be established if, for example, chastisement of the child is not reasonable: see *B v Harris* 1990 SLT 208, discussed *supra* pp 185 ff. A serious lacuna in the list of Sch 1 offences was uncovered in *F v Kennedy* 1988 SLT 404 where no Sch 1 offence was committed if a child under the age of 12 had been the victim of lewd, indecent or libidinous practices but had not suffered physical injury. Similarly, if a child had been the victim of a homosexual offence, no Sch 1 offence was committed unless the child had suffered physical injury. This was because Sch 1 had not been appropriately amended when s 7 of the Sexual Offences (Scotland) Act 1976 had been repealed and replaced by s 80(7) of the Criminal Justice (Scotland) Act 1980. This serious situation was remedied by para 51 of Sch 15 to the Criminal Justice Act 1988 which made the relevant amendments to Sch 1. These amendments have been held to be retrospective: *Harris v E* 1989 SLT (Sh Ct) 42. However, the need for reform of this ground of referral is obvious.
3 1983 SLT 626.
4 *S v Kennedy* 1987 SLT 667.

e) the child is, or is likely to become, a member of the same household as a person who has committed a Sch 1 offence; or

f) in the case of a female child, she is a member of the same household as a female who has been the victim of the crime of incest which was committed by a member of the same household; or

g) the child has failed to attend school regularly without reasonable excuse. Where a child was expelled from school, the ground was held not to be established without evidence of the alleged misconduct which had led to the expulsion;[1] or

h) the child has committed an offence. This is the ground upon which most referrals are brought. The Social Work (Scotland) Act 1968 proceeds on the basis that when a child commits a criminal offence this is merely symptomatic of the child's failure to develop social skills. This failure will often be the result of dysfunctionalism in the child's family. The child who commits an offence is therefore in need of care not punishment.[2] In exceptional cases, for example, very serious crimes such as murder or where the child has committed an offence with an adult, the child may be prosecuted in the High Court or sheriff court. But as a general rule, where a child has committed an offence, his case will be referred by the reporter to a children's hearing to determine whether he or she is in need of compulsory measures of care. In *Merrin v S*,[3] the Inner House held that before this ground can be used the child must have reached the age of criminal responsibility *ie* be aged 8 or over. The case proceeds in exactly the same way as the case where a referral is made on any other of the s 32(2) grounds. This welfare-based approach to the problem of juvenile crime has been the most controversial aspect of the Social Work (Scotland) Act 1968;[4] or

i) the child has misused a volatile substance by deliberately inhaling, other than for medicinal purposes, that substance's vapour ie glue sniffing; or

j) the child has absconded from a place of safety or the control of a

1 *D v Kennedy* 1988 SCLR 31.

2 See generally, *Report on Children and Young Persons* (the Kilbrandon Report) Cmnd 2306 upon which the Social Work (Scotland) Act 1968 was based.

3 1987 SLT 193. In the present writer's view there is force in the dissenting judgment of Lord Dunpark who emphasised that the child need only have *committed* an offence: cf been *guilty* of an offence.

4 Further discussion of this ground is outwith the scope of a text book on family law. For important studies on the operation of the system see, for example, Martin and Murray *The Scottish Juvenile Justice System* (1982); Asquith *Children and Justice* (1983).

person under whom he has been placed by a supervision requirement;[1] or

k) the child is already in the care of the local authority and his behaviour is such that special measures are needed for his adequate care and control.

Procedure in referrals

Where a case is referred by the reporter to a children's hearing, the child is under a obligation to appear[2] and it is the reporter's responsibility to secure the child's attendance.[3] A parent has not only a right to attend at all stages of the hearing[4] but must, as a general rule, attend the proceedings when the child's case is being considered.[5] When the parents and child appear, it is the chairman's duty to explain to the child and the parent the grounds of referral. If the parents and the child accept that the grounds of referral exist, the hearing will then consider how best to dispose of the case.[6] But if the parent and the child do not accept the ground, unless they are prepared to discharge the referral, the hearing must direct the reporter to make an application to the sheriff for a finding whether the grounds of referral are established.[7] An application to the sheriff must also be made if the child is too young to understand what is involved and is unable to accept the ground;[8] however, if the ground is accepted by the child's parents, the sheriff may dispense with the hearing of evidence if satisfied that in all the circumstances it would be reasonable to do so.

The application is heard by the sheriff in chambers within 28 days of being lodged. Again the child must be present[9] and the child and parents can be legally represented.[10] If the sheriff decides that none of the grounds of referral has been established at the date of the proceed-

---

1 On supervision requirements, see *infra* pp 247 ff.
2 Section 40(1): a case can be considered in the absence of the child if the ground for referral is concerned with a Sch 1 offence or if it would be detrimental to the child to be present: s 40(2).
3 Section 40(3). The hearing can issue a warrant for the detention of the child in a place of safety for up to 7 days: if the hearing cannot dispose of the case, the child can be detained for a further 21 days: further extensions of detention may be granted by the sheriff: see ss 40(4)–(9).
4 Section 41(1).
5 Section 41(2): parents' attendance is not necessary if the hearing thinks it is unreasonable or unnecessary.
6 Sections 42(2)(a) and 43.
7 Section 42(2)(c).
8 Section 42(7): *JF v McGregor* 1981 SLT 334.
9 Section 42(3).
10 Section 42(4).

ings in the sheriff court,[1] he will dismiss the application and discharge the referral.[2] If, however, the sheriff is satisfied on the evidence before him, that any of the grounds of referral has been established, he will remit the case to the reporter to make arrangements for the children's hearing to consider and determine the case.[3] As a general rule there is no need for corroboration.[4] However, when the ground of referral is that the child has committed an offence, the sheriff must apply to the evidence the standard of proof required in criminal procedure and corroboration is therefore required.[5] Where the child is alleged to be a victim of a Sch 1 offence, the sheriff can proceed to determine whether or not the ground exists, even if criminal proceedings are pending against the alleged perpetrator of the offence.[6] If the child and the parents accept a ground during the proceedings, the sheriff may dispense with hearing evidence relating to that ground and deem the ground to be established.[7]

If a child fails to attend the hearing of the application, the sheriff can issue a warrant for the child's detention in a place of safety for up to fourteen days.[8] If the sheriff finds the grounds of referral established, he can issue a warrant for the child's detention in a place of safety for up to three days, if this is necessary in the child's interests or he will run away before the children's hearing sits to consider the child's case.[9]

Disposal of the case

If the parents and child have accepted the grounds of referral or if the grounds of referral have been established in proceedings before the sheriff, the children's hearing will then consider how they should dispose of the case.[10] The hearing will have the social background report and any other relevant information. If the hearing considers that further investigation is necessary into the child's circumstances, the case can be continued to a subsequent hearing.[11]

1 *Kennedy v B* 1973 SLT 38.
2 Section 42(5).
3 Section 42(6).
4 Section 1(1) of the Civil Evidence (Scotland) Act 1988.
5 Section 42(6).
6 *Ferguson v P* 1989 SLT 681.
7 Section 42(6A).
8 Section 42(3) as amended by s 25(1) of the Law Reform (Miscellaneous Provisions) (Scotland) Act 1985.
9 Section 42(6) as amended by s 25(3) of the Law Reform (Miscellaneous Provisions) (Scotland) Act 1985.
10 Section 43(1).
11 Section 43(3).

The children's hearing must proceed on the course which, in its view, is in the best interests of the child.[1] If they feel that no further action is required, the children's hearing can discharge the referral.[2] If, however, the children's hearing decides that the child is in need of compulsory measures of care, they can make 'a supervision requirement' requiring the child–

a) to submit to supervision, for example, by a probation officer or social worker, in accordance with such conditions, for example, as to residence, which the children's hearing may impose; or

b) to reside in a residential establishment named in the requirement, for example, a community home or a List D school, and be subject to such conditions, for example, as to access, or placement with foster parents with a view for adoption which the children's hearing may impose.[3]

A supervision requirement ceases to have effect after the child reaches the age of eighteen.[4] However the supervision requirement should not continue any longer than is necessary in the interests of the child and, if a local authority takes the view that the requirement should cease to have effect, it can refer the case to their reporter for review by a children's hearing who can terminate the requirement if they think this would be the proper course.[5] Moreover, a supervision requirement cannot remain in force after a year unless it has been reviewed by a children's hearing.[6] The child and his parents also have the right to a review of the requirement.[7] On review, the children's hearing may continue the requirement or terminate it.

The child or the parents may appeal to the sheriff in chambers against the decision of the children's hearing.[8] An appeal is competent not only in relation to the making of the supervision requirement itself but also as to any of the conditions laid down, for example, as to

1 Section 43(1).
2 Section 43(2).
3 Section 44(1).
4 Section 47(2): supervision or guidance can be extended beyond the age of 18 if the child is prepared to accept it.
5 Section 47(1).
6 Section 48(3).
7 Section 48(4): they can do so after 3 months from the making or variation on review of the requirement or 6 months after a review which had continued the requirement: s 48(4)(a)(b) and (c). A review can take place at any time if a local authority so recommends: s 48(2); and a reporter is entitled to arrange a review, if a supervision requirement has not been reviewed during the previous 9 months: s 48(4A), inserted by s 29 of the Law Reform (Miscellaneous Provisions) (Scotland) Act 1985.
8 Section 49(1): the appeal must be made within 21 days of the decision of the children's hearing.

access.[1] If the sheriff is satisfied that the decision of the children's hearing is not justified, for example, if the hearing failed to consider a matter which was relevant to the case,[2] he will remit the case with the reasons for his decision to the children's hearing to reconsider their decision or he can discharge the referral:[3] but the sheriff cannot give the hearing directions on the steps they should take when reconsidering the case.[4]

For these purposes, parent includes the child's guardian.[5] 'Guardian' includes persons who have custody or charge or control over the child.[6] However, to be a guardian the person concerned must have *de facto* custody of the child at the time of proceedings before the children's hearing or sheriff court.[7]

Safeguarding the child's interests

In any proceedings before a children's hearing or in an application before the sheriff court for a finding that the grounds of referral exist or an appeal to the sheriff against a decision of a children's hearing, in addition to any existing power to appoint a *curator ad litem*, the chairman or sheriff may if there is a conflict of interest between the child and the parents, appoint an independent person to safeguard the child's interests.[8] The safeguarder's report can be used by the sheriff as a check on the sheriff's view that he had formed of the evidence.[9]

Appeals

There is an appeal to the Court of Session, by way of stated case on a point of law or in respect of any irregularity in the conduct of a case, from any decision of the sheriff.[10] On deciding the appeal, the Court of Session shall remit the case to the sheriff for disposal in accordance with such directions as the Court may give.[11]

1 *Kennedy v A* 1986 SLT 358.
2 *D v Sinclair* 1973 SLT (Sh Ct) 47. Cf *C v Kennedy* 1987 GWD 18–661.
3 Section 49(5).
4 *Kennedy v A* 1986 SLT 358: there can be an appeal to the sheriff against the hearings' decision at the rehearing: s 51(2).
5 Section 30(2).
6 Section 94(1) as amended by para 9 of Sch 1 to the Law Reform (Parent and Child) (Scotland) Act 1986.
7 *Kennedy v H* 1988 SLT 586.
8 Section 34A. The safeguarder's appointment should not extend beyond the initial disposal of the proceedings in which he or she was appointed: *Cato v Pearson* 1990 SLT (Sh Ct) 75.
9 *Kennedy v M* 1989 SLT 687.
10 Section 50(1). There is no appeal from the Inner House of the Court of Session to the House of Lords.
11 Section 50(3): see, for example, *Kennedy v A* 1986 SLT 358.

The effect of a supervision requirement

A child who is subject to a supervision requirement is deemed to be in the care of the local authority for certain important purposes.[1] Consequently, in reaching any decision relating to the child, first consideration must be given to the child's welfare[2] and the child's case must be reviewed by the local authority at least every six months.[3] However, the local authority must operate within any conditions imposed by the children's hearing, for example, in relation to access, unless or until the conditions are varied or terminated by the hearing when reviewing the requirement. Where a children's hearing makes it a condition of a supervision requirement that the child be kept in secure accommodation in a named residential establishment, the child remains there only for

> 'such time as the person in charge of that establishment, with the agreement of the director of social work of the local authority required to give effect to the supervision requirement, considers it necessary that [the child] do so'.[4]

Parents or guardians do not lose their parental rights in respect of a child who is subject to a supervision requirement. Thus, for example, not only does a court have jurisdiction to determine custody disputes in relation to such children, but the parent retains title to sue.[5] However this is of little value, for even if the parent is awarded custody or access, the courts have insisted that the parent's *exercise* of these rights are restricted by the local authority's powers to ensure that the child receives the compulsory measures of care which are required. Thus, for example, even if a father has the custody of and/or a right of access to the child, the courts will not allow him to enforce those rights if the local authority took the view that it was not in the interests of a child

1 Section 44(5).
2 Section 20.
3 Section 20A.
4 Section 58A(3). This is only possible where (a) the child is likely to abscond and if he absconds, it is likely that his physical, mental or moral welfare will be at risk or (b) he is likely to injure himself or other persons unless he is kept in secure accommodation. On the complex provisions relating to residence in secure accommodation see ss 58A–G, as amended by s 26 of the Law Reform (Miscellaneous Provisions) (Scotland) Act 1985.
5 *W v Glasgow Corpn* 1974 SLT (Notes) 5; *Aitken v Aitken* 1978 SLT 183; *D v Strathclyde Regional Council* 1985 SLT 114; *Borders Regional Council v M* 1986 SLT 222. Similarly, a child's grandparents have title to apply for parental rights under s 3 of the Law Reform (Parent and Child) (Scotland) Act 1986: however, even if granted, they cannot be exercised while the supervision requirement remains in force: *M v Lothian Regional Council* 1990 SLT 116.

who was subject to the supervision requirement to see his or her father. The only remedy available to the father would be to seek a review by the children's hearing of the supervision requirement and argue that the requirement be terminated or varied to include conditions allowing the father access.[1]

The reason why parental rights do not automatically cease when a supervision requirement is made is because in many cases it is desireable that the child should continue to live or, at least, to retain links with his or her family. If, however, contact with the parents or guardian is not in the child's interests, the local authority can, if grounds exist, assume parental rights by a s 16 resolution, as a child who is subject to a supervision requirement is deemed to be in the care of the local authority, for, inter alia, that purpose.[2] Thus, if as result of a finding that a child is in need of compulsory measures of care, a children's hearing makes a supervision requirement, the way is open to a local authority to assume parental rights – provided a s 16 ground exists – when it is in the child's best interests to do so.

CONCLUSION

The Social Work (Scotland) Act 1968 gives extensive power to state agencies to act to protect children who are in need of care. The system of children's hearings is not only a bold attempt to introduce a welfare based approach to the problem of juvenile crime but also provides personnel with expertise and experience to make decisions which are in the best interests of children who, because of the dysfunctionalism of their family or otherwise, are in need of care. However, the danger of such paternalistic legislation is that insufficient weight is given to the rights of the parents and children themselves. By insisting that a hearing cannot proceed unless the parents and child accept the grounds of referral or where they do not, the grounds are established to the satisfaction of a judge, the present system at least recognises the existence of the rights of parents and children. But at a time when, as a result of unemployment, drug abuse, mental illness and marital breakdown, families are increasingly unable to cope and children are becoming more and more vulnerable, the utility of the provisions of the Social Work (Scotland) Act 1968 should not be underestimated.

1 *Aitken v Aitken* 1978 SLT 183; *D v Strathclyde Regional Council* 1985 SLT 114. Nor is an access order available as that procedure only applies when access to a child who is subject to a s 16 resolution has been terminated: ss 17A and B, see *supra* p 239.
2 Section 44(5): *Lothian Regional Council v S* 1986 SLT (Sh Ct) 37; see also *Central Regional Council v B* 1985 SLT 413.

Index

Abandonment
dispensation with agreement to adoption, 224
Abduction
child of,
Hague Convention, 210–211
international aspects, 208–211
Abortion
child, performed on, parental rights, 191–192
consent to, 148–149
first trimester, sought in, 148
grounds for, 148
offence, 148
prohibition of inducement of, 148
time limit, 149
Access
parental rights, 184
welfare principle, 185, 205–206
Accommodation
cohabitees, of, 96–98
matrimonial home. *See* MATRIMONIAL HOME
Adherence
marriage, legal consequences of, 41
Adoption
agency, 213–214
forbidden degrees of relationship, 22–24
generally, 212–213
order,
court's refusal to make, 228
effect of, 212
registration of, 228
parental agreement,
dispensation with,
abandoning child, 224
cannot be found, 223
generally, 221–222
incapable of giving agreement, 223
neglecting child, 224
parental duties, failure to discharge, 224
persistent ill-treatment, 225

Adoption—*continued*
parental agreement—*continued*
dispensation with—*continued*
serious ill-treatment, 225
freeing child, 220–222
generally, 219–220
unreasonable withholding of, 225–228
procedure, 218–219
prospective adopters, 215–217
welfare of child, 214–215
Adultery
defences in divorce action,
collusion, 106
condonation, 105–106
lenocinium, 103–104
meaning, 102
physical requirements of, 102
standard of proof, 102–103
Affinity
forbidden degrees of relationship, 22–25
Age
capacity to marry, 21–22
criminal liability, of, 170
Agency
adoption, 213–214
Agreement
adoption, to. *See* ADOPTION
financial provision, for, 144–145
Aliment
child, legal rights of,
action for, 173–174
child, meaning, 171
form of, 174–175
importance of, 170
obligation to, 170, 171–172
parent, child's obligation to, 175
income support, relationship with, 53–55
interim, 52–53
marriage, legal consequences of,
award, nature of, 51–52
common law, 47–48

Aliment—*continued*
  marriage, legal consequences of—*continued*
    defences, 50–51
    extent of obligation, 48–50
    nature of obligation, 48–50
    parties living together, where, 51
    procedural matters, 52–53
    spouse, duty owed by, 2
    variation of, 52, 175
Allowance. *See* PERIODICAL ALLOWANCE
Ancillary action for parental rights. *See* PARENTAL RIGHTS
Appeal
  child in care, in respect of, 249
Artificial insemination from donor
  establishing parentage, 151–152

Behaviour
  divorce, grounds for, 107–109
Blood test
  parentage, to establish,
    accuracy of, 153
    consent to, 154–156
    deceased person, in respect of, 156
    evidence,
      importance of, 153–154
      refusal to admit, 156–157
    exclusionary result, 153
    minor, on, 154
    pupil, on, 154, 155
    refusal of, 156
  See also DNA PROFILING

Capacity
  child, of, 148
  minor, of, 165
  pupil, of, 164
Capacity to marry. *See* MARRIAGE
Capital sum
  order for payment of, 123–124
Care
  child in. *See* CHILD IN CARE
  child in need of. *See* CHILD
Child
  abduction of. *See* ABDUCTION
  access, 184–185
  active capacity, lack of, 148
  born handicapped, action in delict, 149
  care, in. *See* CHILD IN CARE
  care, in need of,
    generally, 230
    welfare-based system, 4–5
  curator ad litem. See CURATOR AD LITEM

Child—*continued*
  custody. *See* CUSTODY
  discipline, 185–186
  domicile of, 162
  economic burden of caring for, after divorce, 136–137
  education, 186–187
  illegitimate. *See* ILLEGITIMATE CHILD
  legal rights of,
    aliment,
      action for, 173–174
      child, meaning, 171
      form of, 174–175
      importance of, 170
      obligation to, 170, 171–172
      parent, child's obligation to, 175
      reform of law, 170
    capacity, 148
    contractual obligations, 166–168
    criminal liability, 170
    delict, 168–169
    extent of, 3
    generally, 164
    marriage, 170
    succession, 169
  legitimate,
    current law, 159–160
    illegitimate child,
      distinguished from, 160
      legitimation of, 158
    meaning, 157–158
    preservation of status of, 159
    putative marriage, doctrine of, 158
    void marriage, born during, 158
  medical procedures, 188–193
  minor. *See* MINOR
  names, 193
  parentage. *See* PARENTAGE
  parental rights. *See* PARENTAL RIGHTS
  passive capacity, 148
  physical possession of, 183–184
  religion, 187–188
  tutor. *See* TUTOR
  voidable marriage, personal bar to, 39
  welfare principle. *See* WELFARE PRINCIPLE
Child in care
  compulsory measures,
    appeal, 249
    child's interests, safeguarding of, 249
    children's hearing, 242–243
    disposal of case, 247–249
    generally, 240
    grounds of referral, 243–246

Child in care—*continued*
  compulsory measures—*continued*
    local authority, information to, 241
    place of safety order, 240–241
    referrals,
      grounds of, 243–246
      procedure in, 246–247
    reporter, role of, 241–242
    supervision requirement, 250–251
    generally, 251
  parental rights, assumption of,
    counter-notice procedure, 237
    grounds for, 234–235
    local authority powers, 232–233
    notice of, 235–236
    place of safety order, 233–234
    review of case, 238–239
    welfare principle, 238–239
  reception into care, 231–232
Civil marriage. *See* MARRIAGE
Coat of arms
  succession or devolution of, 160
Cohabitation
  habit and repute, with, marriage by, 16
  See also NON-COHABITATION
Cohabitees
  family accommodation, occupation of,
    89–90
  legal status, 1
Collusion
  defence in divorce action, 106
Compulsory measures of care. *See* CHILD
  IN CARE
Condonation
  defence in divorce action, 105–106
Consanguinity
  forbidden degrees of relationship, 23,
    24–25
Contraceptives
  prescription of, parental rights, 191
Contract
  child, capacity of, 166–168
  engagement as, 6
  marriage, legal consequence of, 43–44
Criminal liability
  age of, 170
Curator
  appointment of, 165
Curator ad litem
  blood sample sought by, 154
  child represented in litigation by, 165–
    166
  meaning, 154*n*

Custody
  arrangements operative prior to div-
    orce, 4
  breakdown of marriage, crucial issue
    on, 199
  common law, at, 208–209
  European Convention, 209–210
  independent application,
    age of child, 195
    Court of Session, to, 195
    generally, 194
    grandparent, by, 195
    sheriff court, to, 195–196
  international aspects, 208–210
  joint, 208
  self-regulation by parents, 4
  traditional liberal approach to title to
    sue, 195
  United Kingdom decrees, 209
  welfare principle as criterion for deter-
    mination, 4, 200–207, 208–209
Damages
  delict, in, 168–169
  wrongful failure to implement promise,
    6
Deceased person
  blood test to establish parentage, 156
Declaration
  de praesenti, marriage by, 14–15
Defective consent. *See* MARRIAGE
Defences
  aliment, claim for, 49–50
  judicial separation, 117
Delict
  child born physically or mentally handi-
    capped, 149
  child's liability in, 168–169
  damages in, 168–169
  marriage, legal consequences of, 44–46
Deportation
  sham marriage entered into to avoid, 34
Desertion
  divorce, grounds for, 110–113
  initial, 110–111
  two years' non-cohabitation, 111–113
Dignity
  succession or devolution of, 160–161
Discipline
  parental rights, 185–186
Divorce
  current law, criticism of, 3
  custody of child. *See* CUSTODY

Divorce—*continued*
financial provision on,
  agreement for, 144–145
  court's discretion, 120–121
  criteria for, 122
  generally, 120–123
  nature of orders,
    capital sum, payment of, 123–124
    generally, 123
    incidental orders, 125–126
    periodical allowances, 124–125
    transfer of property, 125
  principles,
    child of marriage, caring for, 137–139
    economic advantages and disadvantages, 135–137
    financial support, dependence on, 139–140
    generally, 126–127, 142–143
    matrimonial property, sharing of net value, 126–135
    serious financial hardship, 141–143
  procedural matters, 146–147
  reform of law, 121–123
generally, 99–100
grounds of,
  adultery,
    defences,
      collusion, 106
      condonation, 105–106
      lenocinium, 103–105
    meaning, 102
    physical requirements, 102
    standard of proof, 103
  behaviour, 107–109
  desertion,
    generally, 110
    initial, 110–111
    two-years' non-cohabitation, 111–113
  fault-based, 99
  non-cohabitation,
    five years, 115–117
    two years, 111–114
  non-fault, 99
high incidence of, 2–3
history of, 2
irretrievable breakdown of marriage, 100–102
law reform, 119
judicial, introduction of, 2
jurisdiction, 117–118
objectives of good divorce law, 99–100
procedural matters,

Divorce—*continued*
jurisdiction, 117–118
  proof, 118
proof, 118
reform of law, 99–100, 118–119
restrictive right to, 118–119
DNA profiling
generally, 153–154
accuracy of, 153–154
consent to, 154–156
evidence
  importance of, 153–154
  refusal to admit, 156–157
inclusionary result, 153–154
minor, on, 154
pupil, on, 154, 155
refusal of, 156
See also BLOOD TEST
Domicile
child, of, 162*n*
marriage, legal consequences of, 41

Education
parental rights, 186–187
Engagement
breach of promise, abolition of, 6
contract, as, 6
gift, 7–8
property issues, 7
ring, 7–8
wrongful failure to implement promise, damages for, 6
Equality
spouses, of, 1–2
Error
defective consent to marriage as result of, 31–32
Evidence
blood test or DNA profiling to establish parentage,
  importance of, 153
  refusal to admit, 156–157
Exclusion order
matrimonial home, occupancy of, 82–86

Family law
policies underlying most important features, 1–5
recent origin of, 5
Father
consent to abortion not required, 149
parental rights. *See* PARENTAL RIGHTS
See also PARENTAGE

Fear
consent to marriage obtained as result
of, 33
Financial provision on divorce. *See* DIV-
ORCE
Foetus
protection of, 148
Force
consent to marriage obtained as result
of, 32–33
Formal marriage. *See* MARRIAGE
Furniture
matrimonial home, in, 66–69

Gift
engaged couple, between, 7–8
spouses, between, 62
wedding present, 61–62
Grandparent
access, application for, 195
custody, application for, 195
Guardian
meaning, 249

Hague Convention, 210–211
Hardship
financial, suffered as result of divorce,
141–143
Hearing
children's, 242–243
Home
family, cohabitee's rights in respect of,
96–98
matrimonial. *See* MATRIMONIAL HOME
Honour
succession or devolution of, 160–161
Household goods
marriage, legal consequences of, 64–66
Housekeeping
savings from, 70–71
Husband and wife
aliment, duty of, 2
corporeal moveables bought by,
generally, 63–64
household goods, 64–66
matrimonial home,
furniture, 66–69
plenishings, 66–69
gifts between, 62
importance of law of, 1
legal equality of, 1–2
matrimonial home. *See* MATRIMONIAL
HOME
See also MARRIAGE

Ill-treatment
dispensation with agreement to adoption, 225–227
Illegitimate child
alleviation of legal position of, 4
current law, 159–163
law reform, 162–163
legitimate child distinguished from, 161
legitimation of, 158
Income support
aliment, relationship with, 53–55
generally, 46
Impotency. *See* INCURABLE IMPOTENCY
Incidental order
divorce, financial provision on, 125–126
Incurable impotency
meaning, 37–38
voidable marriage as result of, 37–39
**Independent application for parental
rights.** *See* PARENTAL RIGHTS
Information
local authority, to, 241
Insurance policy
marriage, legal consequences of, 71–72
Interdict
matrimonial, 93–96
Intoxication
defective consent to marriage as result
of, 31
Irregular marriage. *See* MARRIAGE

Judicial separation
defences, 117
grounds for, 117
Jurisdiction
divorce, action of, 117–118

Law reform
divorce, 119
illegitimacy, 162–163
marriage by habit and repute, 19
minor, legal capacity of, 168
pupil, legal capacity of, 168
succession, 59
Legal consequences of marriage. *See*
MARRIAGE
Legal impediments to marriage. *See*
MARRIAGE
Legal rights
child, of. *See* CHILD
marriage, arising on, 1
succession, 55–56
Legitimate child. *See* CHILD

Lenocinium
defence in divorce action, 103–105
Local authority
child in care. *See* CHILD IN CARE
circumstances of child, investigation
and report on, 199–200
committal of child to care of, 197–198

Maintenance
matrimonial home, of, 81
Marriage
capacity to marry,
forbidden degrees of relationship,
adoption, 23–24
affinity, 23–24
consanguinity, 23, 25
generally, 22
policy reasons for prohibited
degrees, 25
generally, 21
non-age, 21–22
parties of same sex, 26–27
prior subsisting marriage, 27–30
child, capacity of, 170
defective consent,
error, 31–32
fear, 32–34
force, 32–34
generally, 30
intoxication, 31
mental defect, 30–31
mental illness, 30–31
sham marriage, 34–36
divorce. *See* DIVORCE
formalities of,
formal,
civil, 10–11
civil preliminaries,
advantages of, 13
marriage notice, 8–10
marriage schedule, 10
purpose of, 13
generally, 8
irregularities, effect of, 12
religious, 11–12
generally, 8
non-compliance with, 8, 20
regular,
civil, 10–11
civil preliminaries,
advantages of, 13
marriage notice, 8–10
marriage schedule, 10
purpose of, 13

Marriage—*continued*
formalities of—*continued*
regular—*continued*
generally, 8
irregularities, effect of, 12
religious, 11–12
getting married. *See* ENGAGEMENT
irregular,
advantages of, 19
cohabitation with habit and repute,
by, 16–18
declaration *de praesenti*, by, 14–15
generally, 14
procedure, 18
promise *subsequente copula*, by,
15–16
recognition of validity of, 14
requirements, 16–18
irretrievable breakdown of, 100–102
legal consequences of,
aliment,
common law, 47–48
defences, 50–51
extent of obligation, 48–50
nature of award, 51–52
nature of obligation, 48–50
parties living together, where, 51
procedural matters, 52–53
relationship between income support and, 46, 53–55
generally, 40
income support,
aliment, relationship with, 53–55
generally, 46
matrimonial home. *See* MATRIMONIAL
HOME
moveable property,
corporeal, bought by spouses,
furniture, 66–69
generally, 63–64
household goods, 64–66
plenishings, 66–69
generally, 60–61
gifts between spouses, 62
housekeeping, savings from, 70–71
insurance policy, 71–72
money, 69–70
securities, 69–70
wedding presents, 61–62
obligations,
contract, 43–44
delict, 44–46
personal effects,
adherence, 41

Marriage—*continued*
legal consequences of —*continued*
personal effects—*continued*
domicile, 41
name, 42–43
nationality, 41
sexual relations, 42
succession,
generally, 55–56, 58–59
legal rights, 56–57
prior rights, 56–57
taxation, 46
matrimonial home. *See* MATRIMONIAL
HOME
matrimonial interdict, 93–96
nullity, declarator of,
grounds for,
incomplete marriage schedule, 13
incurable impotency, 36–39
prior subsisting, 27–30
putative, doctrine of, 158
rape within, 42
sham, 34–36
void,
absence of consent, for, validation of,
36
capacity to marry,
forbidden degrees of relationship,
adoption, 23–24
affinity, 23–24
consanguinity, 23–24
generally, 22
policy reasons for prohibited
degrees, 25
generally, 21
non-age, 21–22
parties of same sex, 26–27
prior subsisting marriage, 27–30
child conceived or born during, 158
defective consent,
error, 31–32
fear, 32–34
force, 32–34
generally, 30
intoxication, 31
mental defect, 30–31
mental illness, 30–31
sham marriage, 34–36
generally, 20–21
voidable,
generally, 21, 36–37
incurable impotency,
meaning, 35

Marriage—*continued*
voidable—*continued*
incurable impotency—*continued*
personal bar to declarator of
nullity,
children, 39
delay, 39
generally, 38–39
knowledge of impotency, 39
Matrimonial home
financial provision on divorce, 126–135
furniture, 66–69
generally, 73–74
matrimonial interdict, effect of, 93–96
occupation of,
both spouses have legal title or are
tenants, 90–92
generally, 79
one spouse has legal title or is tenant,
generally, 79
maintenance, 81
orders,
exclusion, 82–86
regulatory, 81–82
statutory rights,
nature of, 79–81
third party and, 86–90
upkeep, 81
ownership of,
both spouses, title in name of, 77–78
one spouse, title in name of, 74–77
plenishings, 66–69
tenancy, 92–93
Matrimonial property
division of, 129–130
meaning, 129
See also DIVORCE, FINANCIAL PROVISION
ON
Medical procedures
parental rights, 188–193
Mental defect
defective consent to marriage as result
of, 30–31
Mental handicap
child born with, action in delict, 149
medical operation on child with,
parental rights, 189–190
Mental illness
defective consent to marriage as result
of, 30–31
Minor
active capacity, 165
blood or DNA sample sought from,
154–155

Minor—*continued*
  legal capacity, law reform, 168
  meaning, 154*n*
  representation of, 165
Money
  marriage, legal consequences of, 69–70
Mother
  negligence by, causing handicap to
    unborn child, 149
  rights of. *See* PARENTAL RIGHTS
  See also PARENTAGE
Moveable property
  marriage, legal consequences of,
    corporeal moveables bought by
      spouses,
      generally, 63–64
      household goods, 64–66
      matrimonial home,
        furniture, 66–69
        plenishings, 66–69
      generally, 60–61
      gifts between spouses, 62
      housekeeping, savings from, 70–71
      insurance policy, 71–72
      money, 69–70
      securities, 69–70
      wedding presents, 61–62

Name
  marriage, legal consequences of, 42–43
  parental rights, 193
Nationality
  marriage, legal consequences of, 41
Neglect
  dispensation with agreement to adop-
    tion, 224
Negligence
  delict, liability of child in, 168–169
  mother, by, causing handicap to unborn
    child, 149
Non-cohabitation
  five years, 115–117
  two years, 111–114
Non-married couple. *See* COHABITEES
Non-parentage
  declarator of, 152–153
Notice
  custody application by person not
    parent of child, 197
  marriage, 8–10
Nuclear family
  essential family unit, as, 1

Occupation of matrimonial home. *See*
  MATRIMONIAL HOME

Offence
  abortion, 148
Order
  adoption, 212, 228–229
  exclusion, 82–86
  financial provision on divorce,
    capital sum, payment of, 123–124
    generally, 123
    incidental orders, 125–126
    periodical allowances, 124–125
    transfer of property, 123–124
  place of safety, 233, 240–241
  regulatory, 81–82
Ownership
  matrimonial home, of, 74–78

Parentage
  declarator of, 152–153
  establishing,
    artificial insemination from donor,
      child born as result of, 151–152
    biological criteria determining
      father, 150
    blood test,
      accuracy of, 153
      consent to, 154–156
      deceased person, in respect of, 156
      evidence,
        importance of, 152–153
        refusal to admit, 156–157
      exclusionary result, 153
      minor, on, 154–155
      pupil, on, 154–155
      refusal of, 156
    DNA profiling,
      accuracy of, 153–154
      consent to, 154–156
      evidence
        importance of, 153–154
        refusal to admit, 156–157
      inclusionary result, 153–154
      minor, on, 154
      pupil, on, 154–155
      refusal of, 156
    father,
      biological criteria determining, 150
      presumption, application of, 150–
        151
    reproductive techniques, effect of
      advances in, 150
  non-parentage, declarator of, 152–153
Parental rights
  action in relation to,
    access. *See* ACCESS

Parental rights—*continued*
action in relation to—*continued*
ancillary,
child of marriage, meaning, 198
custody, award of, 199–200
local authority, investigation and
report by, 199
statutory provisions, 198–199
custody. *See* CUSTODY
generally, 194
independent application,
best interests of child, 197
child, meaning, 195
Court of Session, to, 195
generally, 194
grandparent, by, 195
notice of, given to parent, 197
restrictions on award, 196–197
sheriff court, to, 195
joint custody, 208
rubber stamping of arrangements,
207–208
socio-legal studies, findings of, 207
welfare principle,
access, 205–207
child's welfare as paramount consideration, 200–202
innocent spouse, presumption
relating to, 201–202
mother, award of custody to, 202–
204
religious upbringing, 202
status quo, preservation of, 203–
205
statutory provisions, 200
adoption. *See* ADOPTION
aliment, 175–176
care and upbringing of child,
duration of, 179–182
generally, 4, 178–179
nature of,
access, 184–185
discipline, 185–186
education, 186–187
generally, 182–183
medical procedures, 188–193
names, 193
physical possession of child, 183–
184
religion, 187–188
who can exercise, 178–179
child in care. *See* CHILD IN CARE
father, of, 2
meaning, 178–179, 194
mother, of, 2

Periodical allowance
aliment, 175–176
divorce, financial provision on, 124–125
variation of, 145–146
Personal effects
marriage, legal consequences of,
adherence, 41
domicile, 41
name, 42–43
nationality, 41
sexual relations, 42
Physical handicap
child born with, action in delict, 149
Physical possession
child, of, 183–184
Place of safety
order, 233, 240–241
Plenishings
matrimonial home, in, 66–69
Possession
physical, of child, 183–184
Prior rights
succession, 57–58
Promise
breach of, abolition of, 6
subsequente copula, marriage by, 15–16
wrongful failure to implement, damages for, 6
Proof
adultery, of, 102–103
divorce, ground of action, 118
Property
engaged couple, issue arising between,
7
matrimonial home. *See* MATRIMONIAL
HOME
moveable. *See* MOVEABLE PROPERTY
order for transfer of, 123–124
Pupil
blood sample sought from, 154–155
legal capacity, law reform, 168
meaning, 154n
minor distinguished from, 164
passive capacity, 164–165
representation of, 165
will, lacks capacity to make, 169
Putative marriage
doctrine of, 158

Rape
marriage, within, 42
Regular marriage. *See* MARRIAGE
Regulatory order
matrimonial home, occupancy of, 81–
82

Relationship
  adoption, by, 23, 24
  affinity, by, 23, 24–25
  consanguinity, by, 23, 24
  forbidden degrees of, 22–25
Religion
  parental rights, 187–188, 202
Religious marriage. *See* MARRIAGE
Reporter
  role of, 241–242
Reproductive techniques
  advances in, effect on establishing parentage, 150

Schedule
  marriage, 10
Securities
  marriage, legal consequences of, 69–70
Separation. *See* JUDICIAL SEPARATION
Sex
  parties of same, capacity to marry, 26–27
Sexual relations
  marriage, legal consequences of, 42
Social security
  child's entitlement to benefits, 213
Spouse. *See* HUSBAND AND WIFE
Statutory rights
  matrimonial home,
    nature of, 79–81
    third parties, 86–90
Succession
  child, capacity of, 169
  coat of arms, 160
  dignity, 160
  generally, 56–59
  honour, 160
  law reform, proposals for, 59

Succession—*continued*
  legal rights, 56–57
  prior rights, 57–58
  title, 160
Supervision
  child in care, 250–251

Taxation
  marriage, legal consequences of, 46
Tenancy
  matrimonial home, of, 92–93
Third party
  engagement present from, 8
  matrimonial home, statutory right of occupation, 86–90
Title
  matrimonial home, to. *See* MATRIMONIAL HOME
  succession or devolution of, 160–161
Tutor
  appointment of, 165
  blood sample sought by, 155
  meaning, 154*n*

Void marriage. *See* MARRIAGE
Voidable marriage. *See* MARRIAGE

Wedding present
  marriage, legal consequences of, 61–62
Welfare principle
  access, 185, 205–206
  adoption, 214–215
  child in care, 237–239
  custody, 4, 200–207, 208–209
  medical treatment, 191–192
Wife. *See* HUSBAND AND WIFE
Will
  pupil lacks capacity to make, 169